Making Strategy Work

In the face of accelerating turbulence and change, business leaders and policy makers need new ways of thinking to sustain performance and growth.

Wharton School Publishing offers a trusted source for stimulating ideas from thought leaders who provide new mental models to address changes in strategy, management, and finance. We seek out authors from diverse disciplines with a profound understanding of change and its implications. We offer books and tools that help executives respond to the challenge of change.

Every book and management tool we publish meets quality standards set by The Wharton School of the University of Pennsylvania. Each title is reviewed by the Wharton School Publishing Editorial Board before given Wharton's seal of approval. This ensures that Wharton publications are timely, relevant, important, conceptually sound or empirically based, and implementable.

To fit our readers' learning preferences, Wharton publications are available in multiple formats, including books, audio, and electronic.

To find out more about our books and management tools, visit us at whartonsp.com and Wharton's executive education site, exceed.wharton.upenn.edu.

MAKING STRATEGY WORK
Leading Effective Execution and Change

Lawrence G. Hrebiniak

Ideas. Action. Impact.
Wharton School
Publishing

Library of Congress Publication in Data: 2004111039

Publisher: Tim Moore
Editorial Assistant: Richard Winkler
Development Editor: Russ Hall
Marketing Manager: Martin Litkowski
International Marketing Manager: Tim Galligan
Cover Designer: Chuti Prasertsith
Managing Editor: Gina Kanouse
Project Editor: Christy Hackerd
Copy Editor: Amy Lepore
Senior Indexer: Cheryl Lenser
Compositor: The Scan Group, Inc.
Proofreader: Carol Bowers
Manufacturing Buyer: Dan Uhrig

Ideas. Action. Impact.
**Wharton School
Publishing**

© 2005 by Pearson Education, Inc.
Publishing as Wharton School Publishing
Upper Saddle River, New Jersey 07458

Wharton School Publishing offers excellent discounts on this book when ordered in quantity for bulk purchases or special sales. For more information, please contact U.S. Corporate and Government Sales, 1-800-382-3419, corpsales@pearsontechgroup.com. For sales outside the U.S., please contact International Sales at international@pearsoned.com.

Printed in the United States of America
Third Printing July, 2005

ISBN 0-13-146745-X

Pearson Education LTD.
Pearson Education Australia PTY, Limited.
Pearson Education Singapore, Pte. Ltd.
Pearson Education North Asia, Ltd.
Pearson Education Canada, Ltd.
Pearson Educación de Mexico, S.A. de C.V.
Pearson Education—Japan
Pearson Education Malaysia, Pte. Ltd.

Ideas. Action. Impact.
**Wharton School
Publishing**

C. K. Prahalad
THE FORTUNE AT THE BOTTOM OF THE PYRAMID
Eradicating Poverty Through Profits

Yoram (Jerry) Wind, Colin Crook, with Robert Gunther
THE POWER OF IMPOSSIBLE THINKING
Transform the Business of Your Life and the Life of Your Business

Scott A. Shane
FINDING FERTILE GROUND
Identifying Extraordinary Opportunities for New Ventures

Bernard Baumohl
THE SECRETS OF ECONOMIC INDICATORS
Hidden Clues to Future Economic Trends and Investment Opportunities

Sayan Chatterjee
FAILSAFE STRATEGIES
Profit and Grow from Risks that Others Avoid

Robert Mittelstaedt
WILL YOUR NEXT MISTAKE BE FATAL?
Avoiding the Chain of Mistakes That Can Destroy Your Organization

Mukul Pandya, Robbie Shell, Susan Warner, Sandeep Junnarkar, and Jeffrey Brown
NIGHTLY BUSINESS REPORT PRESENTS LASTING LEADERSHIP
What You Can Learn from the Top 25 Business People of our Times

Oded Shenkar
THE CHINESE CENTURY
The Rising Chinese Economy and Its Impact on the Global Economy, the Balance of Power, and Your Job

Lawrence G. Hrebiniak
MAKING STRATEGY WORK
Leading Effective Execution and Change

113124

CONTENTS AT A GLANCE

CONTENTS

DEDICATION

In memory of Donna, who left us much too soon

INTRODUCTION

This book focuses on a critical management issue: Making strategy work or executing strategy effectively.

Theories and advice about the requisites of good planning and strategy formulation abound in management literature. A vast array of planning models and techniques has been paraded before managers over the years, and managers for the most part understand them and know how to use them effectively.

The problem with poor performance typically is not with planning, but with doing. That is, strategies often aren't implemented successfully. Making strategy work is more difficult than strategy making. Sound plans flounder or die because of a lack of execution know-how. This book focuses on execution—the processes, decisions, and actions needed to make strategy work.

What differentiates this book from others, beyond its emphasis on a critical management need? I'm excited about the present approach to execution for the six following reasons.

LEARNING FROM EXPERIENCE

This book is based on data. It borrows from the experiences of hundreds of managers actually involved in strategy execution. There are multiple sources of data, which ensures complete coverage of execution-related issues. This book doesn't rely on the armchair musings of a few people relating unconnected anecdotes; it is based on real-world execution experiences, problems, and solutions—including mine over the last two decades.

WHAT YOU NEED TO LEAD

The focus of the book is on the knowledge, skills, and capabilities managers need to lead execution efforts. Its content is action- and results-oriented.

Most organizations recruit, train, and retain good managers; they are staffed by good people—even great people. Most managers are motivated and qualified people who want to perform well.

Even good people, however, can be hampered by poor incentives, controls, organizational structures, and company policies or operating procedures that inhibit their ability to execute and get things done. Even great leaders, in top management positions, will fail if they're not well versed in the conditions that affect execution success. Managers need to understand what makes strategy work. Intuition and personality simply aren't sufficient, given such a complex task. This book focuses on this knowledge and the capabilities and insights leaders need for execution success.

THE BIG PICTURE

In this book, I develop a unifying, integrated approach to execution. I focus on the big picture, as well as the nitty-gritty of the execution process and methods. I spell out a logical approach to execution and the relationships among key execution decisions.

This book not only identifies these key factors and their relationships, but also goes into detail on each of the factors needed for execution success. It provides an important, integrated approach to execution and dissects the approach to focus on its key elements, actions, or decisions. This book then provides both an overview of the execution process and an in-depth reference manual for key aspects of this process.

EFFECTIVE CHANGE MANAGEMENT

Leading successful execution efforts usually demands the effective management of change, and this book integrates important change-management issues into its treatment of execution.

This book discusses power, influence, and resistance to change. It focuses on real and practical change-related issues—such as whether to implement execution related changes quickly, all at once, or in a more deliberate and sequential fashion over time. I tell you why "speed kills" and explain how large, complex changes can severely hurt execution outcomes. I focus on the details of cultural change and the organizational power structure, and how they can be used to make strategy work.

APPLYING WHAT YOU LEARN

This book practices what it preaches. The final chapter shows how to apply the logic, insights, and practical advice of preceding chapters to a real, huge, and pervasive problem: Making mergers and acquisitions (M&A) work.

M&A strategies often flounder or fail; my last chapter explains why this is the case and how to increase the success of M&A efforts by applying the book's approach to execution. I also highlight the utility of the book's advice and guidelines when trying to make M&A efforts successful. I feel it is only fitting and proper to end an execution book on a positive and useful note—by showing how practical execution can be in confronting an important and pervasive real-world issue and how it can save management a lot of time, effort, and money.

THE BOTTOM LINE

Sixth and finally, the reasons above—taken together—distinguish this book significantly from other recent works, such as Bossidy and Charan's Execution (Crown Business, 2002). This book covers more of the important factors and decisions related to successful execution. It offers an empirically-based, integrative, complete approach to making strategy work and focuses more extensively on managing change than other publications dealing with implementation.

The bottom line is that my book greatly adds to and follows logically Bossidy and Charan's Execution. It is an important and necessary addition to the toolkit of managers looking to execute strategy and change effectively.

ON A FINAL NOTE

Leading execution and change to make strategy work is a difficult and formidable task. For the six reasons I have listed, I believe this task can be made more logical, manageable, and successful by the present book's approach and insights.

A FEW THANKS

An undertaking such as the present one is challenging and difficult because of its complexity. I alone assume responsibility for the book's content, its interpretation of data and facts, and its conclusions. Still, while the ultimate responsibility is mine, there are a number of people who helped me in my task, and I would like to recognize them for their contributions. Brian Smith of the Gartner Research Group helped immensely with the creation of the online research survey, and contributed important technical support. Cecilia Atoo of Wharton was a real stalwart as she typed the manuscript, created figures and tables, and otherwise helped meet my demands and those of the copyeditors. Many thanks are due to my editor, Tim Moore, as well as Russ Hall, Christy Hackerd, and others at Pearson Prentice Hall who helped me develop the manuscript into its present form. The anonymous reviewers who provided valuable feedback and suggestions for improving the manuscript also deserve recognition for their efforts. Finally, special thanks are due to my son, Justin, and my muse, Laura, whose encouragement, friendship, and support were constant sources of motivation to me.

1

Strategy Execution Is the Key

Introduction

Two decades ago, I was working with the Organizational Effectiveness Group in AT&T's new Consumer Products division, a business created after the court-mandated breakup and reorganization of the company in 1984. I remember one particular day that made an impression on me that would last for years.

I was talking to Randy Tobias, the head of the division. I had met Randy while doing some work for Illinois Bell, and here we were talking about his division's strategic issues and challenges. Randy later moved into the chairman's office at AT&T and then became a successful CEO of Eli Lilly, but his comments that day years ago were the ones that affected me most.[i]

Here was a new business thrust headlong into the competitive arena. Competition was new to AT&T at the time. Competitive strategy for the business was nonexistent, and Tobias was laboring to create that elusive original plan. He focused on products, competitors, industry forces, and how to position the new division in the marketplace. He handled expectations and demands from corporate as he forged a plan for the business and helped position it in the AT&T portfolio. He created a strategic plan where previously there had been none, a Herculean task and one well done at the time.

On that day, I recall asking Randy what was the biggest strategic challenge confronting the business. I expected that his answer would deal with the problem of strategy formulation or some competitive threat facing the division. His answer surprised me.

He said that strategy formulation, while extremely challenging and difficult, was not what concerned him the most. It was not the planning that worried him. It was something even bigger and more problematic.

It was the execution of strategy that concerned him above all else. Making the plan work would be an even bigger challenge than creating the plan. Execution was the key to competitive success, but it would take some doing.

I, of course, sought further clarification and elaboration. I can't remember all of his points in response to my many questions, but here are some of the execution challenges he raised that day, referring to his own organization. He mentioned the following:

- The culture of the organization and how it was not appropriate for the challenges ahead
- Incentives and how people have been rewarded for seniority or "getting older," not for performance or competitive achievement
- The need to overcome problems with traditional functional "silos" in the organization's structure
- The challenges inherent in managing change as the division adapted to new competitive conditions

This was the first elaboration of execution-related problems I had ever heard, and the message has stayed with me over the years. It became clear to me that day that:

EXECUTION IS A KEY TO SUCCESS

It also struck me in those early days with AT&T that, although execution is a key to success, it is no easy task. Here was a company with an ingrained culture and structure, a set way of doing things. For the company to adapt to its new competitive environment, major changes would be necessary, and those changes would be no simple cakewalk. Obviously, developing a competitive strategy wouldn't be easy, but the massive challenges confronting the company made it clear to me early on that:

MAKING STRATEGY WORK IS MORE DIFFICULT THAN THE TASK OF STRATEGY MAKING

Execution is critical to success. Execution represents a disciplined process or a logical set of connected activities that enables an organization to take a strategy and make it work. Without a careful, planned approach to execution, strategic goals cannot be attained. Developing such a logical approach, however, represents a formidable challenge to management.

Even with careful development of an execution plan at the business level, execution success is not guaranteed. Tobias's strategic and execution plans for the Consumer Products division were well thought out. Yet troubles plagued the division's progress. Why? The problem was with the entire AT&T corporation. The company was about to go through a huge metamorphosis that it simply was not equipped to deal with and make work. Execution plans at the business level founder or fail if they don't receive corporate support. AT&T was, at the time, a slow-moving behemoth in which change was vehemently resisted. Well-prepared and logical plans at the Consumer Products business level were hampered by a poor corporate culture. Tobias' insights and potentially effective execution actions were blunted by corporate inertia and incompetence.

Although execution is critical to strategic success, making strategy work presents a formidable challenge. A host of factors, including politics, inertia, and resistance to change, routinely can get in the way of execution success.

Fast forwarding to the present, I just finished a few weeks working with managers from Deutsche Post, Aventis Pharmaceutical, and Microsoft, talking to them about execution problems. I also just participated in a Wharton executive program on strategic management and was debriefing with a few of the participants.

The major point cutting through all the conversations is the importance and difficulty of executing strategy. Two decades after my conversation with Randy Tobias, managers are still emphasizing that execution is a key to success. They are arguing that making strategy work is important and is more difficult than strategy making. Plans still fail or wither on the vine because of poor execution.

The striking aspect of all this is that managers apparently still don't know a great deal about the execution of strategy. It is still seen as a major problem and challenge.

Management literature has focused over the years primarily on parading new ideas on planning and strategy formulation in front of eager readers, but it has sorely neglected execution. Granted, planning is important. Granted, people are waking up to the challenge and are beginning to take execution seriously.

Still, it is obvious that the execution of strategy is not nearly as clear and understood as the formulation of strategy. Much more is known about planning than doing, about strategy making than making strategy work.

Is execution really worth the effort? Is execution or implementation truly a key to strategic success?

Consider one relatively recent comprehensive study of what contributes to company success.[ii] In this study of 160 companies over a five-year period, success was strongly correlated, among other things, with an ability to execute flawlessly. Factors such as culture, organizational structure, and aspects of operational execution were vital to company success, with success measured by total return to shareholders. Other recent works have added their support to this study's finding that execution is important for strategic success, even if their approach and analysis are less rigorous and complete.[iii] These works then, in total, support the view I've held for years:

SOUND EXECUTION IS CRITICAL—A FOCUS ON MAKING STRATEGY WORK PAYS MAJOR DIVIDENDS

Despite its importance, execution is often handled poorly by many organizations. There still are countless cases of good plans going awry because of substandard execution efforts. This raises some important questions.

If execution is central to success, why don't more organizations develop a disciplined approach to it? Why don't companies spend time developing and perfecting processes that help them achieve important strategic outcomes? Why can't more companies execute or implement strategies well and reap the benefits of those efforts?

The simple answer, again, is that execution is extremely difficult. There are formidable roadblocks or hurdles that get in the way of the execution process and seriously injure the implementation of strategy. The road to successful execution is full of potholes that must be negotiated for execution success. This was the message two decades ago, and it still is true today.

Let's identify some of the problems or hurdles affecting implementation. Let's then focus on confronting the obstacles and solving the problems in subsequent chapters of this book.

MANAGERS ARE TRAINED TO PLAN, NOT EXECUTE

One basic problem is that managers know more about strategy formulation than implementation. They are trained to plan, not execute plans.

In most MBA programs I've looked at, students learn a great deal about strategy formulation and functional planning. Core courses typically hone in on competitive strategy, marketing strategy, financial strategy, and so on. The number of courses in most core programs that deal exclusively with execution or implementation? Usually none. Execution is most certainly touched on in a couple of the courses, but not in a dedicated, elaborate, purposeful way. Emphasis clearly is on conceptual work, primarily planning, and not on doing. At Wharton, there is at least an elective on strategy implementation, but this is not typical of many other MBA programs. Even if things are beginning to change, the emphasis still is squarely on planning, not execution.

Added to the lack of training in execution is the fact that strategy and planning in most business schools are taught in "silos," by departments or disciplines, and execution suffers further. The view that marketing strategy, financial strategy, HR strategy, and so on is the only "right" approach is deleterious to the integrative view demanded by execution.

It appears, then, that most MBA programs (undergrad, too, for that matter) are marked by an emphasis on developing strategies, not executing them. Bright graduates are well versed in strategy and planning, with only a passing exposure to execution. Extrapolating this into the real world suggests that there are many managers who have rich conceptual backgrounds and training in planning but not in "doing." The lack of formal attention to strategy execution in the classroom obviously must carry over to a lack of attention and consequent underachievement in the area of execution in the real world.

If this is true—if managers are trained to plan, not to execute—then the successful execution of strategy becomes less likely and more problematic. Execution is learned in the "school of hard knocks," and the pathways to successful results are likely fraught with mistakes and frustrations.

It also follows logically that managers who know something about strategy execution very likely have the advantage over their counterparts who don't.

If managers in one company are better versed in the ways of execution than managers in a competitor organization, isn't it logical to assume, all other things being equal, that the former company may enjoy a competitive advantage over the latter, given the differences in knowledge or capabilities? The benefits of effective execution include competitive advantage and higher returns to shareholders, so having knowledge in this area would clearly seem to be worthwhile and beneficial to the organization.

LET THE "GRUNTS" HANDLE EXECUTION

Another problem is that some C-level and other top-level managers actually believe that strategy execution or implementation is "below them," something best left to lower-level employees. Indeed, the heading of this section comes from an actual quote from a high-level manager.

I was working on implementation programs at GM, under the auspices of Corporate Strategic Planning. In the course of my work, I encountered many competent and dedicated managers. However, I also ran across a few who had a jaundiced view of execution. As one of these managers explained:

> "Top management rightfully worries about planning and strategy formulation. Great care must be taken to develop sound plans. If planning is done well, management then can turn the plans over to the grunts whose job it is to make sure things get done and the work of the planners doesn't go to waste."

What a picture of the planning and execution process! The planners (the "smart" people) develop plans that the "grunts" (not quite as smart) simply have to follow through on and make work. "Doing" obviously involves less ability and intelligence than "planning," a perception of managerial work that clearly demeans the execution process.

The prevailing view here is that one group of managers does innovative, challenging work (planning) and then "hands off the ball" to lower levels for execution. If things go awry and strategic plans are not successful (which often is the case), the problem is placed squarely at the feet of the "doers," who somehow screwed up and couldn't implement a perfectly sound and viable plan. The doers fumbled the ball despite the planners' well-designed plays.

Every organization, of course, has some separation of planning and doing, of formulation and execution. However, when such a separation becomes dysfunctional—when planners see themselves as the smart people and treat the doers as "grunts"—there clearly will be execution problems. When the "elite" plan and see execution as something below them, detracting from their dignity as top managers, the successful implementation of strategy obviously is in jeopardy.

The truth is that all managers are "grunts" when it comes to strategy execution. From the CEO on down, sound execution demands that managers roll up their sleeves and pitch in to make a difference. The content and focus of what they do may vary between top and middle management. Nonetheless, execution demands commitment to and a passion for results, regardless of management level.

Another way of saying this is that execution demands *ownership* at all levels of management. From C-level managers on down, people must commit to and own the processes and actions central to effective execution. Ownership of execution and the change processes vital to execution are necessary for success. Change is impossible without commitment to the decisions and actions that define strategy execution.

The execution of strategy is not a trivial part of managerial work; it defines the essence of that work. Execution is a key responsibility of all managers, not something that "others" do or worry about.

PLANNING AND EXECUTION ARE INTERDEPENDENT

Even though, in reality, there may be a separation of planning and execution tasks, the two are highly interdependent. Planning affects execution. The execution of strategy, in turn, affects changes to strategy and planning over time. This relationship between planning and doing suggests two critical points to keep in mind.

Successful strategic outcomes are best achieved when those responsible for execution are also part of the planning or formulation process. The greater the interaction between "doers" and "planners" or the greater the overlap of the two processes or tasks, the higher the probability of execution success.

A related point is that strategic success demands a "simultaneous" view of planning and doing. Managers must be thinking about execution even as they are formulating plans. Execution is not something to "worry about later." All execution decisions and actions, of course, cannot be taken at once. Execution issues or problem areas must be anticipated, however, as part of a "big picture" dealing with planning and doing. Formulating and executing are parts of an integrated, strategic management approach. This dual or simultaneous view is important but difficult to achieve, and it presents a challenge to effective execution.

Randy Tobias had this simultaneous view of planning and doing. Even as he was formulating a new competitive strategy for his AT&T division, he was anticipating execution challenges. Competitive strategy formulation wasn't seen as occurring in a planning vacuum, isolated from execution issues. Central to the success of strategy was his early identification and appreciation of execution-related factors whose impact on strategic success was judged to be formidable. Execution worries couldn't be put off; they were part and parcel of the planning function.

In contrast, top management at a stumbling Lucent Technologies never had this simultaneous view of planning and execution.

When it was spun off from AT&T, the communications, software, and data networking giant looked like a sure bet to succeed. It had the fabled Bell Labs in its fold. It was ready to hit the ground running and formulate winning competitive strategies. Even as the soaring technology market of the late 1990s helped Lucent and other companies, however, it couldn't entirely mask or eliminate Lucent's problems.

One of the biggest problems was that management didn't anticipate critical execution obstacles as they were formulating strategy. Its parent, Ma Bell, had become bureaucratic and slow moving, and Lucent took this culture with it when it was spun off. The culture didn't serve the company well in a highly competitive, rapidly changing telecom environment, a problem that was not foreseen.

An unwieldy organizational structure, too, was ignored during Lucent's early attempts at strategy development, and it soon became a liability when it came to such matters as product development and time to market. More agile competitors such as Nortel beat Lucent to market, signaling problems with Lucent's ability to pull off its newly developed strategies.

One thing that was lacking at Lucent was top management's having a simultaneous view of planning and doing. The planning phase ignored critical execution issues related to culture, structure, and people. The results of this neglect were extremely negative, only magnified by the market downturns in 2000 and thereafter.

EXECUTION TAKES LONGER THAN FORMULATION

The execution of strategy usually takes longer than the formulation of strategy. Whereas planning may take weeks or months, the implementation of strategy is usually played out over a much longer period of time. The longer time frame can make it harder for managers to focus on and control the execution process, as many things, some unforeseen, can materialize and challenge managers' attention.

Steps taken to execute a strategy take place over time, and many factors, including some unanticipated, come into play. Interest rates may change, competitors don't behave the way they're supposed to (competitors can be notoriously "unfair" at times, not playing by our "rules"!), customers' needs change, and key personnel leave the company. The outcomes of changes in strategy and execution methods cannot always be easily determined because of "noise" or uncontrolled events. This obviously increases the difficulty of execution efforts.

The longer time frame puts pressure on managers dealing with execution. Long-term needs must be translated into short-term objectives. Controls must be set up to provide feedback and keep management abreast of external "shocks" and changes. The process of execution must be dynamic and adaptive, responding to and compensating for unanticipated events. This presents a real challenge to managers and increases the difficulty of strategy execution.

When the DaimlerChrysler merger was consummated in 1998, many believed that the landmark deal would create the world's preeminent carmaker. Execution since has been extremely difficult, however, and the six years after the merger have seen many new problems unfold. The company has faced one crisis after another, including two bouts of heavy losses in the Chrysler division, a series of losses in commercial vehicles, and huge problems with failed investments in an attempted turnaround at debt-burdened Mitsubishi Motors.[iv] Serious culture clashes also materialized between the top-down, formal German culture vs. the more informal and decentralized U.S. company. Angry shareholders at the 2004 meeting created and mirrored internal dissent and issued an ultimatum to Jurgen Schrempp to turn things around fast.

The six years after the merger presented problems unforeseen at the time of the merger. Execution always takes time and places pressure on management for results. But the longer time needed for execution also increases the likelihood of *additional* unforeseen problems or challenges cropping up, which further increases the pressure on managers responsible for execution results. The process of execution is always difficult and sometimes quarrelsome, with problems only exacerbated by the longer time frame usually associated with execution.

EXECUTION IS A PROCESS, NOT AN ACTION OR STEP

A point just made is critical and should be repeated: Execution is a process. It is not the result of a single decision or action. It is the result of a series of integrated decisions or actions over time.

This helps explain why sound execution confers competitive advantage. Firms will try to benchmark a successful execution of strategy. However, if execution involves a series of internally consistent, integrated activities, activity systems, or processes, imitation will be extremely difficult, if not impossible.[v]

Southwest Airlines, for example, does many things differently than most large airlines. It has no baggage transfer, serves no meals, issues no boarding passes, uses one type of airplane (reducing training and maintenance costs), and incents fast turnaround at the gate. It has developed capabilities and created a host of activities to support its low-cost strategy. Other airlines are hard pressed to copy it, as they're already doing everything Southwest isn't. They're committed to different routines and methods. Copying Southwest's execution activities, in total, would involve difficult trade-offs, markedly different tasks, and major changes, which complicates the problem of developing and integrating new execution processes or activities. This is not to say that competitors absolutely cannot copy Southwest; indeed, other low-cost upstarts and traditional airlines are putting increasing competitive pressure on Southwest. This is simply arguing that such imitation is extremely hard to do.

Execution is a process that demands a great deal of attention to make it work. Execution is not a single decision or action. Managers who seek a quick solution to execution problems will surely fail in attempts at making strategy work. Faster is not always better!

EXECUTION INVOLVES MORE PEOPLE THAN STRATEGY FORMULATION DOES

In addition to being played out over longer periods of time, strategy implementation always involves more people than strategy formulation. This presents additional problems. Communication down the organization or across different functions becomes a challenge. Making sure that incentives throughout the organization support strategy execution efforts becomes a necessity and, potentially, a problem. Linking strategic objectives with the day-to-day objectives and concerns of personnel at different organizational levels and locations becomes a legitimate but challenging task. The larger the number of people involved, the greater the challenge of effective strategy execution.

I once was involved in a strategic planning project with a well-known bank. Another project I wasn't directly involved in had previously recommended a new program to increase the number of retail customers who used certain profitable products and services.

A strategy was articulated and a plan of execution developed to educate key personnel and to set goals consistent with the new thrust. Branch managers and others dealing with customers were brought in to corporate for training and to create widespread enthusiasm for the program.

After a few months, the data revealed that not much had changed. It clearly was business as usual, with no change in the outcomes that were being targeted by the new program. The bank decided to do a brief survey to canvas customers and branch personnel in contact with customers to determine reactions to the program and see where modifications could be made.

The results were shocking, as you've probably guessed. Few people knew about the program. Some tellers and branch personnel did mention that they had heard about "something new," but nothing different was introduced to their daily routines. A few said that the new program was probably just a rumor, as nothing substantial had ever been implemented. Others suggested that rumors were always circulating, and they never knew what was real or bogus.

Communication and follow-through for the new program were obviously inadequate, but the bank admittedly faced a daunting task. It was a big bank. It had many employees at the branch level. Educating them and changing their behaviors was made extremely difficult by the bank's size. Decentralized branch operations ensured that problems were always "popping up" in the field, challenging employees' attention and making it difficult to introduce new ideas from corporate to a large group of employees.

In this example, the number of people who needed to be involved in the implementation of a new program presented a major challenge to the bank management. One can easily imagine the communications problems in even larger, geographically dispersed companies such as GM, IBM, Deutsche Post, GE, Exxon, Nestlé, Citicorp, and ABB. The number of people involved, added to the longer time frames generally associated with strategy execution, clearly creates problems when trying to make strategy work.

ADDITIONAL CHALLENGES AND OBSTACLES TO SUCCESSFUL EXECUTION

The issues previously noted are serious, potentially impeding execution. Yet there are still other challenges and obstacles to the successful implementation of strategy. These need to be identified and confronted if execution is to succeed.

To find out what problems managers routinely encounter in the execution of strategy, I developed two research projects to provide some answers. My goal was to learn about execution from those most qualified to give me the scoop—managers actually dealing with strategy execution. I could have relied solely on my own consulting experiences. I felt, however, that a more widespread approach—surveys directed toward many practicing managers— would yield additional positive results and useful insights into execution issues.

WHARTON-GARTNER SURVEY

This was a joint project involving the Gartner Group, Inc., a well-known research organization, and me, a Wharton professor. This is a relatively recent project, with data collection and analysis in 2003.

The purpose of the research, from the Gartner introduction, was as follows:

"To gain a clear understanding of challenges faced by managers as they make decisions and take actions to execute their company's strategy to gain competitive advantage."

The research instrument was a short online survey sent to 1,000 individuals on the Gartner E-Panel database. The targeted sample comprised managers who reported that they were involved in strategy formulation and execution. Complete usable responses were received from a sample of 243 individuals, a return rate that is more than sufficient for this type of research. In addition, the survey collected responses to open-ended questions to provide additional data, including explanations of items covered in the survey instrument.

There were 12 items on the survey dealing with obstacles to the strategy-execution process. They focused on conditions that affect execution and were originally developed in conjunction with a Wharton Executive Development Program on strategy implementation. Let's briefly consider this program and the survey it generated, and then we'll look at the items involved.

WHARTON EXECUTIVE EDUCATION SURVEY

I have been running an executive program on strategy implementation at Wharton a number of times a year for about 20 years. I have met hundreds of managers with responsibility for strategy execution, many of whom confronted major hurdles in their attempts to execute strategy successfully. As part of the formal program, managers brought their real-world problems with them. Time was allocated to air out the problems and focus on their solution in the course of the program.

Based on these presentations and my discussions with managers, I developed a list of execution hurdles or challenges to the execution process. I discussed this list with managers, asking them to rank the problems or obstacles in order of importance. Over time, items were modified, added to, or deleted from the list until I settled on 12 items that made sense and had "face" validity. These items, managers felt, clearly had a relationship to strategy execution.

Using the 12 items to gather opinions over a large number of executive education programs provided me with responses from a sample of 200 managers. They provided a ranking of the items' impact on strategy execution. Open-ended responses to questions about execution issues, problems, and opportunities were also collected over time, providing additional valuable data. Coupled with the data collected in the Wharton-Gartner Survey using the same 12 items, I had complete responses from more than 400 managers involved in strategy execution who told me about their execution problems and their solutions to them.

PANEL DISCUSSIONS

In subsequent Wharton executive programs after the data collection, I held informal panel discussions to collect additional insights into what the data were actually saying. I asked managers why, in their opinion, people responded the way they did. "What are the surveys telling us about execution problems or issues?" was the predominant question.

These discussions forced managers to read between the lines and interpret the formal data. They also enabled me to probe into what could be done to overcome the obstacles and achieve successful execution outcomes. Insights were collected, then, not only on the sources of execution problems but their *solutions* as well.

The surveys and follow-up discussions provided data right from "the horse's mouth." These were not idiosyncratic data, the opinions or observations of a few managers or CEOs who, against all odds, "did it their way." The number of managers providing answers, coupled with an emphasis on real problems and solutions, added a strong sense of relevance to the opinions gathered about strategy execution.

THE RESULTS: OPINIONS ABOUT SUCCESSFUL STRATEGY EXECUTION

Table 1.1 shows the results of the surveys. The 12 items are shown, with the respective rank orderings for the Wharton-Gartner Survey and the Wharton Executive Education Survey. (The actual questionnaire, for those interested, appears in the appendix to this book.)

Table 1.1 Obstacles to Strategy Execution

Obstacles	Wharton-Gartner Survey (n = 243)	Rankings Wharton-Executive Education Survey (n = 200)	Either Survey Top 5 Rankings
1. Inability to manage change effectively or to overcome internal resistance to change	1	1	✓
2. Trying to execute a strategy that conflicts with the existing power structure	2	5	✓
3. Poor or inadequate information sharing between individuals or business units responsible for strategy execution	2	4	✓
4. Unclear communication of responsibility and/or accountability for execution decisions or actions	4	5	✓
5. Poor or vague strategy	5	2	✓
6. Lack of feelings of "ownership" of a strategy or execution plans among key employees	5	8	✓
7. Not having guidelines or a model to guide strategy-execution efforts	7	2	✓
8. Lack of understanding of the role of organizational structure and design in the execution process	9	5	✓
9. Inability to generate "buy-in" or agreement on critical execution steps or actions	7	10	
10. Lack of incentives or inappropriate incentives to support execution objectives	9	8	
11. Insufficient financial resources to execute the strategy	11	12	
12. Lack of upper-management support of strategy execution	12	11	

It is obvious that there is strong agreement on some of the items. The importance of managing change well, including cultural change, is first on both surveys. Inability to manage change effectively clearly is seen as injurious to strategy-execution efforts. Although culture was not mentioned explicitly in the item, the open-ended responses and panel discussions placed culture at the core of many change-related problems. To many of the respondents, "change" and" "culture change" were synonymous.

Trying to execute a strategy that conflicts with the prevailing power structure clearly is doomed to failure, according to the managers surveyed. Confronting those with influence at different organizational levels who disagree with an execution plan surely will have unhappy results in most cases.

Poor sharing of information or poor knowledge transfer and unclear responsibility and accountability also can doom strategy-execution attempts. These two items suggest that attempts at coordination or integration across organizational units can suffer if unclear responsibilities and poor sharing of vital information needed for execution is the rule. Again, this makes sense because complex strategies often demand cooperation and effective coordination and information sharing. Not achieving the requisite knowledge transfer and integration certainly cannot help the execution of these strategies.

There is also agreement on the unimportance of some of the items. Both survey groups clearly agreed that a lack of upper-management support and insufficient financial resources were not major problems for strategy execution in their organizations. These results were extremely surprising, so I pursued them further.

Presenting these results to managers in the panel discussions helped clarify the findings. Basically, the story is that top-management support and adequate financial resources are absolutely critical, but that support is primarily manifested during a planning stage, when deciding on execution plans and methods. Commitment to plans of actions and commitment of resources occur as part of planning, so they are "givens," predetermined inputs to the execution process.

Execution plans and activities already have the blessing and approval of top management, and commitment of the requisite resources has already been made. Occasionally, top management may renege on its support during execution, but managers said that this was the exception, not the rule.

This explains, then, why the items dealing with financial support and top management buy-in were rated as only minor execution problems, not serious obstacles. The issues related to support and commitment had already been confronted and resolved, according to the managers interviewed. They definitely are saying, however, that had the blessing of top management not been attained, execution success would be far less probable, if not impossible, to achieve. Given that buy-in and financial support were a reality and in place, the focus could turn to other execution tasks and activities.

It is important to note, too, that top management and financial support are seen by managers as different issues than the power issue previously reported as significant for execution. Power has a broader and more pervasive influence than financial allocations, although there clearly is some relationship. Even after the approval of an execution project and the attendant budget allocations, power and social influence come into play and can affect execution. Managers were adamant in their opinion that, while power certainly includes elements of hierarchy and budgeting, power differences are deeper, more complex, and permeate the entire organization, regardless of hierarchical level.

There are some differences between managers in the two surveys on a few of the items. Having a "poor or vague strategy," for example, was ranked as the second biggest execution obstacle by the Wharton Executive Education group, but it was ranked fifth by the Wharton-Gartner managers. "Not having a model or guidelines to guide strategy execution efforts" was ranked as the second biggest obstacle by the Executive Education group but was seventh in the Wharton-Gartner Survey. There were also small perceived differences on the importance of organizational structure or design in the execution process.

Why the differences? It may be due in part to the makeup of the samples in the two surveys. The Wharton-Gartner Survey tapped the opinions of managers, some of whom, we can infer, were successful in execution and some of whom weren't. Surely, some of the individuals sampled were successful in their implementation efforts, meaning they weren't having problems.

In contrast, many of the managers in the Executive Education Survey attended the Wharton program because they were having actual execution problems. They came to the program to help solve them and to overcome real implementation obstacles. Their focus was clearly on righting or avoiding execution mistakes. They could see problems, say, with organizational structure or not having a model to guide execution efforts, whereas managers in the Wharton-Gartner Survey may have already overcome those problems and, hence, ranked them lower in importance. Whatever the reason, there were some differences between the two groups.

POOR EXECUTION OUTCOMES

There was strong agreement between the research groups on the impact of the execution problems on performance results. In addition to "not achieving desired execution outcomes or objectives," managers in the surveys ranked a few additional results of poor execution methods as being highly problematical. These include the following:

- Employees don't understand how their jobs contribute to important execution outcomes.
- Time and money are wasted because of inefficiency or bureaucracy in the execution process.
- Execution decisions take too long to make.
- The company reacts slowly or inappropriately to competitive pressures.

These are not trivial issues. Execution problems can cost the organization dearly. Time and money are wasted, and a company can face serious competitive setbacks because of an inability to respond to market or customer demands. Execution problems must be addressed, but which ones and in what order?

MAKING SENSE OF THE DATA AND GOING FORWARD

Given the responses from managers just noted, what does all this mean? What really affects execution? What should we focus on in subsequent chapters of this book?

The first thing I did to answer these questions was to include all items that were ranked fifth or higher in either or both samples of managers. If either or both groups felt that strongly about an execution obstacle, I felt that the item deserved consideration. The far right-hand column in Table 1.1 shows checkmarks by these items.

Second, I looked to the open-ended responses, panel discussions, and my own notes taken during the Wharton programs and panel discussions to flesh out the items in Table 1.1. This proved to be enlightening. I determined easily that "managing change" included managing cultural change to many of the respondents, a point emphasized earlier. The impact of culture itself on execution and company performance was often emphasized, even though culture was not one of the 12 survey items. Managers basically said that culture was an underlying explanatory element in responses dealing with incentives, power, and change, items that were included in the survey. Some argued strongly for the importance of culture as a separate factor affecting execution success.

From these discussions and open-ended responses, I learned why there were many strong comments for certain items, such as the need for an execution model or plan. If a plan existed to guide execution efforts in their company, managers did not rank it as a significant problem. If such a plan didn't exist, it was considered to be a major shortcoming that gave rise to yet additional problems in the execution process.

I read and heard the lamentations of many about execution problems that arise from poor strategy or inadequate planning. Vague strategies cannot easily be translated into the measurable objectives or metrics so vital to execution. Unclear corporate and business plans inhibit integration of objectives, activities, and strategies between corporate and business levels. Poor strategies result in poor execution plans. Points such as these derived from the panel discussions and open-ended responses provided helpful insights into the meaning of the survey items and the factors affecting execution.

Finally, managers told me about the importance of controls or feedback in the execution process. What they were emphasizing is the importance of strategy reviews that provide feedback about performance and allow for changes in execution methods. These points are consistent with the importance of managing change and organizational adaptation, issues already discussed, but the managers' additional emphasis on the importance of controls, feedback, and change were duly noted.

After carefully examining all the data, I then tried to "cluster" the items logically to see which obstacles to successful execution seemed to "stick together." Here is my take on what the data seem to be saying.

THE EXECUTION CHALLENGE

There are eight areas of obstacles or challenges to strategy execution. Or, to put it positively, there are eight areas of opportunity: Handling them well will guarantee execution success. The areas relating to the success of execution are as follows:

1. Developing a model to guide execution decisions or actions
2. Understanding how the creation of strategy affects the execution of strategy
3. Managing change effectively, including culture change
4. Understanding power or influence and using it for execution success
5. Developing organizational structures that foster information sharing, coordination, and clear accountability
6. Developing effective controls and feedback mechanisms
7. Knowing how to create an execution-supportive culture
8. Exercising execution-biased leadership

HAVING A MODEL OR GUIDELINES FOR EXECUTION

Managers need a logical model to guide execution actions.

Without guidelines, execution becomes a helter-skelter affair. Without guidance, individuals do the things they think are important, often resulting in uncoordinated, divergent, even conflicting decisions and actions. Without the benefit of a logical approach, execution suffers or fails because managers don't know what steps to take and when to take them. Having a model or roadmap positively affects execution success.

STRATEGY IS THE PRIMARY DRIVER

It all begins with strategy. Execution cannot occur until one has something to execute. Bad strategy begets poor execution and poor outcomes, so it's important to focus first on a sound strategy.

Good people are important for execution. It is vital to get the "right people on the bus, the wrong people off the bus," so to speak. But it's also important to know where the bus is going and why. Strategy is critical. It drives the development of capabilities and which people with what skills sit in what seats on the bus. If one substitutes "jet airplane" for "bus" above—given today's high-flying, competitive markets—the importance of strategy, direction, and the requisite critical skills and capabilities necessary for success are emphasized even more.

Strategy defines the arena (customers, markets, technologies, products, logistics) in which the execution game is played. Execution is an empty effort without the guidance of strategy and short-term objectives related to strategy. What aspects of strategy and planning impact execution outcomes the most is a critical question that needs answering. Another critical question deals with the relationship between corporate- and business-level strategies and how their interaction affects execution outcomes.

MANAGING CHANGE

Execution or strategy implementation often involves change. Not handling change well will spell disaster for execution efforts.

Managing change means much more than keeping people happy and reducing resistance to new ideas and methods. It also means knowing the tactics or steps needed to manage the execution process over time. Do managers implement change sequentially, bit by bit, or do they do everything at once, biting the bullet and implementing change in one fell swoop? The wrong answer can seriously hamper or kill execution efforts. Knowing how to manage the execution process and related changes over time is important for execution success.

THE POWER STRUCTURE

Execution programs that contradict the power or influence structure of an organization are doomed to failure. But what affects power or influence? Power is more than individual personality or position. Power reflects strategy, structure, and critical dependencies on capabilities and scarce resources. Knowing what power is and how to create and use influence can spell the difference between execution success and failure.

COORDINATION AND INFORMATION SHARING

These are vital to effective execution. Knowing how to achieve coordination and information sharing in complex, geographically dispersed organizations is important to execution success. Yet managers are often motivated *not* to share information or work with their colleagues to coordinate activities and achieve strategic and short-term goals. Why? The answer to this question is vital to the successful execution of strategy.

CLEAR RESPONSIBILITY AND ACCOUNTABILITY

This is one of the most important prerequisites for successful execution, as basic as it sounds. Managers must know who's doing what, when, and why, as well as who's accountable for key steps in the execution process. Without clear responsibility and accountability, execution programs will go nowhere. Knowing how to achieve this clarity is central to execution success.

THE RIGHT CULTURE

Organizations must develop execution-supportive cultures. Execution demands a culture of achievement, discipline, and ownership. But developing or changing culture is no easy task. Rock climbing, white-water rafting, paint-gun battles, and other activities with the management team are fun. They rarely, however, produce lasting cultural change. Knowing what does affect cultural change is central to execution success.

LEADERSHIP

Leadership must be execution biased. It must drive the organization to execution success. It must motivate ownership of and commitment to the execution process.

Leadership affects how organizations respond to all of the preceding execution challenges. It is always at least implied when discussing what actions or decisions are necessary to make strategy work. A complete analysis of execution steps and decisions usually defines what good leadership is and how it affects execution success, directly or indirectly.

CONTROLS, FEEDBACK, AND ADAPTATION

Strategy execution processes support organizational change and adaptation. Making strategy work requires feedback about organizational performance and then using that information to fine-tune strategy, objectives, and the execution process itself. There is an emergent aspect of strategy and execution, as organizations learn and adapt to environmental changes over time. Adaptation and change depend on effective execution methods.

As important as controls and feedback are, they often don't work. Control processes fail. They don't identify and confront the brutal facts underlying poor performance. Adaptation is haphazard or incomplete. Understanding how to manage feedback, strategy reviews, and change is vital to the success of strategy execution.

These are the issues that impact the success or failure of strategy-execution efforts. Coupled with the issues previously mentioned (longer time frames, involvement of many people, and so on), these are the areas that present formidable obstacles to successful execution if they are not handled properly. They also present opportunities for competitive advantage if they are understood and managed well.

The last words, "managed well," hold the key to success. Knowing the obstacles or potential opportunities is necessary but not sufficient. The real issue is how to deal with them to generate positive execution results. The major significant point or thrust of this chapter is that execution is not managed well in most organizations. The remainder of this book is dedicated to correcting this woeful situation.

THE NEXT STEP: DEVELOPING A LOGICAL APPROACH TO EXECUTION DECISIONS AND ACTIONS

So where and how does one begin to confront the issues just noted? Which execution problems or opportunities should managers consider first? What decisions or actions come later? Why? Can an approach to strategy execution be developed to guide managers through the maze of obstacles and problematical issues just identified?

The next chapter begins to tackle these questions. It presents an overview, a conceptual framework to guide execution decisions and actions. Managers need such a model because they routinely face a bewildering set of decisions about a host of strategic and operating problems, including those dealing with execution. They need guidelines, a "roadmap" to steer them logically to execution success.

Priorities are also needed. Tackling too many execution decisions or actions at once will surely create problems. "When everything is important, then nothing is important," is a clear but simple way of expressing the issue. Priorities must be set and a logical order to execution actions adequately defined if execution is to succeed.

Having a model, finally, also facilitates a "simultaneous" view of planning and doing. All execution actions cannot be taken at once; some must precede others logically. A good overview or model, however, provides a "big picture" that enables managers to see and anticipate execution problems. Execution is not something that others should worry about later. Planning requires anticipating early on what must be done to make strategy work.

Development of a logical overview is a step that has been ignored by practitioners, academics, and management consultants alike. Execution problems or issues typically have been handled separately or in an ad-hoc fashion, supported by a few anecdotes or case studies. This is not sufficient. Execution is too complex to be approached without guidelines or a roadmap.

Managers cannot act in a helter-skelter fashion when executing strategy. They can't focus one day on organizational structure, the next on culture, and then on to "good people," only to find out that strategy is vague or severely flawed. They need guidelines, a way to see and approach execution and the logical order of the key variables involved. A roadmap is needed to guide them through the minefields of bad execution decisions and actions. Managers require a "big picture" as well as an understanding of the "nitty-gritty," the key elements that comprise the big picture.

The next chapter tackles the essential task of providing this overview by showing the order and logic of key execution decisions. It begins to confront the obstacles identified in this chapter as it lays out this sequence of decisions or actions. These decisions and actions simultaneously define the areas needing additional attention in later chapters of this book. Having a model of execution is vital to making strategy work, so let's take this important and necessary step.

SUMMARY

- Execution is a key to strategic success. Most managers, however, know a lot more about strategy formulation than execution. They know much more about "planning" than "doing," which causes major problems with making strategy work.

- Strategy execution is difficult but worthy of management's attention across all levels of an organization. All managers bear responsibility for successful execution. It is not just a lower-level task.

- Part of the difficulty of execution is due to the obstacles or impediments to it. These include the longer time frames needed for execution; the need for involvement of many people in the execution process; poor or vague strategy; conflicts with the organizational power structure; poor or inadequate sharing of information; a lack of understanding of organizational structure, including information sharing and coordination methods; unclear responsibility and accountability in the execution process; and an inability to manage change, including cultural change.

- Knowing execution hazards (opportunities) is necessary but not sufficient. For successful execution to occur, managers need a model or a set of guidelines outlining the entire process and relationships among key decisions or actions. A "roadmap" is needed to help with the order of execution decisions as managers confront obstacles and take advantage of opportunities.

- This overview of execution is vital to success and is developed in the next chapter. Subsequent chapters can borrow from this model and focus more specifically on aspects of it to achieve positive execution results.

ENDNOTES

i. For those interested in an informative memoir about Randy Tobias's career, his many experiences (especially as CEO of Eli Lilly), and his views on effective leadership, I suggest you read *Put the Moose on the Table* by Randall Tobias with Todd Tobias, Indiana Press, 2003.

ii. William Joyce, Nitin Nohria, and Bruce Roberson, *What (Really) Works,* Harper Business, 2003.

iii. See Jim Collins, *Good to Great,* Harper Business, 2001; Larry Bossidy and Ram Charan, *Execution,* Crown Business, 2002; and Amir Hartman, *Ruthless Execution,* Prentice Hall, 2004.

iv. "Daimler CEO Defends Strategy, Reign," *The Wall Street Journal,* May 6, 2004.

v. For a good discussion of how a series of integrated activities, activity systems, or processes thwarts imitation and leads to competitive advantage, see Michael Porter's "What is Strategy" in the *Harvard Business Review,* November-December, 1996.

2

Overview and Model: Making Strategy Work

Introduction

Chapter 1 emphasized the fact that strategy execution is extremely difficult. It also argued that most managers know much more about planning or strategy making than about "doing" or making strategy work.

There are many obstacles to execution that, taken together, present a formidable challenge and contribute to poor execution, as the preceding chapter indicated. One of these is that managers often suffer from not having a conceptual framework or a model to guide execution efforts.

The lack of a model, blueprint, or template to shape execution decisions or actions is a major obstacle to making strategy work. Managers need a roadmap to guide execution. "Tell us what to do, when, and in what order," is the request. Without a guide or model, execution efforts simply cannot proceed in a logical way. Without a model, it is difficult to develop a sound plan of execution.

Managers often tell me that they thirst for a good blueprint for execution. They also tell me that anecdotes or "war stories" aren't enough. Stories and anecdotes about execution are always interesting, and they sometimes hold implications for the practice of management. Yet stories and anecdotes alone simply cannot explain the complex issues affecting the execution of strategy that were identified in the preceding chapter. Making strategy work requires more than a handful of managerial sound bites. It requires a template to guide thought and effort in a logical, systematic way.

The purpose of this chapter is to provide a conceptual framework or model of the strategy-execution process. The goal of this chapter is twofold. First, it provides a guide to execution, a "big-picture" view showing how key decisions and actions relate to each other in a logical way. Chapter 1 identified the eight key issues or challenges that affect execution. Rather than immediately handling each of the issues separately, as if each were totally independent of the others, the intention presently is to show first how the issues are *interdependent*—how they relate to each other—and how they come together to define a coordinated approach to execution. This is an important first step in attacking the complexities involved in making strategy work.

Second, this chapter identifies the critical topics or factors that will be considered in detail in subsequent chapters. Presenting a logical overview of execution is the present goal, with the needed details coming later.

Before presenting this blueprint or model, it is necessary to emphasize two points relating to its use.

COMMON VS. UNIQUE EXECUTION SOLUTIONS

The first point is that the guide to execution that follows can be applied across the board in virtually all organizations and industry settings. It is meant to provide a useful overview of execution decisions and actions to help management in an industrial- or consumer-products company or a service business. It can provide guidance to the president of a large university or the head of a nonprofit organization. The overview can help the CEO of a large or small company.

The model presents an approach that identifies common critical execution issues that, if ignored, will lead to execution difficulties. This alone is valuable. This "25,000-foot view" offers an important integrative perspective to help the reader understand the logic of the entire execution process as it plays out consistently in different organizations.

It is also necessary to note, however, that the importance of specific decisions or actions in the model can vary from organization to organization. Each strategy and its demands are in some way unique, given such factors as company culture, history, competition, growth patterns, competencies, and previous successes and failures. Consequently, different organizations may need to place emphasis on different parts of a common roadmap at a given point in time. Execution problems and solutions can vary, even among organizations using the same model or set of guidelines.

These differences in no way negate the value of the general model and its execution guidelines. The model provides the structure, the "menu," that identifies key execution decisions or actions that all organizations must confront and handle. That the importance of certain decisions and actions varies among organizations at any point in time in no way detracts from the importance of the menu and its overview of execution needs. The menu lists the choices that managers must analyze as they face and solve their execution problems.

A NEED FOR ACTION

The execution of strategy takes place in the real world of management. It is concerned not only with questions of "why" but also of "how." Managers are rewarded for "doing" as well as "knowing," "snowball throwing" as well as "snowball making."[i] This places the constraint of "action" on any approach to executing strategy, if it is to be useful.

For an approach to be action oriented, it must emphasize variables that can be manipulated or changed. Effective managerial action assumes that key variables are under a manager's control; without this, there is nothing to manage. It is important to lay out an approach to execution that focuses as much as possible on measurable, manipulable factors and that has a direct relation to managerial action and decision-making.

To be action oriented, a model must also be prescriptive. It must tell us what should be done, when, why, and in what order. A model is action oriented and useful if it identifies how execution decisions should logically be made.

In the real world, aberrations from a logical model can always be found. As is emphasized in Chapter 4, for example, strategy should logically affect the choice of organizational structure. Structure, that is, should reflect and be consistent with the strategy an organization is pursuing.

Does structure always follow strategy logically in the real world? Do certain structural units or divisions occasionally become so powerful that they reverse the model and drive the choice of strategy? The answers, of course, are "no" and "yes," respectively.

But aberrations from a model do not negate it or its usefulness. It still is important to know what should be done, when, why, and in what order.

A good model helps us understand why and where aberrations actually occur so that corrections or changes can be made. In the preceding example, structure affected strategy because of the influence of a "powerful" unit. Power, that is, can affect execution, with good and bad results. It is vital, then, to understand power and include its effects when using the model. The existence of power does not negate the validity or usefulness of the model. Aberrations from the template must be explained, but they certainly don't destroy its basic logic or utility.

This chapter can now turn to an overview of strategy execution. It addresses many of the obstacles and concerns noted in Chapter 1 as it develops a logical, action-oriented approach to execution.

These obstacles and concerns will be analyzed separately and in depth in later chapters. The purpose presently is to show how they relate to each other in the execution process.

A MODEL OF STRATEGY EXECUTION

Figure 2.1 presents a model of the strategy-execution process.[ii] A few general observations are in order before getting into its details.

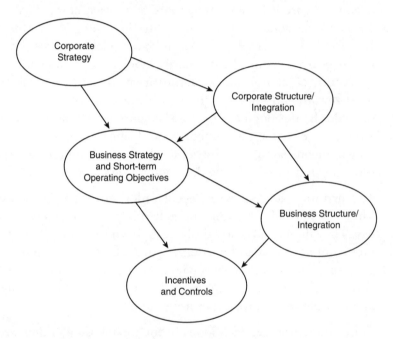

Figure 2.1   Executing Strategy: Key Decisions and Actions

First, strategy is important. Managers in the surveys mentioned in Chapter 1 identified "poor or vague strategy" as a major impediment to sound execution. A clear, focused strategy is necessary for effective execution.[iii] One cannot talk of execution without focusing first on sound strategy formulation. Strategy formulation and execution are separate, identifiable activities or processes. Yet they are highly interdependent. Good planning aids the execution process. Similarly, poor planning begets poor implementation.

Some managers may disagree and argue that good execution can compensate for bad strategy or poor planning. My experience, however, generally proves otherwise. Executing bad strategy is usually a losing proposition. Poor planning usually steers the execution process into troubled waters that become increasingly difficult to navigate. It should not be surprising, then, that Figure 2.1 includes corporate and business strategy formulation in an overview of strategy execution.

Second, Figure 2.1 shows that there is a logical flow of execution decisions or actions. The arrows in the figure show this flow. Incentives, for example, are last in the model because they must be. Incentives cannot be set until prior decisions about strategy, short-term objectives, and structure are made. Logically, incentives must reward and reinforce the right decisions, which must clearly precede the development of those incentives. Similarly, corporate strategy is of paramount importance. If the strategy of a business unit is inconsistent with (or contradictory to) corporate strategy, the latter must prevail. The dog should wag its tail, not vice versa.

The arrows, then, show a logical order to execution decisions. They show which decisions precede others when executing strategy. They do *not* suggest a unilateral, downward-only flow of communication or a lack of participation. As is stressed often in later chapters, execution involves participation and communication up and down the organization, as well as lateral flows of information and coordination across operating units.

Third, there are feedback loops in the model, though they are not obvious. The "controls" portion of the model comprises feedback and change. Execution is a dynamic, adaptive process, leading to organizational learning. For learning and change to occur, feedback about performance against strategic and short-term objectives is necessary. It must come from managers at all levels: from the C-level suites, from regional or district offices, and from people dealing with customers or walking around on the production floor.

An effective model of execution emphasizes both action and reaction. It must be dynamic, allowing for feedback and adaptation. The present model is not static by any means, a notion I wish to stress strongly at the outset.

CORPORATE STRATEGY

The model in Figure 2.1 begins with corporate strategy. GE, ABB, Citicorp, and Becton Dickinson have corporate strategies, and their many businesses also formulate strategy in a search for competitive advantage in their respective industries. The University of Pennsylvania has a "corporate" planning function, while its colleges or "businesses" create plans to deal with their own competitive settings.

Corporate strategy is concerned with the entire organization, focusing on such areas as portfolio management, diversification, and resource allocations across the businesses or operating units that make up the total enterprise. In a corporation, the levels of strategy and associated tasks would look like the following:

Level	Examples of Issues or Tasks
Corporate strategy	■ Portfolio management
	■ Diversifications, including vertical integration
	■ Resource allocations across businesses
Business, divisional, or SBU strategy	■ Which products and services to offer
	■ How to compete
	■ Achieving competitive advantage in an industry
	■ How to differentiate the firm in a given market
Strategy within businesses	■ Functional plans

This book will simply use the terms "corporate" and "business" strategy. The former refers to or reflects decisions for the total enterprise, decisions or actions that cut across businesses (divisions, colleges, strategic business units [SBUs]), whereas the latter represents strategy for the businesses and major operating units within them.

The present model, again, begins logically with corporate strategy. At this level, decisions are made as to what businesses or industries should make up the corporate portfolio. Diversification via acquisition adds organizations to the portfolio, and divestitures eliminate them. Vertical integration typically increases not only the number of companies in the portfolio, but also the number of industries in which the corporation competes. Corporate choices clearly affect the number of operating companies or units in the organization.

Corporate strategists also must decide how to allocate resources across the businesses or operating units, given differences in competitive conditions and growth possibilities across industries. This resource allocation or investment process is critical because it affects strategy execution at both the corporate and business levels.

What decisions or actions affect the execution of corporate strategy? Figure 2.1 and the preceding discussion suggest that there are two key areas to focus on when executing corporate strategy: corporate structure and business strategy. Let's consider each in turn.

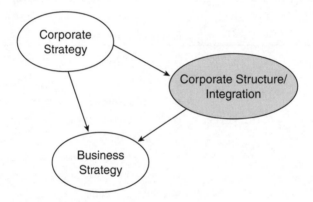

CORPORATE STRUCTURE

Corporate structure, the second element in the model, refers to the organizational units created in response to the demands of corporate strategy. Organizational structure depicts the major pieces or operating units that make up the entire enterprise. Figure 2.1 indicates that the creation of organizational structure is important to the execution of corporate strategy. What is the logic here?

To answer the question, consider the case of diversification as a corporate growth strategy. Mergers and acquisitions are a big business. In 2003, $1.2 trillion in mergers were consummated by investment banks. This is below the figure in the record year of

2000 when close to $3 trillion in mergers were arranged, but it still is significant. The sad truth, however, is that corporate mergers often don't work. Between 1985 and 2000, 64 percent were marked by a drop in shareholder value. What accounts for this poor showing?

Consider just one example: related diversification in the banking industry, where acquisitions and consolidation have been routinely occurring. Bank A buys Bank B, the stated goal usually being increased size, market penetration, and the benefits that follow logically from scale, such as the synergies or economies generally associated with scale. For example, announcement of the intended Bank of America–Fleet merger on March 18, 2004, creating the third largest bank in the United States, defined the goals of the mega-merger. Predictably, they included cost reductions, elimination of redundancies, scale economies related to size, and better customer service.

To achieve synergies and scale economies, however, the banks must be melded into one organization. Duplications must be eliminated. One marketing group, smaller than the combined groups of the separate banks, can do the same work much more efficiently. Similarly, elimination of some bank branches can make the structure leaner and less costly, but with the same capacity to service the market. Finally, one set of back-room operations can replace the original two separate operations, doing the same work with larger scale and resultant efficiencies.

To execute the bank's strategy of related diversification, then, structural change is necessary. Execution of corporate strategy relies in part on the appropriate structure to support it. The failure of so many mergers in banking and other industries to deliver on their promises suggests that these structural changes simply haven't been done well.[iv] To be sure, other factors come into play when explaining poor performance, such as the premium prices paid for acquisitions. Still, given the nature of this form of diversification, structural integration is vital, and poor integration will lead to poor performance. Structure does affect the execution of corporate strategy.

Consider next a strategy of vertical integration. One company buys another company that has proven its worth in a competitive industry. The company is bought because of its capabilities or its record as a moneymaker, a solid foundation for the strategic corporate decision.

An actual case still receiving a great deal of attention years later is Disney's acquisition of ABC. This was a case of forward integration, as a content producer (movies, animated features) bought a TV station to control distribution for its product. The acquisition seemed to make sense: Content that lacks distribution is virtually worthless, but a distribution capability is nothing if access to solid content is missing. The acquisition of ABC by Disney thus seemed like a good marriage of content and distribution.

But what comes next? What is needed to execute the vertical-integration strategy? One important decision deals with organizational structure. Corporate can leave its acquisition as a separate, independent profit center, or it can meld it into an existing division or function. The former choice lets the acquired company continue to function as it did before as a viable force in its own industry. The latter makes it a captive unit, part of a functional area or existing business.

Disney faced a tough structural choice after it bought ABC. Should it meld it tightly into the Disney structure, exert control, and increase its say over how ABC operates? If so, ABC might be seen as a pawn of Disney. This would upset ABC's management and perhaps drive away other content producers (such as Dreamworks) who perceive that giving business to ABC only feeds a major competitor's ample treasury.

On the other hand, letting ABC function independently as a profit center might mean that ABC could reject Disney's content, especially "dogs," movies or shows that Disney would try to foist on ABC because no other networks or cable stations were interested. Also, as an independent, ABC could show "leading-edge" or adult programming that conflicts with Disney's wholesome, family orientation, thus hurting its corporate image.

What should Disney or any corporation do? What form should the structure take? The answer depends on corporate strategy and its attendant goals. What the acquirer hopes to achieve from vertical integration will drive the structural position of the acquired company. A desire for cost controls or synergies would lead to more control and structural integration of an acquisition. A need for an effective presence and growth in a different competitive market would opt for decentralization and an independent profit center.

Critics of Disney and Michael Eisner argue that the company never extracted the expected synergies from the acquisition of ABC. ABC was given too loose a rein, according to these critics, and the Disney-ABC combination never fulfilled its promises. A strategy-structure fit just never materialized. Other factors again surely affected success of the execution process—such as the price paid and cultural differences—but the lack of structural integration clearly was seen as one of Eisner's and the merger's shortcomings.

The Disney example raises the age-old issue of centralization and decentralization of organizational structure. Over time, the corporation creates or acquires the businesses that make up and define the organization. Some corporate acquisitions become relatively independent, decentralized units competing in different industries. Yet there may be activities or functions that cut across different businesses that allow for centralization, reduced duplication of resources, and the scale economies so often sought by corporate strategists. Different businesses must be sufficiently independent to respond quickly to market demands, competitors' actions, and customer needs. Yet they can't be so independent as to create an unnecessary duplication of resources and destroy all chances for synergies or scale economies across businesses. The corporation, then, must create the right balance of centralization and decentralization to execute its strategy and achieve its strategic goals.

Looking at the real world provides countless examples of trying to achieve this structural balance. GE, Philip Morris, GM, Johnson and Johnson (J&J), Microsoft, Citicorp, Merck, Glaxo-Smithkline, and so on, are characterized by corporate-level shared resources that define the "corporate center." Simultaneously, they are decentralized around business units that compete in different industries, product markets, or geographical areas, usually with large amounts of autonomy and local control in a decentralized structure. Similarly, universities are marked by decentralized units (colleges) but have centralized staff functions such as HR that service all colleges to avoid duplication and generate cost savings.

How a company is organized clearly depends on and is related to corporate strategy. Structure is important to the execution of corporate strategy, a point fleshed out in greater detail in Chapter 4.

NEED FOR INTEGRATION

The integration component of corporate structure noted in Figure 2.1 refers to the methods used to achieve coordination across the units comprising organizational structure.

Decisions about structure result in different units focusing on different tasks or specialties. To achieve a unity of effort and combine the activities of these diverse units, formal attention to integrative methods or mechanisms is needed. Business processes that coordinate corporate and business activities or focus on coordination of corporate center functions with business operations are included under the heading of structural integration.

Consider, again, the vertical integration case. To make the strategy of vertical integration work, processes and methods are needed to coordinate the flows of work and materials between supplier and user divisions within the company. Transfer pricing mechanisms must be developed to facilitate internal buy-and-sell transactions. Methods to facilitate information sharing and knowledge transfer also must be developed to facilitate coordination and cooperation. These processes and mechanisms are part of the integration function noted in Figure 2.1.

Consider, too, the case of the global organization. Central to the success of many global strategies is effective integration or coordination. Citibank must coordinate programs and services to its multinational customers worldwide. Work directed toward these large global players must be coordinated across countries or regions. Yet the services performed globally cannot violate local regulations or norms or ignore local economic problems and opportunities. Processes of integration are needed worldwide to deal with this complexity and achieve a strong competitive position.

Asea Brown Boveri (ABB) competes globally in 65 different businesses with approximately 1,300 companies that make up the corporation. A critical task challenging its global approach is the integration of a strategy across many regions or countries. To execute strategy, heavy investments are made in its IT system ("Abacus"), global managers, and a worldwide matrix organization in an attempt to facilitate the needed integration. Integration across structural units and geography is vital to making ABB's strategy work.

A critical final point here is that effective integration or coordination simply cannot occur if task responsibilities and accountabilities are unclear. The data reported in Chapter 1 clearly and unequivocally show that execution programs, processes, and activities will founder or fail if responsibilities for them are muddled or unclear. This is a basic but critical prerequisite for making strategy work.

Much more will be said about organizational structure and its role in strategy execution in Chapter 4. The methods of achieving structural integration or coordination are handled in Chapter 5. These are important topics that need additional exposition. Recall from Chapter 1 that managers surveyed listed a lack of understanding of organizational structure as an obstacle to successful strategy execution. They also mentioned the importance of sharing information and coordination mechanisms for execution success. In fact, managers said emphatically that the structural integration required for sound execution is a vital concern and a formidable execution obstacle if not done well. Consequently, detailed attention will be devoted to these and related structural issues in Chapters 4 and 5. For now, the point of the examples in this overview of execution is to stress that:

> *Corporate strategy affects the choice of organizational structure. Alternatively, organizational structure is important to the execution of corporate strategy. To execute strategy effectively, managers must make sound decisions about structure and develop methods or processes to achieve the needed integration of structural units.*

Business Strategy and Execution of Corporate Strategy

Figure 2.1 shows that the businesses must create strategies of their own, and this represents the next element of the model. At the business level, strategy is focused on products, services, and how to compete in a given industry. Emphasis is on industry analysis and industry forces external to the organization as the business attempts to position itself for competitive advantage. Attention is also paid to internal resources and capabilities as the business tries to create skills and competencies that differentiate it from competitors. In essence, business strategy deals with how to compete and gain advantage in a given market, and much has already been written on the topic.

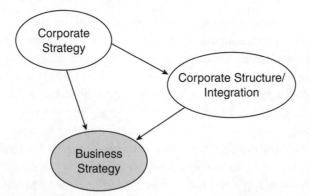

What I wish to stress presently in our model of strategy execution is that business strategy is important to the execution of corporate strategy.

Business strategy is important in its own right because it helps achieve competitive advantage and profitability for the business unit and, ultimately, the entire organization. But business strategy is also important to the execution of corporate strategy, a role not often assigned to it by those interested in execution. Indeed, business strategy and corporate strategy are interdependent; each affects and is affected by the other.

Consider the corporate portfolio strategies developed by the Boston Consulting Group (BCG), GE, Novartis, and others and the familiar terms that have been generated by these approaches: "cash cows," "stars," "pillar" companies, "dogs," and so on. These are familiar names given to business units in a corporate portfolio, but they also describe the role the businesses must play to successfully implement the corporate strategy.

"Cash cows" in the BCG matrix, for example, generate cash. Corporate "milks" them and uses their cash to feed and grow other business units, such as "stars" with growth potential. Corporate needs the "cash cows" to grow parts of its portfolio, consistent with its strategy. What would happen if "cash cows" did not meet corporate expectations? What if they fail to produce the requisite cash nourishment for the internal funding of growth and acquisition? Clearly, funds would have to come from elsewhere; otherwise, corporate strategy could not be executed successfully.

The point is that business-level strategy is vital to the success of corporate strategy. Business strategies are important to the successful execution of corporate plans and the attainment of corporate goals. Similarly, corporate and business strategies must be integrated effectively to achieve desired levels of company performance. Chapter 3 expands upon and clarifies these important points. Suffice it to say for now, given the purpose of this chapter's overview, that:

> *Business strategy is essential to the successful execution of corporate strategy. Corporate planning assigns roles and goals to business units, the performance of which affects the execution of corporate strategy. Poor strategic performance at the business level detracts from corporate's ability to achieve its strategic aims, while good performance helps make corporate strategy work.*

EXECUTING BUSINESS STRATEGY

The focus in the model thus far has been on the implementation of corporate strategy via choices of organizational structure and the contribution of business-level strategies. We now can begin looking more closely at the execution of business strategies.

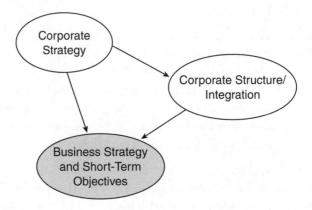

As Figure 2.1 shows, business strategy is affected or constrained by corporate strategy and corporate structure. Even independent, standalone businesses can be constrained somewhat by prior decisions about corporate strategy and structure. The development of business strategy, while dependent primarily on industry forces and business capabilities, will reflect these constraints.

Business strategy is constrained and affected first by resource allocations and the demands of corporate strategy. Resources are allocated to businesses as a function of their role in the corporate portfolio, as emphasized previously. If businesses don't meet corporate expectations in terms of performance, it follows logically that their resource allocations will suffer. These allocations (or lack thereof) clearly will affect a business's ability to execute its future strategies. Even relatively independent businesses are constrained by corporate demands for profitability and contributions to the overall company.

Business strategy is also constrained by prior corporate decisions about organizational structure, as Figure 2.1 shows. Centralization of structural units (such as R&D) constrains a business because it doesn't control needed resources locally, but must rely on a corporate function located elsewhere in the organization. The business is dependent on the centralized resource without control over it, which affects decision-making. Still, though faced with this structural constraint, businesses must formulate and execute strategies to contribute to organizational performance.

There are many examples of the constraints that corporate strategy and structure place on business strategy. Operating units in the old AT&T depended very much on the processes and outcomes of Bell Labs, a corporate R&D unit. Divisions or companies within GE are fairly independent, but corporate center or central functional area activities constrain businesses nonetheless.

Deutsche Post has expanded greatly of late, adding companies such as DHL to its roster of new acquisitions. Although DHL is a separate profit center, it certainly is bound and constrained by corporate strategy and structure, including central functions that service all business units. Even in J&J, one of the most decentralized companies in the world, a few centralized functions place some constraints on SBU decision-making autonomy.

Beyond the constraints posed by the corporate level, there are two aspects of a business strategy that affect its execution: (1) the type of strategy and the "demands" it places on the organization, and (2) the need to translate strategy into short-term, measurable objectives. Handling these issues well will drive execution success.

"DEMANDS" OF BUSINESS STRATEGY

Business strategy creates "demands" that must be satisfied to ensure successful execution. Cost-leadership or low-cost strategies, for example, create demands on organizational investments, resources, and capabilities that are vital to achieving low-cost status. Capital investments in technology and manufacturing are required to drive down the variable cost of goods sold. Demands for standardized products and high production volume must be met to achieve economies of scale and scope. Incentives must be developed that reward cost reductions; otherwise, people will not perform consistent with the demands of the low-cost strategy.

Consider for a moment the remarkable run that Wal-Mart had for years (and still has) in the area of cost reduction. Emphasis was on volume and quick turnover, with little investment in inventory. Investment in information technology assured superior inventory control. These investments also created dependencies among suppliers for up-to-date sales and customer information, which increased Wal-Mart's power over them. Reward systems focused on reducing "shrinkage" and lowering other costs. Sales and advertising expenses were benchmarked against the industry, with resulting costs always below industry average. Development of a "hub-and-spoke" delivery system and investments in warehousing reduced logistical costs. Wal-Mart, in effect, invested money and energy into creating capabilities and activities that supported its low-cost strategy and, in total, were difficult for competitors to imitate.

Nucor provides another good example from a very unattractive steel industry. Nucor's investments clearly supported its strategy. It invested in new steel-making technologies to control costs and quality. It also made a ton of investments in its people, developing HR policies and incentive plans that differentiated it in a stodgy industry and made imitation by larger, slower competitors rather difficult.

The key point here is that strategies demand certain investments and the development of organizational capabilities or resources if successful execution is to result. And different strategies demand different investments and the development of different capabilities. Chapter 3 goes into more detail on these points. For now suffice it to say that:

> Business strategy creates demands for organizational investments in technology, people, and capabilities. These investments must be made and the appropriate skills developed to successfully execute a business strategy.

INTEGRATING STRATEGY AND SHORT-TERM OPERATING OBJECTIVES

To execute business strategy, Figure 2.1 also indicates that strategic plans and objectives must be translated into short-term operating objectives. Long-term goals must generate short-term metrics, measures of performance that relate logically to the business plan.

Most managers in complex organizations face and deal with local, short-term issues. The focus is on what's needed daily, weekly, monthly, or quarterly, as managers confront the usual problems and opportunities associated with customers, competitors, and employees. It is impossible, even at the highest levels of a business, to manage effectively armed only with a strategic plan. Key issues, elements, and needs of the business strategy must be translated into shorter-term objectives and action plans, and this translation process is an integral and vital part of the execution of strategy. Short-term thinking is okay if it's tied to long-term, strategic thinking.

Because the translation of strategy into short-term operating objectives is so important to the execution of business strategy, it must be controlled and orchestrated. Without this control, managers and workers at mid- and lower-level positions may be focusing on the wrong things. A differentiation strategy based, in part, on improved customer service will fail if short-term concerns focus primarily on cost and the avoidance of additional expenses, including those related to customer service. Similarly, if business strategies are changing and adapting to industry forces over time, execution of the new strategies will suffer if short-term objectives and performance metrics don't change and continue to emphasize decisions, actions, and measures "we've always had or relied on in the past." A business simply must ensure that everyday objectives and performance metrics are consistent with its strategic goals and plans.

As basic as this point is—that strategy must be translated into short-term metrics—this translation is often incomplete or faulty. Short-term objectives or metrics in use often are not related logically to business strategy.

As a follow-up exercise after completing my Wharton program on executing strategy, top managers, responding to a challenge from me, have occasionally gone back to their companies and had managers below them ask their subordinates two simple, related questions: "What activities and objectives do you routinely pursue (in your department, unit, and so on), and what business strategy do these activities and objectives support?" The answers are often surprising, I've been told, with people down through the organization unaware of how everyday objectives, activities, or performance metrics relate to business strategy. There are even cases in which everyday activities and efforts are *inconsistent* with business strategy, placing successful execution in jeopardy.

How does a business achieve the needed consistency? A number of methodies related to management-by-objectives programs or their offshoots, such as the Balanced Scorecard or Enterprise Performance Management Systems, exist to help managers integrate long- and short-term business objectives.[v] How these programs aid this integration is presented in greater detail in Chapter 3. For now, the present position and emphasis can be summarized as follows:

> *Business strategy must be translated into short-term operating objectives or metrics in order to execute the strategy. To achieve strategic objectives, an organization must develop short-term, measurable objectives that relate logically to, and are consistent with, business strategy and how the organization plans to compete.*

Business Structure

Figure 2.1 shows next that business structure is also important to the execution of business strategy.

Much of the theory and practice in the area of organizational design has been devoted to business structure, the next component of our overview. This design work has focused primarily on the structure of businesses and the coordination of work across units within the business. This stream of work has provided us with valuable insights into these aspects of organizational design and need not be reviewed exhaustively here.

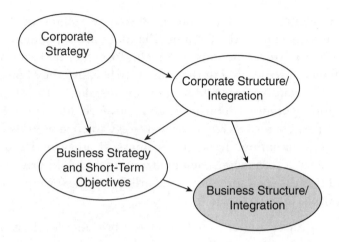

Figure 2.1 shows the place of business structure in the execution of strategy. First, similar to the case at the corporate level, strategy again drives the choice of structure. Business-level strategy and its logical offshoots—short-term operating objectives—affect the choice of business structure.

In a sense, it is necessary now to talk about organizational "designs" or "structures." Different businesses in the same company can face very different competitive situations and thus have a need for different structures. Imposing the same structure on all businesses or divisions simply because they are part of the same organization is not a logical and appropriate way to determine structure. Corporate should avoid this execution error at all costs. Figure 2.1 does show that corporate structure can constrain business structure. To reiterate an example used previously, a centralized R&D unit creates a dependency on the corporate unit and affects coordination between businesses and the corporate staff. Still, this is a vastly different situation than corporate imposing the same structure on all its businesses. Business structure should reflect, and be driven primarily by, the nature of business strategy.

GE Capital and Jet Engines represent two different divisions or companies under the GE umbrella. Both are dependent somewhat on centralized functions and staff. To argue, however, that both should be structured in the same way because they both, after all, are GE companies would be a major mistake. Both companies are in totally different industries, and both face different industry and competitive forces. Each has a strategy to cope with its own competitive situation. It is the business strategy and the different industry forces facing each company that should drive the choice of business structure, not some arbitrary rule for consistency laid down by the corporate level.

Issues raised under structure at the business level again include the degree of centralization vs. decentralization, as a business must adopt its structure to its strategy the same way corporate does. Structure does make a difference to business performance. It does affect costs and other outcomes. The strategy-structure relationship, consequently, along with the costs and benefits of that relationship, will be discussed in depth in Chapter 4.

Integration again comes into play at the business level, just as it did at the corporate level. Once again, structure defines the major functions or operating units that make up the business. Once more, the issue is one of coordination or integration, as businesses develop processes or methods of achieving lateral coordination across these major operating units or functions.

In geographically dispersed businesses, managing across organizational units is of paramount importance. Coordinating work flows, transferring relevant knowledge effectively from one part of the business to another, and achieving integration so as to meet business objectives are necessary ingredients for successful performance. A focus on knowledge transfer, information sharing, and effective integration or coordination is vitally important, as the survey data in Chapter 1 showed rather convincingly.

Consider a large consulting company such as McKinsey. Clearly, one of its needs for continued effectiveness is the transfer of knowledge and information sharing across offices around the world. Helping clients in one location or industry demands the sharing of information about previously developed processes and methods from other locations and industries. Managing across specialized areas of expertise and transferring knowledge effectively is absolutely essential to the execution of McKinsey's strategy.

Size and geographical dispersion are not the only challenges to effective communication and coordination. Different units and functional areas within a business are often characterized by differences in goals, perceptions, and time frames for action. They often have very different cultures. Conflicts often occur across functions such as marketing, production, and R&D because of these differences in goals and perceptions, as every practicing manager knows. Integration of these diverse, differentiated units ("silos") to achieve superordinate goals is certainly a challenging task, but it is central to the successful execution of business strategy. These issues are confronted in detail in Chapter 5. For now, suffice it to say that:

> *Lateral communication and managing across organizational boundaries are important to successful strategy execution. Transferring knowledge and achieving coordination across operating units within a business are vital to strategic success. Information sharing and integration methods can increase the flexibility of structure and the organization's ability to respond to execution-related problems.*

INCENTIVES AND CONTROLS

The picture of strategy execution is not yet complete because the creation of strategy, objectives, structure, and coordinating mechanisms is not sufficient to ensure that individuals will adapt their own goals to those of the organization. Some method of obtaining individual and organizational goal congruence is required. Prior decisions and actions can be negated by a lack of commitment among individuals charged with execution. Execution will suffer if people are rewarded for doing the "wrong" things. Execution will fail when no one has skin in the game.

Feedback on performance is also needed so that the organization can evaluate whether the "right" things are indeed being accomplished in the strategy-execution process. Feed-back is absolutely essential to organizational change or adaptation over time.

In essence, what is required is the careful development of incentives and controls, the last component of the model in Figure 2.1.

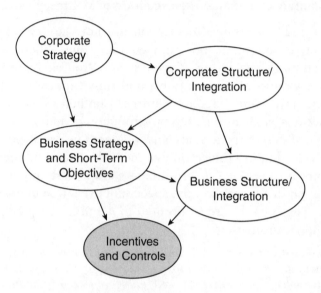

Incentives and controls are together in Figure 2.1 because they represent the "flip sides" of decisions and actions concerned with performance. On one hand, incentives motivate or guide performance; on the other, controls provide feedback about whether desired performance outcomes are being attained. Controls allow for the revision of incentives and other execution-related factors if desired goals are not being met.

INCENTIVES

Incentives must reinforce strategic and short-term objectives. Individual and group rewards are an important aspect of strategy execution because they control performance with respect to desired strategic and short-term outcomes. It truly is critical that the organization rewards the "right things," including previously defined strategic and short-term objectives.

Organizations always seem to be grappling with the right incentives to facilitate strategy execution. For example, more and more CEOs can be seen striking deals that tie pay to performance. Paul

Anderson, CEO of Duke Energy, has a contract under which he is paid only with company stock. GE CEO Jeffrey Immelt is paid in "performance share units," which will become stock shares if performance measures related to cash flow and shareholder value are met. The intention, of course, is to forge a concern with long-term, strategic performance that leads to increased shareholder value.

Many companies are beginning to question "related-party transactions" that pose the risk of "conflicts between a company official's two roles: representative of the shareholder and an individual seeking to get the best deal for himself.[vi] This is the "agency" problem revisited, the concern being that managers' rewards should be tied to the right things, including shareholder value and other strategic and short-term objectives.

In addition to reinforcing attention to desired objectives, the model in Figure 2.1 also indicates that incentives must support key elements of business structure. In a matrix organization, for example, incentives must support the two-boss structure. If only one boss controls rewards, the "grid" or dual nature of the matrix structure is compromised, even destroyed. Similarly, incentives that reward only individual performance will have deleterious effects on the effectiveness of group- or team-based approaches to integration or coordination.

Incentives, then, are central to any plan of execution. They tell people what's important and what to emphasize. Thorndike's age-old law of effect definitely is still salient: Behavior that is reinforced tends to be repeated.[vii] Successful execution requires that incentives reward the right things.

CONTROLS

Controls round out the final element of our model in Figure 2.1. Controls represent a feedback loop. They provide information about the achievement of objectives that derive from strategy and other aspects of our model of execution. This feedback is important because strategy execution is an adaptive process. Managers rarely get everything right; fine-tuning of plans, objectives, and implementation methods is more often the rule than the exception.

Ineffective market and customer surveillance, poor information about organizational performance, and a company's inability or reluctance to act on feedback received from the marketplace surely spell disaster for strategy-execution efforts. Without good controls in place, effective change and adaptation are not possible. Recall that the survey data presented in Chapter 1 showed emphatically that the ability to manage change is an extremely critical execution need. Change is not possible, however, if feedback mechanisms do not exist. The market surveillance and information flows back to the organization upon measurement of performance are critical for change and adaptation. Thus, the final element of the present model, treated in depth in Chapter 6 stresses that:

> Incentives must support the key aspects of the strategy-execution model. They must reinforce the "right" things if execution is to succeed. Controls, in turn, must provide timely and valid feedback about organizational performance so that change and adaptation become part and parcel of the execution effort.

CONTEXT OF EXECUTION DECISIONS

The model of strategy execution just presented lays out the major elements or stages in the process and focuses on the logical connections and order among them. It identifies the broad areas that demand management attention and decisions if execution is to succeed. The task in later chapters is to flesh out the key issues or decisions inherent in each of the elements or stages of the model.

However, the overview is not yet complete. Managers' opinions about execution problems noted in Chapter 1 suggest that an additional set of factors must be considered when trying to make strategy work: namely, the context within which execution decisions and actions take place.

THE EXECUTION CONTEXT

The execution decisions or actions noted in Figure 2.1 take place within an organizational or environmental context. This context is important because it can affect execution processes and outcomes. Consistent with the views reported by managers in Chapter 1, there are four contextual factors that deserve attention when explaining the success of the execution decisions and actions just considered in the model: (1) the change management context, (2) the culture of the organization, (3) the organizational power structure, and (4) the leadership context (see Figure 2.2).

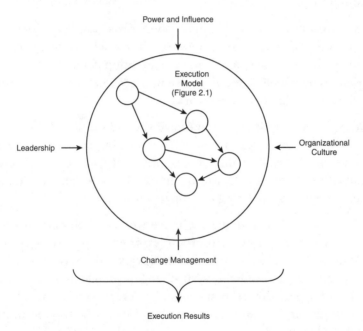

Figure 2.2 Context of Execution Decisions

The four items are not independent; they relate to one another in many ways. The four areas—power, culture, change, and leadership—clearly affect and are affected by each other. One can safely argue that, when all four are in sync, the prognosis for execution success is very positive. Yet, for purposes of analysis and understanding, each is important enough to deserve separate attention.

Managers must understand each of the four well before they can understand their interdependence and interactive effects.

MANAGING CHANGE

Much attention has been devoted to managing change in organizations. Strategy execution, of course, often involves change. Execution may demand changes in job responsibilities, organizational structure, coordination methods, people, incentives, or controls. These changes may be vital to the success of execution outcomes.

Yet we know that individuals often resist change. They may not buy into the execution program. They might actually try to sabotage the changes and cause execution-related efforts to fail. Managing change effectively, then, is obviously an important ingredient in making strategy work.

Despite its importance, there are vast differences in organizational capabilities when it comes to managing change. Some companies do it well, while others' attempts at major changes are absolute disasters. Cultural change is especially difficult, often challenging or negating execution efforts.

That the ability to manage change well is a hallmark of successful execution is only reinforced strongly by the present data. Managers in the surveys and interviews discussed in Chapter 1 reported that problems with change management constitute the single biggest threat to successful strategy execution. This clearly is an extremely important topic, and it will be treated in depth in Chapter 7.

CULTURE

A great deal has been written about organizational culture and rightfully so, for culture affects much of what goes on (and doesn't go on) in organizations. Culture can affect the problems or opportunities managers actually notice or focus on. Culture helps define the performance outcomes that are held dear by organizational members.

Culture defines how work gets done, what rewards are valued, how mistakes or errors are treated, and what management styles are appropriate. Subcultures within organizations or across operating units certainly affect attempts at lateral communication and coordination. Figure 2.2 shows the impact of culture, an important context factor affecting execution.

Perhaps, most importantly, culture reflects and affects the drive and ownership that individuals feel for execution-related goals and activities. When managers are committed to execution success and they feel ownership of the means to successful outcomes, the prognosis for making strategy work is most positive.

When Edward Zander took over as CEO of Motorola, replacing Christopher Galvin, one of his biggest problems was confronting and changing Motorola's go-slow culture, characterized by complacency and little sense of urgency. The company's long tradition of engineering excellence and market leadership had created a laid-back culture where everything is okay, on the right track always.

According to Zander, however, things aren't okay. Motorola is no longer the market leader it once was. A sense of complacency and a "not to worry" culture are no longer appropriate. They can no longer be tolerated. A new culture is needed to facilitate the execution of new strategies, and this represents a major challenge for Zander.[viii]

Culture, admittedly, is a "soft" variable, hard to measure and put your hands around. Still, we all know it when we see it. I have worked in companies in the same industry whose cultures were light years apart. Though focused on the same markets and customers, the companies' methods, managerial styles, rewards, and control processes were quite different. The companies had "different feels" to them. Managers acted differently. The cultures were quite divergent, and they affected how work was done, including how strategy was executed.

Some companies are just "loaded" with culture that one can immediately discern. In my work with Microsoft, GE, J&J, and Centocor, the culture was clearly felt in a short period of time. One could easily see the drive, the results orientation, ownership, and commitment to task and to coworkers. One could see how people aimed high, trying to improve performance and achieve innovation.

Organizational culture affects the execution of strategy. Inappropriate cultures must be changed if they don't support execution efforts. But change is difficult to achieve, as was just mentioned. Consequently, Chapter 8 is devoted to the critical topic of managing culture and change.

THE ORGANIZATIONAL POWER STRUCTURE

Power is social influence, the ability to influence others to do something. Power usually can be described in terms of dependency.

If an individual or unit within an organization solves the critical problems facing an organization or is able to control important scarce resources, the dependency of others results in power differences. The individual or unit relied upon can exercise social influence. One such exercise among top managers is the formulation of strategy. Those in power identify external needs or opportunities, define new markets and customers, and determine company direction. Power, then, affects the creation of strategic plans and goals.

Power differences don't only affect the formulation of strategy; they also affect key execution decisions and outcomes. Those in power decide on resource allocations to individuals and organizational units that affect execution efforts. If those in power resist or don't support an execution plan, the success of the plan clearly is jeopardized.

Power is social influence, and that influence can materialize in different ways. Managers can influence others directly, relying on hierarchy or position. They can influence others indirectly by "persuading" them via reliance on expertise or logic to act in a certain way. However it's done, power and the exercise of influence clearly can affect execution.

Power thus is an important contextual factor in the execution of strategy, as Figure 2.2 indicates. Chapter 1 notes that understanding the power structure was rated by managers as an important ingredient in the execution process. Both the survey and interview data indicate strongly the folly of trying to execute a strategy that conflicts with the existing power structure. Consequently, a chapter is devoted to this important topic (Chapter 9).

THE LEADERSHIP CLIMATE

People are vital to execution success. Clearly, their motivations, capabilities, commitments, and ability to create and follow through on plans of action will affect the success of execution efforts.

Among the characteristics or qualities of people who have received a great deal of attention is leadership. Recent popular books have played up the importance of leadership for the execution of strategy.[ix] They have consistently stressed the characteristics of great leaders, including their personality traits (quiet, self-effacing, and demanding) and ability to choose and motivate followers.

I, too, argue that leadership is critical to the successful execution of strategy (see Figure 2.2). My focus, however, concentrates more on the context of leadership than on the actions of a few great individuals. I'm concerned with the climate created by leaders at all levels of an organization (not just the top) that affects strategy execution. How leaders create this climate or context is the critical issue here.

It is important to focus on the climate that leaders create. The responses from managers in the surveys reported in Chapter 1 emphasized the central role of the leadership climate. My own experiences reinforce the notion that it is important to focus on the reactions of followers to the context or climate that leaders create. Most managers up and down the organization, after all, are both leaders and followers. They create and react to climate, which again suggests its role in execution.

Leadership, of course, is pervasive. It affects or reflects a host of things, including the management of change, culture, and the exercise of power or influence. Because of this centrality, I discuss leadership and, relatedly, "people" effects on execution, in a number of chapters. The importance of leadership for execution will be duly expanded upon and emphasized, although a separate chapter is not dedicated to the topic.

NEED FOR A DISCIPLINED APPROACH

My argument in this chapter has been that a disciplined approach to execution is needed to make strategy work. A reliance on a few sound bytes, anecdotes, or stories is not sufficient. Chapter 1 revealed the complexity and difficulty of the strategy-execution process and the obstacles it confronts. Only an integrated, disciplined approach can cut through this complexity and achieve execution success.

Managers need to see the "big picture," an overview of key decisions or actions that, in total, represent a template, model, or guide to effective execution. They must understand the contextual forces that affect the workings of this model. Decisions about structure, incentives, coordination, and controls, after all, do not occur in a vacuum. They take place in a setting or climate that itself can affect execution outcomes.

Managers responsible for making strategy work must keep a model like the one discussed in this chapter firmly in mind. Having such a model allows one to take a disciplined approach to the execution task. It lays out the order and logic of execution decisions and action. With such an approach, one can see the variables that are essential to the development of a solid execution plan.

The overview in this chapter has identified the decisions and actions that need additional attention and analysis, as each is central to execution success. So, let's start looking more specifically and in greater detail at the topics suggested in this chapter.

SUMMARY

This chapter has presented an overview of the strategy-execution process. It emphasizes the following:

- Strategy execution is difficult and is not easily explained by managerial sound bytes or the idiosyncrasies of a few successful managers.

- A logical model and a disciplined approach are needed to understand the strategy-execution process. Emphasis must be on what to do, when, why, and in what order. This chapter initiates this logical overview of strategy execution. No model is perfect or all-inclusive, of course. Still, managers interested in execution must start somewhere. They need a blueprint for analysis and action. The reasons why execution succeeds or fails can only be understood by having a benchmark against which to analyze execution decisions and actions.

- The key ingredients defining strategy execution include decisions about strategy, structure, coordination, information sharing, incentives, and controls. These decisions take place within an organizational context, aspects of which include power, culture, leadership, and the ability to manage change. An understanding of the interactions among key execution decisions and contextual forces is necessary to understand how to make strategy work.

- Subsequent chapters will consider components of the execution model and organizational context in greater detail. Having provided the big picture or overview in this chapter, additional attention can now turn to specific topics or factors and how they affect execution.

ENDNOTES

i. The terms "snowball making" and "snowball throwing" are used in McKinsey and Company to denote conceptual planning and knowledge creation ("snowball making") and the application of the knowledge to solving client problems and generating revenues ("snowball throwing"). I personally don't know if the terms are still in use, but my McKinsey informants assure me that these were actual descriptive terms used for years in the consulting giant.

ii. An earlier version of this model can be found in L.G. Hrebiniak and W.F. Joyce's *Implementing Strategy,* Macmillan, 1984.

iii. See, for example, William Joyce, Nitin Nohria, and Bruce Roberson's *What (Really) Works,* Harper Business, 2003.

iv. See "The Case Against Mergers," *Business Week,* October 20, 1995. Numerous recent articles in *The Wall Street Journal* and elsewhere have also enumerated the problems of specific mergers.

v. See, for example, Robert Kaplan and David Norton's *The Balanced Scorecard,* Harvard Business School Press, 1996.

vi. "Many Companies Report Transactions with Top Officers," *The Wall Street Journal,* December 29, 2003.

vii. Edward Thorndike, *The Elements of Psychology,* A.G. Seiler, 1905.

viii. "Ed Zander Faces a Go-Slow Culture at Motorola," *The Wall Street Journal,* December 17, 2003.

ix. Jim Collins, *Good to Great,* Harper Business, 2001; M. Useem, Leading Up, Crown Business, 2001; M. Useem, *The Leadership Moment,* Three Rivers Press, 1998; E. Locke, *The Essence of Leadership,* Lexington Books, 1991.

3

The Path to Successful Execution: Good Strategy Comes First

Introduction

It all begins with strategy.

It is impossible to discuss execution until one has something to execute. Central to the model of execution presented in Chapter 2 is strategy, at both the corporate and business levels. Strategy is the driving force, the first essential ingredient in the execution process.

That strategy is so important and fundamental to execution efforts should hardly be surprising. Logically, it follows that poor inputs to the execution process will result in poor outputs. Execution outcomes can be hurt severely by problems that arise from faulty strategy formulation or poor strategy. It is vital to eliminate as many problems as possible in the strategy-formulation stage, as they will surely emerge to haunt, test, even destroy the execution process.

There is a connection between planning and doing. The purpose of this chapter is to clarify this link and show how strategy creation affects strategy execution.

IS THE IMPACT OF STRATEGY OVERRATED?

The major obstacles to execution noted in Chapter 1 included poor or vague strategy as a significant barrier to effective execution. Managers indicated that lack of a sound strategy often causes major difficulties. Their point was that bad strategy begets poor execution. Of course, even good strategies can suffer from poor execution plans and processes. But bad or ill-conceived strategies virtually guarantee poor results, despite execution efforts.

Strategy clearly is important to the managers who provided their views on execution in this research. Still, there are some who argue that strategy may not be the first critical step to competitive success. Jim Collins, for example, in a very popular book, tells us that strategy did not "separate the good-to-great companies from the comparison companies" in his research.[i] Both sets of organizations had well-defined strategies, he asserts, so strategy didn't account for greatness.

Yet his own examples seem to contradict his point. Nucor's strategy, for instance, couldn't have been more different than that of Bethlehem Steel. Nucor was a first mover, the initial adopter of the thin slab casting process for producing flat-rolled steel developed by SMS in Germany. Nucor had highly developed technological capabilities, including the ability to construct new mills and then run them efficiently. It was entrepreneurial, willing to take technical and financial risks. Its HR policies, flat organizational structure, meritocracy based on performance, and ample at-risk reward structure supported its strategy and clearly differentiated it in the steel industry.

Did Bethlehem, the counterpart company to Nucor in Collins' work, also have a solid, well-defined strategy? Hardly, in my opinion. For years it was a slow mover, turtle-like in adopting the new technologies of integrated Japanese and European steel makers. A low-cost strategy wasn't supported at all by its HR policies, a tall, bureaucratic organizational structure, or labor-management relations. Strategic inertia and risk avoidance allowed a nimble competitor like Nucor to outmaneuver it and become the most profitable, low-cost producer in the industry. Nucor's strategy and capabilities clearly made a difference.

Similarly, Gillette developed a differentiation strategy by investing in new, radical technology to support product innovation, while its competition didn't. Philip Morris recovered from a bad bout of diversification, including the Seven-Up acquisition debacle, better than its competition. Its strategic focus on food (Kraft/General Foods) and economies of scope in brand management and other functional areas gave it a competitive edge. Pitney Bowes followed a disciplined strategy of related diversification and its counterpart didn't, fueling its successful performance.

Collins' examples clearly seem to support a case *for* the importance of strategy in helping to make companies great, not a lack of importance. Coupled with the opinions of managers in Chapter 1's surveys regarding poor strategy being a significant barrier to execution, the impact of strategy as a critical variable for organizational performance is only reinforced. The importance of a sound strategy cannot be overrated.

Returning to the impact of strategy on execution, the main focus here, it can be said unequivocally that:

> *Bad strategy begets poor execution. Ill-conceived strategies virtually guarantee poor execution outcomes. Execution truly does begin with a good strategy.*

But what are "good" and "bad" strategies? What characterizes "good" planning and differentiates it from "bad" planning? Most managers know quite a bit about strategy and planning and far less about execution, a point emphasized previously. So, the present purpose isn't to teach good planning or to repeat what most managers already know about competitive strategy.

The goal at present is to look at those elements or aspects of planning and strategy that cause the most problems for execution. With this in mind, let's emphasize four points or issues, critical aspects or properties of strategy and planning that affect subsequent efforts at execution and the success of those efforts. The four issues are as follows:

1. The need for sound planning and clear, focused strategies at both the corporate and business levels.
2. The vital importance of integrating corporate and business strategies and conducting strategy reviews.

3. The need to define and communicate clearly the key operational components of strategy and the measurement of execution results.

4. The importance of understanding the "demands" of strategy, their effects on the development of organizational resources and capabilities, and the impact of the resources and capabilities on execution.

ISSUE #1: THE NEED FOR SOUND PLANNING AND A CLEAR, FOCUSED STRATEGY

This is not a book about strategy formulation; the focus is on executing strategy and making strategic plans work. Nonetheless, a focus on formulation and the development of clear strategies is necessary because of the impact on execution outcomes. This is true for both corporate and business planning, especially in the latter case in which business strategy is so vital to the development and maintenance of competitive advantage.

CORPORATE-LEVEL PLANNING

Strategic planning at the corporate level is primarily involved with portfolio decisions and resource allocations across businesses. The former includes decisions about diversification and the array of industries in which the corporation feels comfortable competing. These components of corporate strategy, along with some of their key issues or questions, are noted in Table 3.1.

Table 3.1 Corporate Level Strategy

Key Components	Major Decisions or Issues
Portfolio analysis	Right "mix" of businesses Cash generators and cash users Positioning the company for growth Stable returns vs. risk-taking and high returns Eliminating "deadwood"
Diversification	Analysis of industry attractiveness Return on invested capital Integration of acquisitions

Key Components	Major Decisions or Issues
Resource allocations to businesses	Internal vs. external sources of investment capital
	Performance expectations of different businesses
	Review of business performance and future allocations of resources

The thrust of Table 3.1 is that corporate planners must make sound strategic and financial decisions to grow their company. Investments in new businesses must be preceded by a thorough analysis of the corporate portfolio, including the mix of cash generators and cash users. Decisions about diversifications should be made only after careful analysis of the attractiveness or profit potential of target industries. Resource allocations must take into account the levels of risk that corporate leaders and stakeholders can comfortably assume. Sound corporate strategic planning is vital to overall organizational performance.

Corporate strategy must be clear and sound. If corporate planning is poor or ill conceived, the effects on strategy execution and corporate and business performance are many and potentially fatal. Resources won't be available or sufficient to sustain growth. The "right" business decisions can be thwarted or compromised by corporate mistakes. Needed resources won't be forthcoming for businesses that potentially could grow into stars in the corporate portfolio. Cash generators could be overtaxed or "milked" too extensively by corporate, seriously hampering future cash-generation capabilities. Diversifications could fail because of poor corporate planning, affecting the entire organization.

AT&T: BAD CORPORATE STRATEGY?

In Chapter 1, I presented AT&T two decades ago as a lumbering giant whose corporate strategy negatively affected the development of new businesses at the time. Recently, in May 2004, the occasion of C. Michael Armstrong's retirement after 40 years as a business leader, a new controversy about more recent strategic decisions made by Armstrong at AT&T in 1997 have come to the fore.[ii]

In 1997, Armstrong, as chief of AT&T, made a $100 billion bet on the cable market, figuring that he could use cable to bundle a host of new products for consumers. But the bet failed. Why? Why did AT&T have to sell off its cable business to Comcast, making Armstrong look like a failed CEO?

Armstrong's argument in May 2004 was that AT&T was done in by fraud at WorldCom and other players in the long-distance market. These competitors, he argued, were fraudulently pumping up their numbers, showing higher demand and lower costs than AT&T. This, of course, made AT&T look bad. Wall Street felt that AT&T was losing its market position, and it consequently didn't give the company time to execute its long-distance and cable-related strategy. Armstrong was forced to break up AT&T, a decision that a host of stakeholders mercilessly beat him up for making.

Was it poor strategy and/or poor execution? In their book, Larry Bossidy and Ram Charan say, "Yes, it was." They argue that AT&T couldn't keep up with faster, more nimble rivals, that Armstrong made some bad critical "people" choices, that AT&T's strategy "was disconnected from both external and internal realities," and that its culture "could not execute well enough or fast enough" to make AT&T's strategy work.[iii]

Who is right? Was Armstrong duped by lying competitors? Was he, in fact, doing sound industry and competitor analysis in arriving at his strategic conclusions, only to be duped by the fraudulent misinformation put out by competitors? Or was his plan of execution flawed? Did he simply make a bunch of strategic mistakes in the areas of planning and strategy execution?

The case is interesting and compelling because it presents data that allow conflicting interpretations and explanations. On one hand, Ralph Larson, a former AT&T board member and chief executive of J&J, says that Armstrong did a superb job in setting the company's strategic direction. On the other hand, critics such as Bossidy and Charan point to major mistakes, including those involved with strategy execution.

Who's right? You can decide for yourself, but the deck seems to be stacked against a slow-moving AT&T organization that even a capable executive like Armstrong had a hard time changing. For present purposes, let's say that the case illustrates a number of key points:

- Corporate strategy must be clear and sound. Poor planning will waste resources and kill execution plans and processes. Poor strategy begets poor execution.

- Corporate strategy formulation and execution are difficult. They depend on data about industry forces, competitors, and company capabilities. Getting the wrong data can hurt planning and execution efforts.

- Market misinformation exists, and management must sift through the informational lies and chaff to get at the kernels of truth that drive strategic decisions. Life at the top isn't easy. Bad strategic decisions based on poor information suggest managerial shortcomings.

Another point should be obvious from the AT&T example and the decisions noted in Table 3.1; namely, that corporate strategy affects how businesses operate. Corporate resource allocations affect the execution of business strategies. Reviews of business performance by corporate personnel suggest an important control function that affects company direction. Sound corporate planning is essential to the integration of corporate and business plans. This integration of plans is vital to the successful execution of strategy at both the corporate and business levels.

In the following section, I return to the integration of corporate and business strategies because of its impact on successful execution. First let's consider the importance of business planning and business strategy for subsequent efforts at execution.

BUSINESS STRATEGY

Good planning and sound strategy are also vital at the business level. Business strategy, too, must be focused and clear. The goal is to develop a strategy that leads to competitive advantage in an industry or market segment. Strategy formulation here depends upon a company's ability to understand its industry and competitors and to develop resources and capabilities that lead to a favorable competitive position.

Figure 3.1 shows the external and internal analyses needed to develop a sound business strategy and achieve competitive advantage. At the business level, it is absolutely essential that management perform an in-depth analysis of the following:

- Industry/market forces
- Competitors, actual and potential, including their strategies and capabilities
- The company's own resources and capabilities, including those that represent a distinctive or core competence

	Key Issues
Industry Analysis	• Size/Concentration of Industry • Number of Strategic Groups (Market Segments) within Industry • Power of Buyers or Customers • Power of Suppliers to Industry • Number of Substitute Products • Rivalry within Industry
Competitor Analysis	• Competitors' Resources and Capabilities • Competitors' Size and Market Power • Competitors' Strategies • Competitors' Previous Offensive and Defensive Moves
Resources and Capabilities	• Our Own Resources, Tangible and Intangible • Our Competitive Capabilities • Existence of a Core Competence – Do we have one? • Competitors' Resources and Capabilities

Figure 3.1   Business Strategy Formulation

These analyses tell management what's possible or doable in terms of strategy development. Strategy formulation doesn't occur in a vacuum. An organization must match its capabilities with external opportunities and position itself accordingly to maximize its chances for competitive advantage.

The issues and analyses in Figure 3.1 have been presented and debated more than adequately in the management literature, most notably by Michael Porter.[iv] The point to emphasize presently is that business planning and business strategy and the conditions that affect industry position and competitive advantage can also affect the success of strategy execution. Here are some examples that I've observed over the years.

- **Having market share often facilitates execution.** Market share or size can lead to power over suppliers or buyers if the latter groups become increasingly dependent on a company. Market share can compensate for inefficiencies elsewhere in the organization, such as in systems integration or channel support on the sell side. Having market share certainly is not a total panacea, but it generally is easier to execute strategies with market share and market power behind the execution efforts.

  Witness the success of Wal-Mart. Its power over suppliers has enabled it to execute its vaunted low-cost strategy for years. Or look at the success in the heydays of IBM, Dell, GM, and AT&T when they enjoyed similar market power. It simply is easier to make strategy work when market power is on your side. Pressuring a supplier for price concessions will work if it is extremely dependent on your business. The same tactic will spell disaster in the absence of buyer power. Having market share and market power obviously can support the execution of a business strategy.

- **Entry barriers support strategy execution.** Market share is a formidable entry barrier, but there are others: capital requirements, brand or reputation, distribution channels, patented technologies or processes, service capabilities, customer relationships, and so on. High entry or mobility barriers keep others from entering a company's space and competing with its strategy and operations. High barriers to entry facilitate strategy execution for the protected organization. It is easier to execute a plan when others cannot easily copy what's being done. Like market share, entry barriers don't guarantee execution success. They can, however, insulate execution efforts from challenges, thereby providing support for execution activities.

- **Executing a differentiation strategy in a competitive industry, marked by increased commoditization and strong similarity of product offerings among competitors, is extremely difficult to do.** Global competition, for example, often results in a proliferation of substitute products and more of an emphasis on price as a competitive factor. Execution of a differentiation strategy, given many similar, lower-priced, substitute products, becomes extremely challenging at best. It can be done, as shown by Nucor in the steel industry or Porsche in an increasingly competitive global automotive industry. But it normally is difficult to achieve and sustain differentiated products and services under these conditions. Execution simply is a more formidable challenge.

- **Misreading major competitors' technological capabilities can doom a strategy premised on technological differentiation in the marketplace.** Microsoft, Sony, and Intel are keenly aware of the effects of imitation on the ability to execute a business strategy successfully over time. The more difficult the imitation, the greater the likelihood of execution success.

  I was once told by a manager at Intel that imitation must be assumed, no matter how technologically advanced a new product is. As soon as Pentium 2 was on the market, work began on Pentium 3. When Pentium 3 was introduced, work had already begun on Pentium 4 or even 5. The goal is technological leadership, and even self-cannibalization is preferable to competitive incursions by imitating companies. All effort must be expended to maintain a differentiation edge.

■ **Easy imitation injures or destroys execution efforts.** The value of a competitive strategy at the business level is undermined by easy imitation. This point was mentioned in the preceding examples, but it is worth repeating. One measure of the worth of any strategy is the difficulty competitors will have copying it. The greater the difficulty, the greater the ease of execution.

Recall for a moment the case of Southwest Airlines. It doesn't do a host of things (no meals, no baggage transfer, and so on) that other airlines are doing and can't easily stop doing. Its activities, in total, can't easily be imitated. Execution of its unique strategy is made easier by the ability to thwart imitation. Although Southwest's low-cost, no-frills strategy is currently being challenged by other low-cost carriers, imitation has not come easily or cheaply for the upstarts.

■ **A company's assumption of a core competence when formulating strategy can lead to an execution disaster if the original critical assumption of a competence is wrong.** Quite frankly, I've been amazed by the number of companies I've worked with that assume a core competence and advantage over competitors. I recently asked a top-management team if their company enjoyed a distinctive or core competence and was told that "we have at least seven or eight, maybe more." In truth, given the conditions that spell out a distinctive or core competence,[v] the company had none!

If strategy execution and success depended on these nonexistent capabilities, the company would certainly find itself in a troubled competitive position. The lack of clear core capabilities could be a source of confusion to employees trying to execute the flawed strategy. It could also be frustrating when the strategy reaps few or no benefits for the organization.

Strategy execution can be helped immensely by having distinctive capabilities that competitors cannot easily develop. A technological advantage (as with Microsoft and Intel) or a series of interconnected activities or business processes that are hard to duplicate (as with Wal-Mart and Southwest

Airlines) certainly can provide a strong competitive position. But assuming the impact and importance of these capabilities *when they don't exist* only leads to trouble and disappointment when trying to execute a flawed strategy.

- **Assuming that customers face high "switching costs" and, consequently, an inability or lack of desire to replace a particular product or service with a competitor's product or service can lead to disaster if that assumption is invalid.** Strategy execution will definitely suffer, given such an erroneous assumption.

When Dell first came up with its "direct" model, selling high-end PCs directly to savvy, corporate customers and avoiding resellers and retailers, I was told by some IBM managers that Dell's strategy wouldn't work. The assumption was that IBM's customers faced high switching costs. This simply was not the case. Knowledgeable customers could easily switch to Dell.

The low switching costs enabled Dell to grab market share. The inability of IBM, HP, and Compaq to "go direct" and imitate Dell due to commitment to a business model involving retailers and resellers clearly facilitated Dell's ability to execute its strategy. Trade-offs and channel conflicts reduced the ability to imitate Dell, paving the way for Dell's execution success. Dell, then, was the company that enjoyed switching costs, which helped facilitate execution and achieve positive performance results.

- **Relying on a low-cost position to support price cuts can likewise be disastrous if competitors have more favorable cost positions and are in better position to sustain a price war.** Poor competitor intelligence can lead to poor decisions about competitors' capabilities and can make a strategy based on erroneous information impossible to execute successfully. Assuming a low-cost position that doesn't exist can spell strategic disaster for the executing company.

When Ryanair first entered the lucrative London-to-Dublin market, it came in as a carrier stuck between two strategies: low cost and a differentiated service provider such as Aer Lingus or British Air. It lowered prices, assuming that the other airlines wouldn't engage in a price war. Ryanair was wrong. British Air and especially Aer Lingus undercut its prices. Ryanair had miscalculated its competitors' capabilities and resolve not to give away a profitable route. Being stuck between two strategies and performing neither particularly well, it was driven literally to the brink of disaster and bankruptcy.

■ Ryanair managed not only to survive but also prosper. How? By creating a clearer, more focused strategy. It focused on being a low-cost carrier and in many ways emulated Southwest Airlines and the ways of doing business that full-service airlines couldn't easily copy. Its focused strategy and complementary capabilities allowed it to execute more efficiently and effectively than it ever had been able to do when straddling a strategic fence.

A myriad of other examples exist, but the point should be clear: The key issues noted in Figure 3.1 must be carefully analyzed as part of strategy development. Sound business planning dictates that all relevant data must be analyzed in the strategy-formulation process. Less than thoughtful and thorough analysis can lead to "poor or vague strategy" or inadequate strategic planning, which can hinder or render useless strategy-execution efforts, as managers in the Wharton surveys emphasized. Execution is easier if, borrowing from the classic analysis of Chester Barnard years ago, an organization is pursuing "the right things."[vi] Execution is more difficult, if not impossible, if business strategy is unclear, unfocused, ill-founded, pursuing the "wrong things," or reading the competitive environment incorrectly.

In sum, sound planning and a good strategy are necessary ingredients for the successful execution of strategy. Whatever the strategy—low cost, product differentiation, innovative services—it will only work if it is "sharply defined, clearly communicated, and well understood by employees, customers, partners, and investors."[vii] In IT circles, a popular expression is "garbage in, garbage out." The same is basically true with strategy: Poor, ill-conceived plans breed poor results. Managers cannot execute an unclear, unfocused, or poorly created plan. Strategy drives or affects a great deal; it should be developed carefully.

ISSUE #2: THE IMPORTANCE OF INTEGRATING CORPORATE AND BUSINESS STRATEGIES

Corporate and business strategies must be consistent with and support each other. They must work together, not be in conflict. Achieving this integration or consistency has positive implications for strategy execution, at both corporate and business levels.

The need for consistency and balance of corporate and business strategy is clearly a condition suggested by the preceding discussion of sound planning and the model presented in Chapter 2. Yet my experience, and that of many managers in this research, suggests that this consistency between corporate and business strategies is occasionally elusive and difficult to come by. And inconsistency or conflicts in strategy breed execution problems. Consider just one example previously mentioned—that of portfolio analysis—to see what can go wrong and negatively affect the execution of strategy.

Table 3.2 lists some purposes or goals of portfolio models in strategic planning. These include resource allocations by corporate to its businesses or major operating units. A search for balance in the portfolio suggests that the proper mix of businesses—cash generators and cash users—will help to achieve internal financing and long-term growth. The approaches to portfolio analysis done by companies such as GE or consulting firms such as BCG or McKinsey & Co. highlight this quest for balance and a good mix of businesses.

Table 3.2   Consistency Between Corporate and Business Strategies: The Case of Portfolio Analysis

Purposes/Goals

Resource allocations/internal financing

Portfolio balance

Achieve growth and future profitability

Guide business strategy formulation

Set business performance objectives

Develop criteria for assessment of business performance

Needs or Conditions for Success

Adequate communication between corporate and businesses

Unambiguous role of businesses in the corporate portfolio

Clear, well-defined business strategies

Proper balance of centralization and decentralization of structure

Appropriate business-level incentives based upon measurable performance metrics

Portfolio analysis is also intended to guide strategy formulation at the business level. "Cash cows" or cash generators would likely pursue cost-leadership strategies to take full advantage of their market share and power to increase the flow of funds available for internal distribution or investment. Businesses tagged as high-growth prospects by corporate are likely to attempt to differentiate themselves in some inimitable way, such as via technology, brand, or product performance. Performance metrics can then be developed that are consistent with strategy at the business level, and corporate can use these criteria to measure and assess business performance. "Cash cows" can be evaluated on their cost savings. Differentiators can be evaluated against metrics that logically reflect their basis of differentiation, such as product performance.

So, what can go wrong? Table 3.2 suggests a number of potential problems.

THE ROLE OF THE BUSINESS IS UNCLEAR

Corporate assumes one role, the business another. Corporate treats the business like a "cash cow," but the business sees itself as a potential star that should receive an infusion of capital and not be "milked" dry. Poor planning at the business level doesn't paint a clear picture of business strategy and fails to convince corporate about the business's role in the portfolio.

Different perceptions or assumptions create conflict. A business wants capital to grow, add products, and increase R&D. But corporate sees it differently, treating it as a cash generator or cost center, denying the business the resources it feels it desperately needs. Tensions grow, and the inconsistency between corporate and business perceptions fuels conflict and negatively affects performance. The execution of strategy at both the corporate and business levels is severely compromised.

Before Ciba Geigy merged with Sandoz to form Novartis, it had a portfolio-planning problem with its pigments division. This division was classified as "core" or a cash cow, which affected a host of corporate decisions such as investment levels, return on investment required, and payback period for invested capital.

The high-performance pigment products within the division, however, did not behave as core, commodity-type products. They acted more like "pillar" or high-growth products, capable of generating high returns on investment. Managers in charge of the high-performance pigments bristled at being treated like a commodity division. They saw a different role for their business within Ciba's portfolio than corporate did, which led to both planning and execution difficulties. Managers at the corporate and business levels evaluated the portfolio differently, creating an inconsistent and problematic situation.

INAPPROPRIATE PERFORMANCE METRICS

Because of different assumptions of the business' role, corporate may expect levels of performance (such as cash flows, return on assets) that the business cannot deliver. Poor communication and poor planning processes ensure that corporate and business people do not see eye to eye on key performance measures. The company wants more in terms of performance, but the business feels that those requests are unrealistic. Again, the potential for conflict is high, and the negative consequences for strategy execution are obvious.

A related problem is when corporate holds all businesses accountable for the same performance measures, even though the businesses are in different industries with different competitive conditions.

A good example comes from a large, well-known company with mainly high-tech products. Corporate looked to each business for the same profit growth and return on assets, despite varying competitive conditions across industries. In the business manufacturing capacitors and resistors, however, products were commodities, with competition based primarily on price. Most of the other businesses faced more favorable competitive conditions, making the profit goal a more realistic one. Still, the "different" division was held accountable for the unrealistic goals. It is easy to see how this could cause major problems between corporate and the business and affect the execution of strategy at both levels.

BATTLES OVER RESOURCE ALLOCATIONS

In the cases mentioned previously, there clearly will be differences in resource allocations throughout the corporate portfolio. Some businesses will feel neglected in the allocation process, feeling that other businesses are receiving favorable, but inappropriate, treatment by corporate. Businesses may even feel that organizational structure is wrong, with way too much centralized control over scarce resources and not enough decentralized control with more resources entrusted to the business.

In the example just mentioned, the resistor-capacitor business consistently couldn't make its profit bogey. Allocation of resources to it was negatively affected. It felt it was being cheated by corporate. It also felt that too much corporate control was negatively affecting its ability to respond to its market and competitive conditions. Corporate strategy and goals were seen as inconsistent with business strategy and industry conditions. Tensions grew between the business leaders and corporate staff.

ASSESSMENTS OF BUSINESS PERFORMANCE CREATE ADDITIONAL PROBLEMS

If a business feels that it's been assigned an inappropriate strategy or role in the corporate portfolio, it follows that the business would see the assignment of performance objectives as invalid or unrealistic. From the corporate point of view, the business' performance rating would be low. The business, in turn, would feel it's been mistreated. If incentives such as pay, bonus, or future promotion are based on these "exaggerated" or "invalid" performance metrics, managers at the business level would feel mistreated and violated, causing further tension. The prognosis for future planning is bleak, as business people may feel the need to "lowball," "play games," "change corporate's expectations," or "prove them wrong," according to some managers in this situation I was able to interview.

The point is that there must be a logical consistency between corporate and business strategy. The latter is vital to the successful execution of the former. Corporate expects a certain level or type of performance of businesses in its portfolio. If the businesses see different strategic roles and different performance criteria, the execution of corporate strategy will be jeopardized. If businesses don't perform to corporate's expectations, resource allocations will be affected, thereby injuring the businesses' ability to execute competitive strategy.

The argument can be summarized by the following two statements:

- Corporate strategy can affect businesses' ability to execute strategy and achieve competitive advantage.
- Businesses' performance in the portfolio can affect the execution of corporate strategy, thereby affecting firm-wide performance.

Corporate and business strategies are interactive and interdependent. Resources given to (or withheld from) businesses affect their ability to execute strategy and achieve competitive advantage. The performance of businesses, in turn, affects the implementation of corporate strategy. Businesses' playing (or not playing) their assigned roles in the portfolio will impact the execution of corporate plans and the attainment of company-wide goals.

To avoid problems, adequate communication and interaction between corporate and businesses are absolutely essential. Agreement must be reached on the key elements listed in Table 3.2 to execute strategy successfully. Inconsistencies or conflicts between corporate and business strategies and businesses' roles in the corporate portfolio must be identified. Inability to do so will surely lead to execution mishaps that will affect both business unit and company-wide performance. How can these problems be avoided?

THE STRATEGY REVIEW

One way to improve the requisite communication between corporate and businesses is through a strategy review. While the review is discussed again in Chapter 6 dealing with the control process, it should be mentioned in the present context.

Figure 3.2 depicts a simple graphic of the strategy review. It is a tool that has been used successfully in various forms by GE, Crown Holdings, Allied Signal, Boeing, and other well-known companies. The purpose of the review is fourfold:

1. To discuss the development of corporate and business strategies

2. To integrate strategy at both levels by clarifying roles, responsibilities, and goals for corporate and the businesses

3. To provide a forum for the review and evaluation of business performance

4. To allow for change and adaptation over time to keep strategy and performance metrics current and meaningful

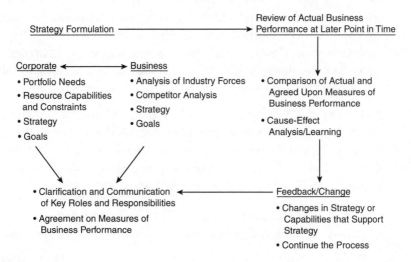

Figure 3.2   The Strategy Review

Basically, what does Figure 3.2 show? It shows, first, a high degree of communication between corporate and business levels. The position of a business within the corporate portfolio is analyzed, including its role or function in the corporate game plan. The support or value-added contribution that the corporate center can provide the businesses is discussed. Also communicated are the resource conditions and constraints under which businesses must perform.

Figure 3.2 shows, second, that agreement is reached on business strategy and operating goals. A business' responsibilities include industry and competitor analysis and the justification of its strategy, given the state of competitive industry conditions. Steps 1 and 2 include necessarily an analysis of past performance, as well as anticipation of future competitive, technological, and economic trends. Discussion between corporate and business leaders focuses on the business' analysis of industry forces and future competitive conditions to reach agreement on the business' strategy and goals.

The important issue here is to focus on the key competitive, technological, and economic conditions that affect business strategy. All too often, the focus of the corporate-business discussion is only on the numbers. Numbers are important but only to a point. The real issues deal with what's behind the numbers. Learning and agreement typically result from discussion and arguments about the conditions or factors that drive the numbers.

I like very much what companies such as J&J and Crown Holdings do in their corporate-business planning sessions. Part of the planning process is purposely spent on discussion of the qualitative factors that underlie quantitative projections. Simple questions drive the discussion, such as the following:

- Where is the business now, and where does it want to be in five years? Explain how the business is going to get there.
- What are the anticipated trends in your industry (technological, competitive conditions), and how can you take advantage of them to improve your business?

Discussions of qualitative issues such as these don't necessarily create a panacea, but they do help the process of agreement. They help corporate and business managers get beyond the numbers and the "low-balling" or posturing that often accompanies an exclusive focus on numbers. Such discussions improve communication and both corporate's and businesses' abilities to see the other's constraints, opportunities, and point of view. The value of these discussions to planning and execution: priceless.

The figure shows, third, that the agreed-upon measures of business performance are used in the reviews of the business' actual performance. There can be no surprises. Corporate is forced to recognize differences in the competitive landscape across industries, allowing potentially for different performance metrics for each business. These metrics, in turn, become the criteria against which business performance is judged at a later date.

Finally, Figure 3.2 shows that the planning and review process is not only interactive but adaptive as well. Corporate and business strategies are reviewed to determine their continued relevance and feasibility, given changes in external conditions and internal capabilities. The strategy review focuses on the roles of the corporate level and the various businesses and how these roles must change over time.

The strategy review is an important step in integrating corporate- and business-level strategies. It helps to foster analysis, communication, and debate between the levels, ensuring that "good" plans are being executed by the organization. Without this clarification of the corporate-business relationship, execution efforts will suffer. My dealings with managers responsible for execution have constantly reinforced the need for a strategy review and the process of communication and interaction demanded by it.

ISSUE #3: THE NEED TO DEFINE AND COMMUNICATE THE OPERATIONAL COMPONENTS OF STRATEGY

The critical first ingredient in an execution plan is strategy. But most people in an organization can't manage armed only with a strategy. Something else is needed to guide daily, monthly, or quarterly performance because many managers operate of necessity in the short term. How do we reconcile and integrate long-term strategic aims with short-term operating plans and objectives?

To execute a strategy successfully, it must be translated into short-term operational metrics that (a) are related to long-term needs, (b) can be used to assess strategic performance, and (c) help the organization achieve long-term strategic goals. Figure 3.3 shows a simplified picture of this translation process.

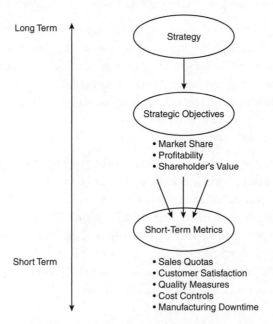

Figure 3.3 Translating Strategy into Short-Term Operating Objectives

Short-term operating objectives represent the grist of the strategic mill. Strategic plans are "ground" or refined into smaller, more manageable pieces, which become the operating criteria to guide short-term behavior. These short-term goals are "strategic" in that they are produced from and related to the long-term, strategic needs of the organization. To achieve long-term goals, it is necessary to manage the short term.

This last statement is important because it highlights a major misconception. Managers often believe that short-term thinking is bad. Emphasis on short-term objectives surely must breed long-term strategic problems. The popular mantra is that managers must become "strategic thinkers," virtually eschewing short-term performance measures.

Nothing could be further from the truth. Short-term operating objectives are vital to strategic performance if they reflect and are integrated with long-term strategic objectives. Execution will suffer if strategic needs are not translated properly into shorter-term metrics and communicated down the organization. If short-term objectives are not logically related to and consistent with strategic plans, the rift between short- and long-term needs will create problems.

INTEGRATING STRATEGIC AND SHORT-TERM OBJECTIVES

Much has been written over the years about the integration of the long and short terms. Early writers focused on management-by-objectives (MBO) programs. They talked about the translation of strategic needs to short-term objectives and the communication it required, but this integrative link never seemed to drive execution or implementation efforts.[viii] MBO programs often came to be seen as paper-creating, bureaucratic burdens rather than facilitators of effective execution. Bill Joyce and I focused on the importance of "managing myopia" in two different publications, stressing the need to integrate long- and short-term objectives.[ix] Although I have had some success in forging this integrative link in companies I've worked with, the integration of long- and short-term metrics has not been achieved effectively in many other organizations I've known.

More recent attempts at this translation and communication process may be seeing greater success. The Balanced Scorecard, for example, provides a framework to translate strategy into operational terms.[x] It helps to develop and communicate short-term objectives in the areas of financials, customer service, internal business processes, and learning and growth, and it attempts to link these objectives to company strategy and long-term goals. The success of the scorecard approach reported by Robert Kaplan and David Norton in a host of companies clearly suggests its impact on strategy execution and making strategy work.

To be sure, the Balanced Scorecard reiterates much of what previous work on the integration of long- and short-term needs espoused and discussed in detail. It is not, by any means, a brand-new thrust or invention in managerial thinking. Still, it is useful in that it is very convincing about the importance of managing the short term well. It does offer a clear view on the needed integration of long- and short-term objectives. This serves to reinforce the message currently being discussed, namely the need to define and communicate the operational components of strategy if successful execution is to be achieved. To realize long-term goals, it is necessary to manage the short term well.

NEED FOR MEASURABLE OBJECTIVES

It is important to emphasize one final point: The operational aspects of strategic and short-term objectives means that these objectives are measurable. They are useful for strategy execution if they measure important results. Strategy must be translated into metrics that are consistent with the strategy and measurable. Only then can the results of execution be adequately assessed. Without these useful metrics, successful evaluation of execution results is not possible.

To be sure, some managers will gripe about and resist a demand for measurability. Staff people especially will argue vehemently that what they do is not measurable. I've heard lawyers in a number of companies insist that "you can't measure what lawyers do." I've worked with IT people who argue that their support services are not quantifiable. I've observed near rebellions in government organizations such as the FTC and Social Security Administration when managers tried to introduce zero-based budgeting and the use of clear, measurable objectives in planning and execution processes.

What can be done when confronting this type of resistance from staff managers or personnel in "soft," nonline functions? Here are some questions that can be used to facilitate the measurability of staff work. The questions come from various companies I've worked with, and I've seen them result in fruitful discussions of value-added and useful metrics of performance.

- If this unit or department were eliminated, what would change? What would be the impact on other units or departments in the company, and how, specifically, would this impact be felt or measured?

- Given two departments like mine, assume that one was highly effective and the other highly ineffective. How could you tell the two apart? With no one telling you who was effective and who was not, how could you identify and differentiate between the two departments?

- How do you, as an internal customer of my staff's services, evaluate what we do? What criteria do you use to judge or evaluate our performance?

Obviously, some jobs or functions are more difficult to measure than others. It may also be that people resist measurement and the accountability it implies. Still, simple questions such as the preceding can "break the ice" and help people see that they indeed are making valuable and measurable contributions to strategic and short-term goals. People can also be made to see that only things that are measurable can be improved or changed. Without measurement, there can be no useful assessment of the worth or contribution of a job or department to the execution of a chosen strategy.

ISSUE #4: UNDERSTANDING THE "DEMANDS" OF STRATEGY AND SUCCESSFUL EXECUTION

The last point to emphasize is that strategy makes "demands" on the development of organizational skills, resources, and capabilities. To ignore these demands surely will result in poor strategy execution and unfavorable performance.

I have long argued this position, that strategy demands the development of specific capabilities if the strategy is to succeed. In one study, Charles Snow and I examined the relationship between strategy and distinctive competence and its effect on organizational performance in 88 companies in four different industries.[xi] The primary hypothesis was simple and straightforward: Companies that developed capabilities or competencies consistent with a chosen strategy would perform better than companies that hadn't achieved this fit between strategy and capabilities. Put another way, we were testing two related points:

1. Strategy demands investment in, and development of, specific capabilities or competencies.

2. Firms making such an investment will perform better than companies in which the requisite capabilities are not developed.

The results of the studies were strong and consistent with expectations. The two points were clearly validated.

Companies that created capabilities to match their strategies outperformed their competitors, looking at return on assets. When the right capabilities or competencies weren't developed to support a strategy, execution suffered and performance outcomes were poor. The demands of strategy had to be met to achieve successful execution.

What are some examples of these demands, and how do they affect execution? Table 3.3 lists some of the demands for two popular generic strategies: low-cost producer and differentiation. I focus on these first because they are well-known approaches to competitive strategy. I've also been able to study companies with varying levels of success in executing these strategies and thus have developed some insights over the years into the factors that affect execution. Companies pursuing these two generic strategies do not always develop each and every item listed in Table 3.3. Still, the trend toward developing and "bundling" resources and capabilities consistent with the strategies has been obvious and striking to me over time.

Table 3.3 The "Demands" of Strategy

Low-Cost Producer	Differentiation
Capital investment in equipment, technology	Effective product engineering
Need for volume, standardization, and repetition	Sound R&D (emphasis on "D")
Focus on economies of scale and scope	Heavy emphasis on marketing and advertising
Development and use of appropriate accounting controls and methods	Concern with quality and quality assurance
Effective MIS or IT systems and processes	Organizational structures favoring effectiveness
Organizational structures favoring efficiency	Getting close to customers
Incentives and controls that support cost reduction	Incentives that support product/service differentiation

LOW-COST PRODUCER

To achieve this position in an industry or market segment, companies usually invest heavily in up-to-date equipment or technology to reduce costs. Computerized production controls and robotics, for example, reduce variable costs of production by replacing labor, a more expensive factor of production. This is readily seen in the automotive industry and other mass-production situations. In service industries, the same trend can be seen. Airlines seek larger planes with fewer, more-fuel-efficient engines to reduce the operating cost per passenger mile. Even movie theaters invest in large, centrally located popcorn machines to serve all the theaters in their multiplex model.

The need under the low-cost strategy—indeed, the holy grail of sorts—is to achieve high volume, standardization, and repetition of work, for these lead invariably to economies of scale and scope, the basis of a low-cost position.

Standardization can lead to yet other decisions—such as a smaller or narrower product line—to help foster volume and large production runs in the quest for scale economies. Some large insurance companies specialize in term insurance, eschewing financial or estate planning and other more elaborate policies, to reduce and standardize product offerings and perform the same tasks over and over again.

Other investments are also suggested in Table 3.3 in companies' quest for a low-cost position. Effective and efficient IT or MIS systems are needed to provide up-to-date information about costs, production, shipments, and inventory. Accounting controls and methods are developed to provide valid information about variable costs in a timely manner. IT systems aid in knowledge transfer so that headway in cost reduction in one part of the organization can be understood and deployed in other, more remote parts of the company. Again, look at the success of companies such as Wal-Mart that have made these IT investments.

Other changes also support the demands of the low-cost strategy. Organizational structure, for instance, must be consistent with strategy. Choice of structure usually focuses on functional structures to maximize repetition, volume, and economies related to scale and scope (see Chapter 4). Incentives are tied to cost reduction to support the strategy and "reward the right things" (see Chapter 6). Again, to achieve a low-cost position, decisions about investments, capabilities, and operations must support and be consistent with that strategy.

DIFFERENTIATION STRATEGIES

Table 3.3 notes the capabilities or decisions needed to support the differentiation strategy. For product companies, I've often found that companies invest heavily in R&D (emphasis on "D") and engineering in order to respond to customers' needs or demands and reconfigure products and services. Emphasis often is on quality, with programs and actions directed toward quality assurance.

Managers in companies pursuing differentiation strategies often talk of "getting close to customers," the manifestation of which takes many forms. "Getting close" may simply mean interviewing customers occasionally or conducting questionnaire surveys, or it might mean making customers part of internal business processes such as new product development or quality assurance programs.

Virtually every company pursuing differentiation strategies in the marketplace relies heavily on marketing efforts. Marketing capabilities are usually developed internally, but even if they are outsourced, internal controls are developed to ensure effective execution of an overall marketing plan. Heavy advertising in targeted market segments usually is an integral part of the marketing efforts.

Organizational structure is designed around goals of effectiveness and performance rather than efficiency in the differentiating firm. While cost clearly comes into play at some point in every organization, the primary thrust is on customer satisfaction, product performance, service, market share, gross margins, and responding quickly to customer or market demands, rather than on pure cost issues. Logically, incentives are developed to support and reinforce these desired outcomes in companies pursuing differentiation strategies.

DEVELOPING THE RIGHT CAPABILITIES

Table 3.3 shows only a partial list of the resources and capabilities that are developed in response to the demands of a strategy. Still, hopefully one point is very clear: The resources or capabilities needed to support and execute a strategy vary with the strategy employed.

What one invests in or nurtures in terms of organizational competencies clearly varies according to how one competes. Cost leadership demands a different set of skills or functional capabilities than the pursuit of a differentiation strategy. Two business units pursuing the two strategies noted in Table 3.3 should look and act very differently because of the requisite development of different resources and capabilities.

To execute strategy effectively, the right capabilities must be developed. The right capabilities, however, vary as a function of the type of strategy being pursued.

This discussion also suggests that caution must be exercised when changing strategies. Imagine a company that for years has pursued a differentiation strategy. Changing economic and competitive conditions over time (globalization, commoditization, and influx of new and larger competitors) dictate that the company must increasingly compete on price, emphasizing the need for a cost-based strategy.

But the company cannot simply or automatically convert to a cost-leadership mode: It has resources and capabilities that do not lend themselves to the execution of a low-cost strategy. For years it has invested in and nurtured skills or competencies that supported differentiation, and these competencies are not the ones that support a competitive strategy based on cost leadership. The company cannot simply expect or demand a change in strategy by fiat, as it doesn't have the appropriate skill set to do so.

Consider the case of Sun Microsystems. Sixteen years ago, this Silicon Valley computer maker decided on a differentiation strategy to separate itself from the pack. It chose to ignore the standard chips and software that other computer makers routinely used. It chose instead to focus on its own high-powered custom inputs. Its machines, then, would be much more powerful—and expensive—than those of its competitors.

The gamble worked remarkably well for years. Sun became the provider of choice in certain market segments, such as servers that support Internet sites and powerful corporate computers. Customers paid more but clearly were happy with Sun's souped-up products. The attempt at differentiation and higher margins clearly was paying dividends.

Changes in the market and other suppliers' capabilities over time, however, soured Sun's prospects. "Standard" chips made by Intel and "standard" software by Microsoft matched the performance of Sun's souped-up, more expensive versions. Rival computer makers could provide the same powerful applications and solutions as Sun but at a much lower price. Standardization and commoditization of what had been powerful, differentiated components and computers in effect eliminated Sun's advantage and put it at a competitive disadvantage compared to lower-priced competitive products.

Sun's sales fell drastically as customers fled to rivals' product offer-ings. In October 2003, Sun's stock price had fallen to approxi-mately $3.50, down from a split-adjusted high of about $65 in the fall of 2000.[xii] Sun's CEO, Scott McNealy, finally let go of his per-sistent adherence to the higher-priced, differentiation strategy and decided that Sun had to change. It had to focus on standardized products and the low end of its market, a move that clearly chal-lenged its long-held business model based on high-end, differenti-ated products.

The challenges facing McNealy and Sun are obvious and ominous. Can Sun become a low-cost producer of standardized products and still make money? Can its new strategy still allow it enough profit to focus on R&D and technology that heretofore had helped differ-entiate it from the competition? Competing in a new, low-end mar-ket segment in which experience and the appropriate capabilities are lacking surely presents many problems and few opportunities.

To be sure, Sun or any other company can meet the demands of a new, price-conscious market. It can acquire a competitor already well versed in cost-leadership skills. It can add a new division or business unit for the low-end market. It can create and develop a new structural unit internally with the requisite competencies for low-cost or price-based competition. It can buy or add the right capabilities.

What it shouldn't do is try to pursue the new strategy with the old capabilities. For years, the company developed the skills or capabil-ities noted on the right side of Table 3.3, and these are not the skills and capabilities needed to compete on the left side of Table 3.3. The bulk of competencies developed for the old strategy of differentia-tion are not fungible and easily applied to a new situation of cost leadership. Care must be taken to avoid setting up a "lose-lose" sit-uation in which the failure of a new strategy is virtually guaranteed by failing to develop the requisite capabilities for success. Different strategies demand different capabilities; trying to execute a new strategy with old capabilities can only lead to major problems.

Can functions *within* a business pursue different goals or functional strategies, such as low cost in manufacturing and differentiation in marketing? Of course. Manufacturing, in fact, typically pursues a low-cost position, a normal quest for efficiency and lower variable costs. But that is not the issue here.

We're talking business strategy and how the entire company positions itself to compete. Manufacturing can pursue low cost. But if the company overall is attempting to differentiate its products and services, the right capabilities must be developed to support the differentiation strategy for successful execution to result. If the low-cost tactics of manufacturing injure the company's ability to attend to customers' needs or demands for product quality, then execution will suffer and corrective action must be taken. If manufacturing resists product development or product extensions that customers want because doing so is costly (stopping the line, retooling, experimentation), the interference with the differentiation strategy must be eliminated. The goals and operations of any functional area cannot be inconsistent with or injurious to business strategy. The demands of the differentiation strategy must be met.

THE DEMANDS OF GLOBAL STRATEGY

Let's consider one more example—the demands of global strategy. This is a hybrid of sorts, as global strategy certainly can include the low-cost and differentiation examples already discussed. Global strategy, however, does make additional demands on management to develop the right resources and capabilities to facilitate effective competition in world markets.

The focus of the present example is the coordinated global strategy. The key word here is "coordinated." Unlike the simple international presence of the multidomestic firm with independent operations in various countries, the coordinated global strategy is more complex.

Competitive advantage under a coordinated global strategy is derived, in large part, from the sharing and leveraging of skills or capabilities across country boundaries. Countries or regions may enjoy comparative advantages such as in labor costs or other factor prices. The trick is to leverage the low-cost position into competitive advantage elsewhere. Or a company may enjoy a technological capability in one part of the world that represents a core competence. Again, the need is to share and integrate the core competence across product lines and country boundaries. Or a company can have a complex web of interdependencies, such as basic or preliminary work on a product is done in one country, sent to another for finishing or advanced development, and then sent to yet other countries for inclusion in a final product that is shipped everywhere. The need here is an ability to manage these interdependencies well.

A company such as Asea Brown Boveri exhibits this complexity and need for coordination in many of its businesses. Work in plants or businesses within countries is coordinated by worldwide business heads and country/regional managers to determine where semifinished and finished products will wind up. Some of ABB's businesses are truly global, whereas others are super local, with the former receiving inputs from ABB units across the globe. Capabilities are needed in the global businesses to ensure worldwide coordination of efforts.

Citibank reminds us that global complexity and the need for coordination are not just characteristics of product organizations but service businesses as well. When servicing large, multinational corporations (MNCs) worldwide, clearly the emphasis must be on coordination of activities and services for MNCs across regional or country boundaries. The trick to getting an MNC's business in Tokyo or Sao Paulo may be the services provided or global finance programs developed in New York or elsewhere. Although Citibank must be aware of differences in bank regulations and processes by country, its main focus in servicing MNCs is clearly global, reflecting interdependencies and coordination across countries.

Table 3.4   Meeting the Demands of a Coordinated Global Strategy

- Concentrate on coordination, the sharing of core competence, and developing economies of scale and scope across countries or worldwide regions.
- Focus on human resources and developing a cadre of effective global managers.
- Rotate key managers through different countries to achieve a global perspective; make sure that promotion and other rewards depend on this experience.
- Emphasize a core language to facilitate communication and create a core traveling staff to help ensure communication and control.
- Implement a matrix organization to ensure a dual, simultaneous focus on both worldwide businesses and a geographical region or country. Provide incentives that support the dual focus of the matrix rather than one side over the other.
- Develop incentives and feedback mechanisms to support cooperation and corporate goals and to avoid the suboptimatization of businesses and geographical areas working at cross purposes.

In these cases, methods of coordinating, sharing, and integrating are important demands of the global strategy. Communication and control across divisional and country boundaries are central to the execution of the strategy.

Table 3.4 shows some of the steps a company can take to meet these demands of the coordinated global strategy. The list is only a partial one, of necessity, but it provides examples of how organizations must develop human, technological, and structural capabilities to achieve the coordination demanded by the global strategy.[xiii]

In sum, managers pursuing low cost, differentiation, or global strategies should make up a list of demands of those strategies similar to those shown in Tables 3.3 and 3.4. Such a focus will identify the key needs or capabilities that are essential to successful execution. If the demands of strategy aren't developed adequately, the execution of the strategy will surely suffer or fail.

A FINAL POINT

The value of a well–thought-out strategy to successful execution cannot be exaggerated. Care taken in strategy development at both the corporate and business levels, and in the integration of those strategic plans, surely results in positive dividends for the organization.

A popular mantra among a handful of managers I've known is that "good execution can overcome bad strategy." In my experience, this is rarely the case. The typical result is that a poor strategy results in poor outcomes. Bad strategy can create major frustrations, as managers work long and hard hours in a futile attempt to execute that which is not executable. Hard work that produces no benefits is exasperating. Vague strategy and constant changes in strategy have the same frustrating results.

Managers who participated in the Wharton surveys were entirely correct when they argued that "poor or vague strategy" leads to execution problems. Attending to the four strategy-related issues noted in this chapter will reduce, if not entirely eliminate, these problems.

SUMMARY

A number of points in the present chapter relate to the success of a company's execution or implementation efforts.

- Strategy is the essential ingredient, the driving force behind execution efforts. Sound planning is essential, then, at both corporate and business-unit levels.

- It is vitally important to integrate corporate and business strategies. This means that effective communication is needed between levels, along with processes that enable decision-makers to reach agreement on strategies, goals, and performance metrics. The strategy review is one method of achieving this integration of corporate and business strategies.

- Long-term strategic needs of the organization must be translated into short-term operating objectives in order to successfully execute strategy. The short term is a key to successful execution; managers routinely spend a lot of time there. It is necessary to have short-term operating objectives that provide measures or metrics that can be used to evaluate execution plans and efforts.

■ Finally, strategy makes demands on organizational resources and capabilities. Development of the appropriate skills and competencies is vital to the successful execution of strategy. Care must be exercised when changing strategy or pursuing different strategies simultaneously, as the skills and competencies needed will vary as a function of strategy pursued.

The focus in this book is on making strategy work. Toward this end, we considered the major obstacles to successful execution in Chapter 1. We've also begun to confront these obstacles. In Chapter 2, the vital importance of a model or template to guide execution decisions and actions was emphasized. In this chapter, key early elements of the model—corporate and business strategy—were discussed to show how the characteristics of strategy and sound planning affect execution outcomes. In Chapter 4, we'll turn to the next key element of our model or template—organizational structure and its impact on strategy execution.

ENDNOTES

i. Jim Collins, *Good to Great*, Harper Business, 2001, p.10.

ii. "Former Chief Tries to Redeem the Calls He Made at AT&T," *The Wall Street Journal*, May 26, 2004.

iii. Larry Bossidy and Ram Charan, *Execution*, Crown Business, 2002, especially pages 179–182.

iv. Michael Porter, *Competitive Strategy*, Free Press, 1980; "What is Strategy?" *Harvard Business Review*, November-December, 1996.

v. See, for example, C. K. Prahalad and Gary Hamel, "The Core Competence of the Corporation," *Harvard Business Review*, May-June, 1990.

vi. Chester Barnard, *The Functions of the Executive*, Harvard University Press, 1938.

vii. William Joyce, Nitin Nohria, and Bruce Roberson, *What (Really) Works*, Harper Business, 2003, p. 16.

viii. See, for example, Steve Carroll and Henry Tosi, *Management by Objectives*, Macmillan, 1973.

ix. L. G. Hrebiniak and W. Joyce, *Implementing Strategy*, Macmillan, 1984; "The Strategic Importance of Managing Myopia," *Sloan Management Review*, Fall, 1984.

x. Robert Kaplan and David Norton, *The Balanced Scorecard*, Harvard Business School Press, 1996.

xi. Charles Snow and L. G. Hrebiniak, "Strategy, Distinctive Competence, and Organizational Performance," *Administrative Science Quarterly*, June 1980.

xii. "Cloud Over Sun Microsystems: Plummeting Computer Prices," *The Wall Street Journal*, October 16, 2003.

xiii. For an additional discussion of the problems and issues involved in executing different types of global strategy, see L. G. Hrebiniak, "Implementing Global Strategies," *European Journal of Management*, December, 1992.

4

Organizational Structure and Execution

Introduction

The model of execution outlined in Chapter 2 shows the central role played by organizational structure. Strategy affects structure, or alternatively, structure is important to the execution of strategy, at both corporate and business levels.

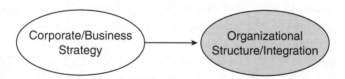

Despite its centrality, the role of structure in strategy execution is sometimes problematic. Managers who participated in the Wharton Executive Education Survey and the panel discussions reported problems with structure in strategy execution. They argued that structure is often set up or changed for the wrong reasons. Design or redesign efforts are handled badly and, not infrequently, are frustrating or doomed to failure. Integration or coordination of diverse structural units is poor or incomplete. The link to strategy when changing structure is unclear or often simply missing. Managers in the Wharton-Gartner Survey reinforced poor interunit information sharing and unclear responsibility as major execution problems.

The purpose of this chapter is to clarify the role and impact of structure in strategy execution. The intent is not to try to summarize the massive volume of work already done on organizational design. Rather, the goal is to consider and clarify the handful of structural issues that are most important for making strategy work.

What are these issues? What are the biggest structural-related problems, challenges, or mistakes when executing strategy? Let's identify them by looking at a few examples.

THE CHALLENGE OF STRUCTURAL CHOICE

GENERAL MOTORS

Let me first stress just how difficult and complex structural choices can be. Take the case of General Motors, whose competitive woes and loss of market share are well known and documented. Foreign carmakers hurt GM badly. Customers deserted the American company in droves because of poor quality. The 1980s and early 1990s saw GM as a stumbling giant, a company in trouble.

The company desperately needed change. Significant improvements were essential in product quality, customer relations, and cost reduction. Another perceived need was an overhaul of organizational structure. Consequently, North American Operations was restructured to comprise two groups: BOC (Buick, Oldsmobile, and Cadillac) and CPC (Chevrolet, Pontiac, and Canada). The old structure, with its car divisions, manufacturing division, and so on was history. Each group was relatively self-contained with its own functional components. The restructuring, however, proved to be a disaster. Why?

Many employees and managers had no idea that such a large-scale change was in the offing. They were shocked when it occurred. Would their jobs change? Would layoffs occur? The uncertainty was unbearable.

The logic of the new structure wasn't clear. What did the groups represent? It wasn't a clear division of big cars vs. small cars. (Some managers told me facetiously that BOC stood for "big ol' cars"!) Why add Canada, or geography, to groups with a product-line or brand focus? (A few managers joked that CPC would some-day be CPSiSi, as Mexico might be added to the group. Gallows humor?) Top management was silent on the connection between strategy and structure. How did the new structure relate to GM's strategy? How would the change contribute to the solution of problems in product quality, costs, and organizational effective-ness? The logic of the restructuring was missing, unclear, or uncommunicated.

The structural change proved to be a failure. Top management per-formed poorly. But in their defense, consider the size and com-plexity of the problems they faced. GM was a huge company at the time, slightly larger than the U.S. Navy, I believe. It had been suc-cessful for years, causing no small amount of inertia. ("We must be doing something right.") The relative independence of the car divi-sions, Body by Fisher, and the manufacturing divisions was engrained in the culture. This made attempts at coordination and the creation of superordinate goals difficult at best.

Roles and responsibilities had become diffused and unclear, in part again because of the company's size. Looking, for example, at product quality, I found numerous groups or functions at the cor-porate, group, divisional, and plant levels that were "responsible for quality." But who ultimately was responsible or accountable? This was unclear to me and most observers. Where should the responsibility and accountability for quality be? Should it be a corporate, group, or functional responsibility in the new struc-ture? These were tough questions that needed answering.

I'm not defending GM, but I'll concede that creating or changing structure in such a large organization is a difficult task. Many companies have made huge mistakes in this area, not just GM. And these companies are run by bright, experienced people. Perhaps some of the poor performance may be attributable to the difficulty of the task itself and not simply managerial incompetence.

JOHNSON & JOHNSON

Take next the case of Johnson & Johnson (J&J). J&J has always been a decentralized company with a huge number of independent businesses or strategic business units (SBUs). It was long felt that decentralization fostered entrepreneurship, motivated managers to perform well in their own "small" companies, and allowed a closeness to the market and customers that was difficult to achieve in more centralized structural forms. Central staff was kept quite small, a further testimony to the company's preferred culture of decentralization and SBU autonomy. And J&J's outstanding performance over the years seemed to reinforce its belief in the benefits of decentralization and the smallness of companies in its portfolio.

There were (and still are) challenges to J&J's structure. One of these was the need for increased coordination across the independent business units. Increases in customer power (such as the rise of large HMOs in the hospital sales businesses) threatened the traditional autonomy and independence of decentralized SBUs serving these markets. Whereas the traditional model had numerous J&J companies selling different products (Tylenol, bandages, diagnostic equipment, and so on) to the same hospital, HMOs comprising many hospitals refused to deal with 10 or 20 different J&J companies when making purchases. They wanted to deal with one source representing all the J&J companies. They wanted J&J to perform the integration or coordination of purchases that individual hospitals previously were forced to do. These larger, more powerful buyers could force J&J to adopt a different operating structure.

Dealing with these new demands was a real challenge to J&J. The task was to coordinate work in areas that traditionally were the bailiwick of separate independent businesses. Increased centralization or corporate control was needed to affect the coordinated selling and delivery of products across units that traditionally had autonomy to do things in their own way. Care was needed so as not to confront and violate a company culture and operating structure premised on decentralization, independence, and local control.

That J&J successfully met this challenge with reengineering and restructuring (for example, a national sales group) says a great deal about its managerial capabilities. The task was not easy, however. Convincing independent SBU managers about the need for increased centralization of sorts, with more controls placed on autonomous units, was an important but delicate task. Changing structure, without threatening a structural "institution" of decentralization and autonomy in decision-making, clearly was a formidable challenge and difficult chore.

CITIBANK AND ABB

Consider, finally, the structural needs and problems of large global players such as Citibank and Asea Brown Boveri (ABB). The issue of centralization and decentralization again comes into play. Global control demands centralization, as the need exists to focus on businesses worldwide and coordinate information flows and knowledge sharing across geographically dispersed units. There is a related need to create synergies or achieve economies of scale and scope, which again calls for centralization and corporate control over certain resources.

But global companies also need decentralization. Businesses must be able to respond to local needs and customer demands in a large, geographically dispersed company. Local autonomy is needed to cope with differences in economic conditions, laws, regulations, or aspects of culture that affect how business is done in different parts of the world.

Companies such as Citibank and ABB are forced to handle these and similar issues. They must create structural forms comprising corporate center staff and decentralized business units to handle global and local needs simultaneously. In both companies, a geographical organization exists side by side with a worldwide product- or service-based organization. Tensions between global and local controls must be handled, and a forum for resolving conflicts between overall company and local needs must be made operational. These and other issues have been and are being handled by Citibank and ABB, using product- and geography-based organizations and matrix structures to achieve effective coordination and integrate global and local needs.

THE CRITICAL STRUCTURAL ISSUES

What do these examples tell us about the structural issues that affect the execution of strategy? There are at least five issues suggested by them that deserve additional consideration. They are as follows:

1. **Measuring the impact of structure.** What are the costs vs. benefits of different structural forms? How are the costs and benefits measured?

2. **Centralization vs. decentralization.** What is the right balance, and what determines it? Included here is the size and role of the corporate center in organizations with both centralized and decentralized units.

3. **The relationship between strategy and structure.** What aspects or elements of strategy drive the choice of structure? How does structure affect the execution of a strategy?

4. **Achieving coordination and information sharing across organizational units.** Integration and knowledge sharing are important to execution, whether between corporate center staff and businesses or across decentralized geographical units of a company.

5. **Clarifying responsibility and accountability.** These basic structural definitions are necessary for effective execution. People must know who's responsible for what, when, and why, for execution to work.

The present model of execution uses two structural terms: organizational *structure* (corporate and business) and *integration*. The former is defined by boxes and lines. It shows the anatomy of an organization and how it groups and uses specialized resources, such as functions or divisions. The remainder of this chapter will consider the first three items in the preceding list as elements of organizational structure and how structural choice depends on strategy.

Structural integration deals with the clarification of responsibilities and the mechanisms or management processes used to make the boxes and lines work. Processes of coordination or the integration of workflows between functional areas are examples of these operating mechanisms. Processes of knowledge transfer across organizational boundaries or units represent another example of structural integration. The last two structural issues in the preceding list, aspects of integration, will be covered in Chapter 5. Other aspects of execution suggested by the preceding examples, such as managing change and culture, will be handled in later chapters.

Let's now consider the first three organizational structural issues in the preceding list. The logic here is that, to understand the role of structure in strategy execution, it is necessary to do the following:

1. First understand the basics of structure, including its costs and benefits.

2. Apply the basics to make better decisions about centralization and decentralization.

3. Tie everything together by looking at the relationship between strategy and structure in the execution process.

The third issue, relating strategy and structure, is the most critical one for execution. Yet to explicate and clarify this issue, the basic elements of structure defined and discussed in the first two issues are absolutely essential. The first two issues represent necessary building blocks for understanding the third issue.

Managers interviewed in the panel discussions and Wharton executive programs stated that basic aspects of structure are often misunderstood. Yet, they stressed, managers are sometimes reluctant to seek advice on basic issues. Consequently, I'll discuss the first two issues as precursors to the critical analysis of the third issue and let the reader pick and choose from among the facts or insights presented, as needed.

STRUCTURAL ISSUE #1: MEASURING COSTS AND BENEFITS OF STRUCTURE

How does structure affect actual costs or measurable benefits? What results can reasonably be expected from different organizational forms?

To answer these questions, let's go back to basics. Picture an organization in the very simple way suggested by the following diagram:

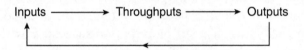

All organizations have inputs: raw materials, staff or employees, patients, financial resources, and so on. All have throughputs: processes or technologies that transform inputs into outputs. Manufacturing firms have mass-production equipment and robots. Hospitals employ different skill sets or techniques (surgery, lab tests, dietary regimes) when working on patients. Universities have "technologies" (Socratic dialogues, case teaching methods) to educate students. Finally, all organizations have outputs (cars, cured patients, educated MBA students).

Using this simple figure, it is possible to argue, first, that organizations can be structured around their throughputs—the processes, technologies, or skill sets (the "means") employed in converting inputs into outputs (the "ends"). The term "process specialization" can be used to emphasize this focus on throughputs or the common processes employed to generate organizational outputs.[i]

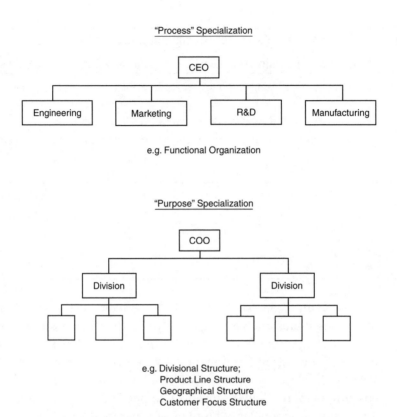

Figure 4.1   Organizational Structure: Process and Purpose Specialization

Figure 4.1 shows the best-known example of process specialization—the common functional organization. Organization by throughput or process breaks the company into functions (manufacturing, R&D, marketing). As Table 4.1 shows, there are benefits and costs associated with the functional structure.

Table 4.1   Costs and Benefits of Process and Purpose Specialization

	Process Specialization/Functions	Purpose Specialization/Divisions
Benefits	■ Expertise of knowledge/a "critical mass"	■ Focus on customer, products, markets
	■ Economies of scale and scope/efficiency	■ Effectiveness
	■ Avoid duplication of scarce resources	■ Fewer coordination problems
	■ "Career" benefits	■ Quick response to industry change
Costs	■ Coordination costs	■ Duplication of scarce resources
	■ Functional myopia	■ Potential loss of economies/efficiency
	■ Loss of "big picture"	
	■ Bureaucracy	

The focus on expertise, with skilled engineers, scientists, or manufacturing managers working closely together, is a positive aspect. Groups of experts often form a "critical mass" that is needed for problem solving and innovation. A group of scientists working together in close proximity, with high levels of interaction and discussion, is more likely to discover something new than that same group split among a large number of separate divisions.

The repetition and standardization of work (such as doing lab tests in hospitals, assembly lines in manufacturing, engineers working on common problems) often lead to efficiency, economies of scale and scope. Duplication of resources is avoided, as personnel in a function can service many customers within the company.

Finally, there may be some "career" benefits when, for example, engineers work with engineers and know that their career path is through engineering. A handful of engineers reporting to a business manager in a small division in Tierra del Fuego may not see such a clear career ladder.

There are costs to the functional organization, as shown in Table 4.1. The most obvious are coordination costs. To service a customer or make a product, it is necessary to coordinate the many and diverse functions. The differences in goals and perceptions that mark different functions' views of work can exacerbate the problems of coordination and detract from a common goal such as customer service or high product quality. It simply is difficult to coordinate work among groups that hold differing views of what's important and what needs attention. Relatedly, the greater the number of diverse functions that need coordination, the more difficult the task and the higher the likelihood of problems.

Another way of looking at this is to talk about "functional myopia."[ii] Functional people get so wrapped up in their own technologies and views of the world that they lose sight of the "big picture." R&D people get so involved in research, new technologies, and the long term that they totally ignore the "mundane" requests for product-line improvements now, in the near term. Science is more exciting and compelling than product revisions or customer demands. Functional myopia clearly exacerbates problems of coordination and unity of effort.

Finally, I've often heard the cry of "bureaucracy" by people who have trouble dealing with functional resistance to new ideas or the speeding up of work. Each function has its own rules and will follow them, the accusation goes, even if organizational work comes to a standstill.

Table 4.1 also shows the benefits and costs of what has been called "purpose" specialization. Purpose specialization simply means organization around "ends," or outputs, in contrast to the focus on "means," or throughputs, or the common functions of process specialization. For our purposes, think of "divisions" in organizations (see Figure 4.1). Strategic business units (SBUs) or product-line organizations also qualify as examples of this type of specialization, but let's focus on divisions to facilitate discussion. Divisional structures that focus on customers (Consumer Products Division), product lines (Mainframe Division), or geography (Asian or North American Division) are common examples of this form of organization.

As is seen in Table 4.1, the costs and benefits of purpose specialization or divisionalization are generally the opposite of those shown under process specialization. Divisions can focus on customers, products, or geographical areas, increasing effectiveness. A dedicated organizational structure allows for quick responses to customer needs or industry changes. There are fewer coordination problems. Even if divisions are organized functionally, the focus derived from attention to one customer (the Government Products Division), product (Mainframe Division), or geographical region (the Asian Division) facilitates and enables coordination around a common goal, customer, or output.

The costs of divisional structures include the duplication of scarce resources. Each division head will argue for control over his or her own resources, staff, or functional groups, leading potentially to large amounts of costly duplication. Similarly, although the functional structure reinforces efficiency and scale economies, smaller divisions may not be able to achieve or sustain these same efficiencies.

It is clear that the purpose/divisional form contributes to effectiveness or "doing the right things" (having the right products or services, meeting customer needs quickly), whereas it may sometimes sacrifice efficiency or "doing things right" (low cost, scale economies).[iii] The process/functional form contributes heavily to "doing things right" but potentially at the expense of "doing the right things" because of the problems noted in Table 4.1.

The actual metrics that can be employed to measure the impact of structure can be summarized under the headings of efficiency and effectiveness.

Efficiency	Effectiveness
• Cost per (unit, patient, student)	• Market Share
• Economies of Scale	• Customer Satisfaction
• Duplication of Resources (Fixed costs, Costs of Staff)	• Revenue Growth
• Coordination Costs (# of people and time spent)	• Time to Market
	• Product Introductions

↓	↓
Functional Structure ("Doing Things Right")	Divisional Structure ("Doing the Right Things")

These prototypical organizational forms and metrics are basic. Still, keeping these basic ideas in mind, along with their costs and benefits, helps immensely when facing difficult structural decisions such as centralization vs. decentralization of organizational structure or relating structure to strategy. Let's apply these basic ideas in the next section of this chapter, where we consider the choice between centralized and decentralized structures.

STRUCTURAL ISSUE #2: CENTRALIZATION VS. DECENTRALIZATION

"You're damned if you do and damned if you don't," lamented a CEO whose company I helped restructure. "If I ask corporate center people where resources should be, they answer 'here, naturally.' Ask the same question of my business heads, and of course, the answer is quite different. They want all resources in their businesses or divisions, not at corporate. As profit centers, they want total control of all functional staff. Corporate is seen as a hindrance, not a help."

This quote reflects a common problem in many organizations—where to put scarce resources or assets. Should R&D or manufacturing be centralized and service all divisions or businesses, or should they be decentralized and under the control of managers who most directly need and use their capabilities? The quote shows that even today there obviously are mixed answers to this question.

Building on the preceding discussion of structural costs and benefits can help with decisions about the location of scarce resources. Should top management opt for the efficiencies of the functional structure, despite its coordination and other costs? Or should it choose to decentralize around product lines, customers, or geography to serve markets more effectively?

The simple answer is that structural choice depends on what is important to management in Table 4.1, strategically or operationally. Given competitive conditions, industry forces, and the company's strategy (see Issue #3 later in this chapter), choices are made between the different structural forms noted in Table 4.1.

Complexity arises because most companies need and use both centralized and decentralized structures. The issue is how to create the right mix.

A Sequential Decision Process

To see the interplay between the need for efficiency and effectiveness in structural choices and understand better the mix of centralization and decentralization, consider the decision process suggested in Figure 4.2. At the corporate level, corporate center staff reports to the CEO, along with the COO, the top operations-oriented manager. The corporate center staff represents functions that service the entire company in the name of consistency of service across all businesses, such as legal, HR, IT. Emphasis is on expertise, efficiency, and avoidance of duplication of key personnel. Corporate center staff thus represents process specialization and centralized company-wide functional support.

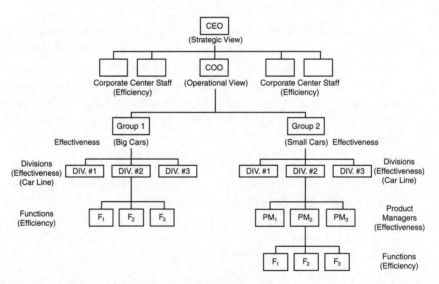

Figure 4.2   A sequential approach to structural decisions.

Reporting to the COO are two groups, structural units representing clusters or group of divisions such as "big cars" and "small cars." The driver here is effectiveness, the assumption being that each group has its own particular strategic or operating needs that must be met. Each group may have different customer demographics, strategies (such as differentiation vs. low cost), and marketing approaches, and the structural separation allows for the recognition of these important differences. The separation into groups could also reflect a size issue. The differentiated groups may represent a way to break down the product lines into smaller, more manageable pieces to facilitate management attention and decision-making.

Both groups are then broken up into divisions, representing a further emphasis on effectiveness. Each division (such as a car line) has its own customers who express brand loyalty and whose unique needs are met by divisional functions and personnel. Cadillac within GM, for instance, has tried to differentiate itself as a division catering to well-to-do customers who might otherwise consider Lexus or Mercedes Benz cars as substitute products. The Cadillac division has its own general manager to focus on the unique strategic and operating needs of that brand of cars. Emphasis is primarily on effectiveness, servicing the desired customer base well.

The next level of analysis shows some differences between divisions in the two groups. Division 2 in Group 1 exhibits a functional structure, reflecting a primary concern with efficiency. In contrast, Division 2 in Group 2 exhibits a product-management structure, reflecting a continued managerial concern with effectiveness. Each product-management unit in Group 2 then is separated into functions, finally showing some concern for efficiency.

Why the differences? Because each division has different strategic and operating needs. A division in Weyerhaeuser that makes newsprint, the commodity paper used in newspapers, needs efficiency and low-cost production to remain competitive and stay in business. A sister division that makes and sells high-grade, high-quality, or high-performance paper products may focus less on efficiency than on effectiveness, employing product represen- tatives who get close to customers and tailor products to their needs. The division selling a commodity product focuses earlier on efficiency than the latter division, whose main focus is on qual- ity and customization of products. The commodity division has thin margins, making efficiency vital to survival. The latter divi- sion's margins are likely much higher because of its differentiated, customized products, giving it a bit more leeway on the cost side.

Large companies such as J&J, ABB, and GE likewise have numer- ous divisions or SBUs with varying strategic and operating needs. Some are organized primarily around efficiency concerns, while others are focused primarily on effectiveness, getting close to cus- tomers and markets. Divisions in the same company simply con- front and solve different strategic and operating problems, giving rise to varying concerns with efficiency and effectiveness.

Decisions about structure, then, can be seen as a sequential process, a logical order of decisions that examines needs for effi- ciency and effectiveness at each descending level of organization. Corporate decides which staff should service all businesses (effi- ciency, centralization), which groups or divisions should be creat- ed to reflect varying market needs (effectiveness, decentralization), and which functional support groups should be in those groups or divisions rather than at corporate (decentralization). Group and division staff, in turn, decides which functions will service all prod- uct lines (centralization) and which functions are unique to each product line (decentralization). And so on. Decisions about cen- tralization/decentralization occur between corporate and business levels and within businesses, reflecting a concern with efficiency and effectiveness and the performance measures previously listed.

Tall vs. Flat Organizations

The sequential decision process doesn't mean to imply that organ- izations need be tall, with lots of layers devoted to different needs or problems. The example in Figure 4.2 was used merely to show how decisions about structure are made logically by looking at each adjacent level of organization. It is not intended to suggest that all organizations need a complex, tall structure. The sequential process certainly can also result in flat structures, which, to many managers, means faster decision-making, less bureaucracy, closeness to the customer or market, and greater flexibility of structure.

GE Capital

Consider for a moment the case of GE Capital. GE is a large, complex organization, marked by different sectors (high tech, service) and businesses within sectors. Traditionally, the business heads reported directly to the CEO. The head of GE Capital reported to Jack Welch for years and was responsible for all segments of the business in that financial services unit. The structure, very basically, looked like this:

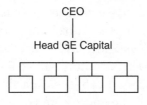

Business Areas

All communications about GE Capital business areas, strategy, functioning, earnings, and so on went through the head of the division or business unit. There were three organizational levels, down to the businesses, with additional levels within each business. The CEO had only indirect access to the business areas within GE Capital, including consumer finance, insurance, commercial finance, and equipment management.

Over time, this structure created some problems. GE Capital grew immensely and, as of this writing, had about $460 billion in assets, one of the largest nonbank financial institutions in the world. Critics, including Jeffrey Immelt, GE's CEO and replacement for Jack Welch, felt that too much was going on in GE Capital's businesses that wasn't easily understood by management or external financial analysts. One article described GE Capital as a financial "black box" that acts as a huge private bank without adequate financial disclosure.[iv] Immelt felt that he didn't have enough contact with or control over what was happening within this black box, and he wanted more direct, unfiltered communication with business elements.

Accordingly, he changed the structure, flattening it. GE Capital was broken up into four separate businesses: GE Commercial Finance, GE Consumer Finance, GE Equipment Management, and GE Insurance. The businesses now report directly to Immelt, thereby flattening the structure while aiming to improve oversight, improve transparency, and streamline and speed up decisions in a very complex business. Eliminating a level of management brings the performance effectiveness of the four businesses closer to top management scrutiny than had been the case.

Not everything was changed by Immelt's bold move. There still are common corporate functions within GE Capital serving all the businesses, such as risk management, capital markets, and tax and treasury. Reliance on the central functions still represents a quest for efficiency, consistency, and expertise that all businesses can tap into and use. The structural move flattening the organization, however, clearly is one driven primarily by the CEO's perceived need to be closer to business performance while improving transparency, communication, and oversight. The new structure of GE Capital, that is, deals with both efficiency and effectiveness but clearly focuses on the latter. The new structure, eliminating a level, looks like this:

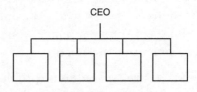

Four Businesses of GE Capital

Flatter structures clearly suggest benefits for organizations and management. They usually eliminate or reduce the problems associated with slow vertical communication. They result in greater decentralization and "job enlargement," as managers close to markets and customers assume more responsibility and make more decisions. They often are described as more "flexible" in their ability to respond more quickly to market changes than their taller counterparts. They increase control and improve transparency and accountability.

It must also be emphasized, however, that flat structures can fail to deliver. They are not an automatic panacea for structural woes. In fact, flat organizational structures potentially create four highly related problems that must be handled for them to produce positive results. These problems are: (a) inertia, (b) inadequate expertise, (c) individuals' not accepting responsibility for decision-making, and (d) creation of lateral communication problems.

Inertia

Flattening an organization may scare some managers or disrupt their routines. Previously, nasty problems could be referred up the hierarchy to one's boss. Flat structures usually have larger spans of control, making such referrals difficult, thus forcing people to act or decide. Some may be reluctant to do things differently and may change slowly, if at all, negatively affecting problem-solving or decision-making.

Inadequate Expertise

For individuals to make the additional decisions required of them in flat organizations, an increase in expertise is usually necessary. Larger spans of control make it difficult to tap into a superior's knowledge. This means that lower-level managers must develop much of the expertise and knowledge that their bosses once controlled. They need the increased knowledge to make decisions and solve problems in a more decentralized setting.

If training and managerial education processes are lacking, the creation of new expertise suffers, as does the ability to solve problems in the flat organization. Flat structures demand greater knowledge and insight from managers and others responsible for more and more decisions over time. Without this expertise, they can actually create decision bottlenecks and poor results.

Not Accepting Responsibility

The inertia and inadequate expertise just discussed clearly can make people reluctant to accept responsibility for new, more complex decisions. Increased closeness to the market and customers, coupled with the "need for speed" and quick reaction to external threats and opportunities, demands that more responsibility be assumed by lower levels in flat structures. Not having the necessary tools and having a fear of failure or a feeling of inadequacy will work against the acceptance of new responsibilities, causing the organization a host of problems.

Lateral Communication Problems

Finally, flattening an organizational structure can create new, lateral communication problems. Let me use an actual example from a company I know well that went through a period in which it tried to "delayer" its structure, to use its term. In this case, results were far from happy and useful. In the words of one functional manager:

> *"Spans of control increased tremendously due to the virtual elimination of an entire level. Of necessity, the company had to become more decentralized. Getting help from the boss is possible when span of control is one to seven; it's virtually impossible when span is one to forty-nine or some such ridiculous number.*
>
> *Decentralization meant that we, this "group of forty-nine," had to communicate laterally with each other rather than go through our bosses as we did in the past. Only then did we realize that so many things were different across previously separate units. The beliefs, values, and operating principles were simply not the same due to past differences in goals, competition, and history of the units. One group talked about margins, contribution, real costs, and value-added measurements that were foreign to people in other units. Perceptions of profit varied, as different groups looked at different expenses to arrive at different net figures. One group mentioned customers' needs frequently, while another had never seen or talked to customers and, hence, couldn't care less about them. There literally was nothing in common to bind people who previously had different bosses and views of the world. A common outlook to help the restructuring was not present.*

*With so little in common, it was extremely difficult to commu-
nicate. I know it sounds unbelievable, being the same company
and all that, but it's true. We couldn't talk to each other!"*

This clearly may be an extreme case, but it helps make the point:
Flat organizational structures have ample benefits if managers
handle the problems of inertia, inadequate expertise, reluctance to
accept responsibility, and new demands for lateral communication. Flat structures are not an automatic cure-all. They work, but
they need adequate managerial attention.

The Corporate Center

The mix of centralization vs. decentralization raises another structural issue that currently is receiving much attention: the size and
role of the corporate center.

The corporate staff's primary functions discussed thus far include
efficiency, or economies of scale and scope, consistency of centralized support services across all businesses or operating divisions, and an avoidance of duplication of resources. Thus, legal or
HR staffs are seen as providing the same consistent services to all
businesses, regardless of their industries, technologies, or customer base.

These clearly represent important services with a definite value
added. A staff of experts helps all businesses of divisions, thereby
sharing expertise and avoiding duplications of effort. Recently,
however, managers are telling me that they see an expanded role for
the corporate center. They see additional tasks or services that can
help strategy execution at both corporate and business levels. What
are some aspects of this expanded role for the corporate center?

A number of tasks for an expanded corporate center have been
suggested. Presently, I'll mention only three:

1. A strategic management function
2. An executive education function
3. "Centers of excellence" functions

Strategic Management Function

This group would advise the CEO and business leaders in a number of areas. Portfolio strategies could be reviewed to maximize strategic and financial goals. This group could help with benchmarking and the development of best practices in strategic planning, the management of information and information flows, and strategy-execution methods.

Recent developments at Crown Holdings suggest this type of centralized function in a strategic management group. A corporate strategy group focuses not only on corporate issues but also integration of corporate and business strategy. An important objective is to create an interactive planning process, integrating both corporate and business unit plans. Processes also focus on integration across geographical regions as well as across businesses. Additionally, the group is charged with the task of identifying and understanding future trends in the industry that could affect business or geographical performance. Clearly, this unit is concerned with more than just efficiency or central support services. As a corporate center group, it is charged with a strategic, educational, and integrative role that affects company performance.

Another important task for this group is to facilitate the strategy review discussed in Chapter 3 and again in Chapter 6. This review is important for corporate-business interactions, the integrity of corporate portfolio models, and the metrics used to evaluate business performance, all of which affect strategy execution.

Executive Education Function

This group would concern itself with the continuing education of management. The knowledge and capabilities of top management are vital to the success of strategy formulation and execution and, ultimately, to a company's ability to achieve competitive advantage. This corporate center group would focus on executive development in generic areas—planning, incentive systems, marketing, leadership, managing change—as well as areas specific to success in a given industry—new product development, customer service, and competitor intelligence. The goal is to create an educational resource that can profoundly affect strategy execution and organizational performance over time.

Recent trends at Microsoft indicate the development of an important executive education function. The growth, size, and increasing complexity of Microsoft suggest the need for such a centralized function. My work with many of their general managers and director-level people has been shaped and supported by a central group focusing on leadership and management development. Separation of the global giant into seven businesses has enabled the company to focus on different industries, competition, and customer needs. But Steve Ballmer, the CEO, and other top managers also correctly recognize that there are critical leadership and management capabilities that cut across the different businesses and consistently affect performance. The task of a new corporate center function in executive education and development is being directed toward these critical leadership and management skills.

More and more companies are creating internal "universities," corporate center groups involved in critical educational tasks. Indeed, in May 2004, there were some 1,600 such company "universities" in the United States, more than the 1,300 or so conventional universities offering undergraduate business degrees.[v] Clearly, the executive education function is becoming an increasingly important task for the corporate center concept.

Centers of Excellence

In a recent project I did with Aventis Behring, management spoke often about "centers of excellence." Under this concept, emphasis was on groups responsible for industry-wide standards of performance in such areas as medical and regulatory systems, preclinical research, clinical quality control, and biometry and statistical services.

The goal of center formation at Aventis and elsewhere is to develop groups that create leading-edge knowledge and processes that result in better enterprise performance and industry leadership. A related goal is the attraction of highly qualified scientific and managerial staff, resources that can help the company innovate and achieve competitive advantage. The focus on leading-edge technology and attraction of the "brightest and best" scientific and management personnel is another step in ensuring that the organization has the requisite resources and capabilities to support strategy execution.

The "new" corporate center, then, would contain the typical functions found in a centralized structure, such as legal, HR, IT, and finance. However, it would also have additional value-added services such as those shown in Figure 4.3. Clearly, this expanded role can have a large impact on strategy-execution activities.

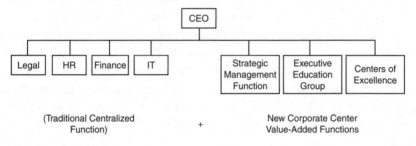

Figure 4.3 The corporate center.

A final caveat is needed here. The new corporate center concept certainly seems to be attractive, offering critical value-added services to help the entire enterprise execute its strategy more effectively. Yet care must be taken when defining the center's role in strategy execution. The center does represent an increased emphasis on centralization of resources and capabilities. If successful execution depends more on the decentralization of businesses and the ability to react quickly and appropriately to customer or market needs, the corporate center concept could become a hindrance to effective strategy implementation.

The important issue to keep in mind is that both centralization and decentralization have costs and benefits. It is necessary to balance the emphasis on the two structural forms so as to attain the desired strategic and operating outcomes for the organization.

STRUCTURAL ISSUE #3: THE STRATEGY-STRUCTURE-PERFORMANCE RELATIONSHIP

In many respects, this issue has already been suggested when considering the first two issues earlier in this chapter. Still, let's be more precise and provide some specific guidelines as to how strategy affects structure in the execution process.

The Demands of Strategy

Chapter 3 discussed the "demands" of strategy and their impact on resources and capabilities. The point then was that strategy demanded the development of certain skills, resources, or capabilities if successful execution was to occur. The latter resources include structure, which must reflect and respond to strategic demands. If structure doesn't reflect the demands of strategy, execution will suffer. Let's look at some examples.

Low-cost Strategy

Cost reduction and containment obviously are central to a cost-leadership or low-cost strategy. Commodity product or highly competitive industries usually are marked by price competition, with price as a "given" or constant. The fixed-price nature of these industries indicates that additional revenues cannot be gained by raising price and must come from lowered costs.

Organizational structure in these cases would favor the efficiencies and scale economies of centralized, functional forms. These forms are characterized by standardization, volume, and repetition, which foster efficiencies from economies of scale and scope. They also reduce unnecessary duplications of resources, further reducing costs. Thus, for the low-cost strategy:

Low-Cost Strategy ⟶	Centralized Functional Structures
• Commodity Products	• Efficiency, Economies of Scale and Scope
• Price Competition	• Standardization, Volume, and Repetition of Work
	• Lack of Duplication of Scarce Resources

Focus Strategies

These strategies usually focus on the customer, geography, or product line. Organizational structure, in turn, reflects the critical focus, usually with emphasis on the divisional form or a similar type of decentralized structure.

Focus Strategy ⟶ Decentralized, Divisional Structure

- Focus on Customer, Geography, or Product

- Dedicated Division and Staff

- Focus on Object of Strategy (e.g. Consumer Products and Government Products Divisions, Mainframe and PC Divisions, Asian Division)

- Minimum Centralized Staff Needed to Support Decentralized Operations

Even with the predominantly decentralized divisional structure, there still may be some centralized staff to achieve efficiencies across the decentralized units. The primary emphasis, however, clearly is on decentralization.

Differentiation Strategies

The key question here deals with the type of differentiation intended or the product or customer characteristics important to differentiation, such as high end of market vs. low-end products, "performance" products directed toward affluent buyers, and so on.

Using high-end (more expensive, higher quality, high performance) products vs. low-end products as an example, the firm would opt for a divisional structure with two businesses or divisions. The low-end division would likely pursue a low-cost strategy, whereas the high-end business would concern itself with satisfying its customers' needs for performance, quality, and "image." Each business would be relatively self-contained, as the resources or capabilities needed to pursue a low-cost strategy will differ from those needed to pursue the high-end strategy (see Chapter 3).

Differentiation Strategy ⟶ Decentralized, Divisional Structure

(High-End vs. Low-End Products)
- Two Divisions (High-end and Low-end)

- Self-Contained, with Different Resources and Capabilities

- Minimum Centralized Staff Needed to Support the Different Businesses

Simultaneous Pursuit of Two Strategies

The last example presents a common case: a company pursuing two or more strategies at once in a given industry. Care must be taken to develop for each strategy an appropriate structure and set of resources or capabilities to allow for successful execution. The divisional structure is ideal in this regard, in that it allows each business to focus on its own industry or market needs, as well as development of its own skills and resources. Using the simple case, again, of high-end and low-end products, we would have two separate divisions:

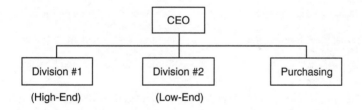

Having two separate, different, decentralized divisions, however, does not automatically rule out centralization and its attendant economies and related benefits. As the preceding figure shows, the two divisions, despite serving two different markets with very diverse customer tastes and product characteristics, still can benefit from centralized purchasing. Economies of one-source, centralized buying can be achieved, despite the major strategic differences between the two divisions. A similar argument for centralized functions may be made in areas such as HR or legal, if the work done is identical across the different divisions based on customer or market.

An emphasis on decentralization is rarely total; the emphasis is usually relative. Some centralization may exist, even in highly decentralized organizations, consistent with the strategy being pursued and the resources required.

Global Strategy

Global competition provides another example of the simultaneous pursuit of two strategies. Companies in global competition must often worry about focusing, at once, on both worldwide product lines and geographical differences in markets. They push products worldwide but also must adapt them, or their marketing and distribution, to local needs, tastes, and customer demographics. A common response here is the matrix structure that helps execute the coordinated global strategy. A "simultaneous" structure, with worldwide product and local geographical components, becomes the design of choice.

Global Strategy ⟶ Matrix Structure

• Need for Coordination

• Dual View: Product and Geography

• Combines Dual Focus on Product and Geography

• Integrates two Divisions or "Purpose" Specialized Units

• Combines Efficiency and Effectiveness

Because the matrix structure is primarily concerned with integration or coordination of diverse functions or units, a more in-depth discussion of it will occur in Chapter 5.

Strategic "Drivers" of Structural Choice

Let's try to synthesize this discussion of the impact of strategy on the choice of structure. Table 4.2 lists the four main strategic drivers of structural choice that were discussed or implied in this chapter. Each will be briefly discussed and summarized.

Table 4.2 Strategic "Drivers" of Structural Choice

1. Type of strategy	
a. Low-cost ———————————→	Centralization, functional structure
b. Focus/differentiation —————————→	Decentralization, divisional structure
c. Coordinated global —————————→	Matrix organization
2. Need for efficiency/effectiveness	
d. Efficiency ————————————→	Centralization
e. Effectiveness ————————————→	Decentralization
3. Market and technological relatedness	
f. If both are high —————————————→	Increased centralization
g. If both are low ————————————→	Increased decentralization
h. If one is low and the other high ———→	Mix of decentralization and centralization
4. Organizational size/growth	
Growth/large size ——————————————→	Increased decentralization (reducing large organization to smaller, more manageable pieces)

1. **Type of strategy.** Structure varies with strategy. Cost leadership usually requires some reliance on a functional structure (process specialization) because of its ability to drive down costs and achieve various economies. The emphasis on standardization, repetition, and volume under this form of organization is totally consistent with the need for efficiency and economies of scale and scope that support the low-cost strategy.

   In contrast, a focus or differentiation strategy usually requires some form of purpose specialization (divisions based on product line, geography, or customer; product- or project-management organizations) to provide the needed focus and attention to customer, geographical region, or product line.

   A coordinated global strategy usually requires a simultaneous focus on worldwide businesses or product lines and different geographical regions or cultures. This typically results in a matrix structure that focuses on both dimensions (business, geography) at once when executing the strategy.

The main point in these examples is that structure is responding to the demands of strategy. Chapter 3 listed some demands of low-cost, differentiation, and coordinated global strategies. To execute the strategies, these demands must be met. The current discussion has been focusing on how structure, with its costs and benefits, responds to and supports strategy, leading to execution success. Type of strategy drives the choice of structure and the desired attendant benefits.

2. **Need for efficiency/effectiveness.** Strategies may focus on efficiency or effectiveness in a quest to gain competitive advantage. The greater the need for efficiency, the greater usually is the reliance on centralization of structure and the cost controls inherent in it. The greater the need for effectiveness, the more likely it is that an organization will opt for a decentralized structure.

Cost-leadership strategies obviously need and rely on cost efficiencies, explaining again why centralized functional structures are critical for strategy execution and organizational success. When strategy focuses on effectiveness in serving different customers or geographical regions with a variety of products and services, emphasis will logically be on decentralization, with different divisional-type structures based on customer, geography, or product line.

3. **Market and technological relatedness.** The degree of "relatedness" is an important strategic driver of structure. It was only implied in previous discussions, so it's important to spend a bit of time clarifying its role in structural choice.

A company may serve a variety of related or unrelated markets. Diversification strategies may focus on expansion into related or unrelated industries. High market relatedness simply means the same or similar customers, distribution channels, pricing, and demand elasticities. Unrelated markets denote differences on these same dimensions. Technological relatedness or unrelatedness refers to the use of the same vs. different technologies, manufacturing processes, or "throughputs" that translate inputs into outputs. Relatedness is important because the greater the degree of market and/or technological relatedness associated with a strategy, the higher the likelihood of centralization in organizational structure. The lower the relatedness, the higher the likelihood of decentralization.

If a company makes different products with the same manufacturing process and equipment, manufacturing will most likely be a centralized function, serving all product lines. If the markets for the products vary, necessitating product changes because of customer, cultural, or geographical differences in usage or taste, the marketing and distribution functions, and perhaps even manufacturing, will be decentralized, reflecting the need to tailor or modify products for the different markets.

Great care must be taken when defining the degree of relatedness before choosing an appropriate structure. Poor or sloppy definition can result in structural choices that lead to execution problems.

This lesson was first driven home to me years ago. An entrepreneur named Howard Head had founded a ski company that had amazing success. Its product was a metal ski—high end, high price, handmade, the "cheater," as it was dubbed, because it made people better skiers. At one point, it was suggested to Head that he enter the low end of the market to capitalize on his brand and extend his product line. A ski, after all, is just a ski, so he might as well saturate the entire market.

Head declined to enter the low-end market. Among the reasons to justify his decision, he considered what this discussion is focusing on currently—degree of market and technological relatedness. He pointed out that metal skis are made differently than cheaper plastic skis. The technology is different: a handmade product vs. injection molding for the plastic ski, a technology Head knew nothing about.

The markets were also different or unrelated, given Head's competencies and marketing approach: a high-end, pricy product vs. a low-end, cheap product; different elasticities of demand and profit margins; different distribution channels (ski-specialty shops vs. mass-market distribution in large retail discount stores); and different service capabilities (the ski pro vs. the discount-store clerk who sells fishing tackle and bowling balls as well as ski equipment).

There were other differences, but the point is clear: though part of the same industry, the low-end and high-end ski markets were vastly different in terms of customers and technology. Entering an unrelated market would demand a different organization with different skills and capabilities. A strategy of unrelated diversification, even within the same industry, would demand a different technology and vastly different sales, distribution, and marketing. Head, of course, could have bought an existing company already in the low-end business, thereby immediately acquiring the needed capabilities and appropriate organizational structure, but he declined to do so. Better to "stick to one's knitting" and continue to do what one knows and does best, was his logical answer.

When Philip Morris bought Seven-Up, it entered an industry that in some respects was similar to tobacco and beer, but in many others was quite different. Some channels of distribution were the same. A sophisticated marketing group could service all industries, it was thought, perhaps achieving economies of scope.

But the industries were also very different. Tobacco and beer strategies had targeted men primarily, but soft drinks had a broader, more diverse market. Industry concentration was different, with Coke and Pepsi dominating the market with their brands and full array of products. Small players such as Seven-Up often "piggybacked" on Coke and Pepsi bottlers, making them dependent on and vulnerable before these giants.

Maintaining Seven-Up as a small niche player seemed like the appropriate structural decision. The soft-drink industry was basically different than the tobacco and beer industries. Decentralization and an independent Seven-Up seemed like the right way to go because of the unrelated aspects of customer, market, and industry forces.

Philip Morris' actions, however, suggested that it saw more elements of related diversification than others did. Expansions of capacity suggested that Seven-Up, like Marlboro and Miller Beer, could gain market share, even in the cola segment. Seven-Up introduced a cola, Like, which proved to be a disaster as it directly confronted Coke and Pepsi and invited retaliation. Actions and expenditures by a centralized marketing and brand management group suggested that Philip Morris saw the need for consistent marketing activities across industries that, it believed, were related in important ways. It seemed to be searching for economies of scale and scope, given this assumption of market relatedness.

The venture failed, and Philip Morris sold Seven-Up at a loss. In part, the problem represented a misread of market relatedness and consequent mistakes in decisions about strategy and structure. Understanding the concepts of market and technological relatedness indeed are important to these choices and to strategic and execution success.

Finally, let's look at the merger of DaimlerChrysler. Is this a related or unrelated diversification? Both companies are in the same industry, but the segments served traditionally by each are clearly different or unrelated. Customer demographics, price points, elasticity of demand, targeted income groups, brand recognition, product quality, and perception of exclusivity vary markedly, suggesting an unrelated diversification by Daimler Benz.

Yet engineering and manufacturing are basically the same. Creating product platforms and sharing design skills suggest some consistency across the two companies. Distribution channels and methods are very similar, save for a few appearance details and customer perks at retail outlets.

So, again, is this a related or unrelated diversification in this "merger of equals"? The answer to this question is currently driving changes in strategy and structure that clearly will impact execution and future sales and earnings performance. Decisions about relatedness will determine how separately or independently each party to the merger operates or, alternatively, how much technological melding or structural combination of the two parties is attempted in the name of synergy. Squabbles reported occasionally suggest that issues related to structure, including responsibility and degree of autonomy, are far from being resolved.

In sum, the greater the market or technological relatedness across products or services, the higher the probability of centralization or sharing the same functions or capabilities. The greater the unrelatedness, the more likely it is to see decentralization of organizational units, as the following suggests:

a) High Market Relatedness — and — High Technological Relatedness — = Centralization

- Same Customers
- Same Distribution Channels
- Same Pricing
- Same Demand Elasticities

- Same Manufacturing
- Same Processes or Technologies
- Use of Same Capabilities or Skills

b) Low Market Relatedness — and — Low Technological Relatedness — = Decentralization

If either market or technological relatedness is high and the other is low, then structure will be a combination of centralization and decentralization. To expand on the preceding examples, a "high-end" and "low-end" product company could have both centralization (common functions) and decentralization (two different divisions). The latter would reflect different customer demographics, pricing, and distribution channels. The former would reflect the need for efficiency and consistency of performance from a function (such as purchasing, manufacturing) that services both high- and low-end products. A mixture of market and technological relatedness will affect organization structure (separate divisions vs. common functions) and its degree of centralized vs. decentralized decision-making.

c) A Mixture of Market and Technological Relatedness (High and Low) — = — A Mix of Centralization and Decentralization

4. **Organizational growth and size.** If a company's growth strategy works, organizational size can increase complexity and the difficulty of coordinating diverse organizational units. The usual response is to reduce large organizational size to smaller, more manageable units. This results in greater decentralization of structure.

Following this logic, strategies that focus on growth—such as diversification and global expansion—usually create the need for increased decentralization over time. The effects of size are usually coupled with the effects of market and/or technological relatedness when diversifying or expanding globally, with increased size usually correlated with a larger number of unrelated markets. Global expansion typically results in product or service modifications to meet divergent customer or geographical needs and tastes and to reflect local capabilities or technological methods.

Still, size warrants at least a separate mention because of its independent impact on structure. Size often demands that big problems be factored into smaller, more manageable proportions and be handled by smaller structural units, resulting in decentralization. This results, for example, in regional offices within the United States, even when products and technologies are exactly the same across the country.

These four conditions or variables in Table 4.2, then, are the strategic "drivers" of structural choice. These are the factors that management must consider and analyze carefully as it ponders structural choice or structural change. An incomplete analysis of these factors can lead to major problems. Structure must respond to and be consistent with the demands of strategy if successful execution outcomes are to result.

SUMMARY

Four key conclusions or takeaways are suggested by the present chapter, beyond the basic point that structure is important to the execution of strategy.

1. The first is that structure affects real costs and benefits to an organization. Different ways of organizing affect outcomes. "Process" specialization or functional structures, for example, positively affect efficiency via standardization, repetition, high volume, and the economies that follow. This type of organization also avoids duplication of resources and efforts, which further reduces costs.

In contrast, "purpose" specialization (divisions, SBUs) loads on effectiveness by organizing around customers, products, or markets. Whereas process specialization enables the organization to "do things right," purpose specialization helps the firm "do the right things." Process specialization may occasionally work against effectiveness, while purpose specialization can increase costs, primarily due to duplication of resources.

2. The second key conclusion follows logically from the first: The right mix of centralization and decentralization must be attained to optimize both efficiency and effectiveness. Centralization results in efficiency and the creation of expertise, an organization-wide asset, resource, or capability. Decentralization results in getting close to customers or markets. Decentralized units must rely and draw on the expertise or knowledge of centralized resources, which can slow responses to customers and markets. Excessive decentralization, however, may injure overall company efficiency and result in a loss of central, core competence. Again, a balance between centralized and decentralized resources must be achieved.

Related to the discussion of centralization is the developing role of the corporate center. No longer just a way to achieve efficiency, a new corporate center concept focuses on adding value to an organization. By focusing on such areas or skills as executive education, strategic management, and worldwide centers of excellence, the corporate center's concerns and contributions far transcend those of basic efficiency and cost control.

3. This chapter also stressed that there are strategic drivers of structural choice. These include: (a) type of strategy (global, low-cost), (b) the need for efficiency or effectiveness, (c) market and technological relatedness, and (d) organizational size/growth. These issues, emanating from strategy and strategic analysis at both the corporate and business levels, affect the choice of structure. High market and technological relatedness, for example, usually argues for increased centralization, whereas low relatedness calls for increased decentralization. Other examples of these "drivers" at work were provided in the chapter, explicating the relationship between strategy and structure.

4. Finally, the chapter suggests that a sequential process of analysis is useful when examining relationships between strategy and structure, as the following figure shows:

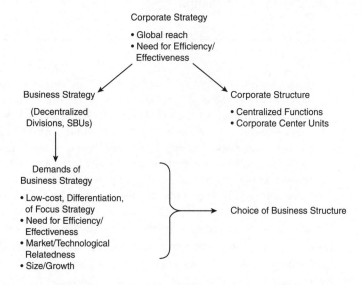

We see that corporate strategy is the lead driver as top management considers such factors as the organization's global reach and the relative need for efficiency and effectiveness. Strategy at this level includes a portfolio approach as decisions are made about what businesses to pursue and which ones to exit. These analyses fuel choice of corporate structure as decisions are made about centralization (centralized functions, corporate center units) and decentralization (business units and the resources they need to operate effectively). Each of the business units, in turn, creates or refines its strategy, which makes demands on the organization and defines the conditions (such as market and technological relatedness) that will drive structural choice at the business level.

Keep in mind that this process reflects a sequential logic. In most organizations, rarely are all of these analyses and decisions made from scratch, sequentially, in every planning cycle. Still, if, for example, strategy should change, this model provides a logical flow against which to consider the possibility of structural change, at both corporate and business levels.

This chapter has looked at structure, the anatomy of the entire organization. Attention can now turn to structural integration and how to coordinate the work of different organizational parts, the substance of the next chapter.

ENDNOTES

i.   Usage of the terms "process" and "purpose" specialization can first be found in the works of early management and organization theorists. For example, see the following: L.H. Gulick and L. Urwick (eds.), *Papers on the Science of Administration,* New York, 1937; James G. March and Herbert A. Simon, *Organizations,* John Wiley, 1958. Process specialization refers generally to a set of skills or processes (such as clerical, manufacturing) that are specialized, repeatable, and performed in the same or consistent ways. Purpose specialization refers to departmentation or ways to break up work into more focused tasks in smaller subunits of the organization.

ii. H.J. Leavitt, "Small Groups in Large Organizations," *Journal of Business,* 1955; *Managerial Psychology,* Chicago, 1958.

iii. The description of efficiency as "doing things right" and effectiveness as "doing the right things" has been discussed or implied by managers and academics alike. Probably one of the earliest and most interesting discussions is by Chester Barnard in *The Functions of the Executive,* Harvard University Press, 1938.

iv. "GE Capital is Split into Four Parts," *The Wall Street Journal,* July 29, 2002.

v.   "But Can You Teach It?" Special Report on Business Schools, *The Economist,* May 22, 2004.

5

Managing Integration: Effective Coordination and Information Sharing

Introduction

Structure refers to the dissection or separation of the organization into operating units: divisions, functions, corporate center groups, and so on, as Chapter 4 just showed. This designation of form and function and the boxes and lines that depict it represent the anatomy of the organization, showing the separate parts and their positions, responsibilities, and relationships.

Creating a structure, however, is only half the story. For organizations to operate effectively, execute strategy, and achieve their goals, integration or coordination is also needed.

The work of diverse and separate organizational units must be coordinated to achieve desired results and a unity or consistency of effort. Structure shows the different parts of an organization and their separate capabilities. Integration or coordination of these parts or units and their capabilities is absolutely vital to the execution of a coherent, focused strategy.

To put it another way, structure paints a relatively static picture of the organization. To be sure, some dynamism and interaction are suggested by flat organizational structures or the "lines" that show relationships among units. One can envision the communication and interaction needed to get work done.

Still, the picture is incomplete. To make the organizational structure work to achieve strategic and short-term goals, we need to add "movement" to the static picture. Processes of integration and information sharing are needed to make the boxes and lines of organizational form come alive and accomplish something of value. Coordination processes are necessary for this vitality and interaction and, ultimately, the execution of strategy.

In the present model of strategy execution (see Chapter 2), strategy affects structure at both corporate and business levels. Structure contains two elements: organizational structure and structural integration.

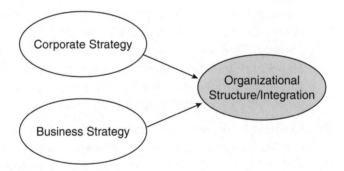

Structural integration provides the requisite coordination of structural parts and information flows among the parts. Creating the right structure is critical, as Chapter 4 stressed. But structural integration is also necessary for the success of execution. The obstacles to effective execution noted in the research surveys in Chapter 1 emphasized the negative consequences of poor integration and inadequate information sharing for execution success. Sharing information effectively and achieving coordination of important structural units are clearly vital to making strategy work.

THE IMPORTANCE OF INTEGRATION

To appreciate the importance of structural integration for execution and organizational performance, let's look at a few examples from some well-known companies.

BOEING

In July 2002, Boeing announced it would be merging its stand-alone space and military businesses.[i] The new business unit is called Integrated Defense Systems, with the emphasis on integration. Why the internal merger?

Boeing believes that bringing these diverse structural units together will facilitate the sharing of expertise. Bringing different assets together will help achieve integration and make it easier to develop coordinated programs and a focused strategy to give the company an advantage when competing for new military business. The goal is to bring different organizational pieces together so that customers don't have to deal with unconnected units. Customers desire integration, and the move is intended to provide it. That effective integration facilitates strategy execution is the operating assumption at Boeing.

ROYAL DUTCH/SHELL GROUP

An interesting but unusual article in the March 12, 2004 *Wall Street Journal* proclaimed that Shell's structure was responsible, in part, for the company's overstatement of its reserves of oil and natural gas.[ii] How can structure "fuel" such over reporting of critical assets? How did the company misjudge its reserves so badly?

Shell's structure is based on a vast empire of independent operating units that, over time, found themselves under two different, but equal, holding companies. Both holding companies have separate boards and separate headquarters in The Hague and London, respectively. The companies and their units enjoy exceptional autonomy, including when estimating oil and gas reserves. They have the leeway to use their own geological methods and financial assumptions to project reserves, the cost of bringing them to market, and the profits that would accrue to the company. To project a unified position on oil and gas reserves and execute a focused, company-wide strategy at Shell, integration of the holding companies is absolutely essential. The problem is that integration apparently failed.

There is a committee of managing directors over the operating companies that is charged with the integration responsibility, but it hasn't done its job. Outlandish forecasts of reserves and future profits from two holding companies competing with each other were never challenged, examined, and integrated. Aggressive reporting of separate, autonomous companies very likely led to the exaggeration of oil and gas reserves. The failure of effective integration mechanisms allowed for mistakes. It also caused the company great embarrassment when it was forced to publicly announce the reduction of reserves on four separate occasions. Poor integration and an incentive system that rewarded overreporting of reserves were the major culprits in this unusual, but real, example.

DELL COMPUTERS

To see the importance of integration and information sharing one more time, consider the meteoric rise of Dell Computers in the late 1990s in the United States. Dell was a player in a PC market that could only be considered unattractive. Intense rivalry among PC makers such as Compaq, IBM, and HP was eroding profits. Common "standards," desired by both PC makers and customers, were adding to the commoditization or standardization of the PC. PC firms looked alike, following the same business model with reliance on resellers or retailers to push their computers. The market power of companies such as Microsoft and Intel allowed these companies to hold up the industry and extract the major portion of profits, leaving the rest for the PC makers to squabble over.

Then along came Dell with a different business model. It would sell direct to customers, especially knowledgeable corporate buyers. In a bold move, it eliminated reliance on resellers. It differentiated itself to its corporate customers by tailoring solutions, loading a company's proprietary software onto its machines, and providing the service that large, knowledgeable buyers were desperately seeking. It changed the way business was done in the PC industry. And competitors couldn't follow Dell's lead easily because of their commitment to resellers whom they couldn't simply eliminate from their business model. The costs—the "tradeoffs"—were too high.

But there was more, a lot more. Dell focused on activities or systems of activities that reduced its costs, improved delivery and customer service, and led to competitive advantage. These activities focused on different parts of the value chain, as the following list shows:

Dell's Activities

Inbound logistics	JIT delivery; close integration with suppliers
Operations	Efficient manufacturing "cells"; customization of product, with integration of customer's propriety software
Outbound logistics	Direct delivery; outsourced materials shipped directly to customers
Service	Close technical support; integration of customer needs; electronic and on-site service

What's so special about these activities? They couldn't easily be imitated by competitors. Imitation of the direct sales model couldn't easily be done without angering long-term, powerful resellers or retailers. In addition, the various activities and processes were integrated into "activity systems" that made imitation even more difficult.[iii] Integration or effective coordination was the key. Procurement processes were integrated with inbound logistics, just-in-time (JIT) delivery systems, and direct delivery of components from suppliers to customers. Close contact with and geographical proximity to suppliers reduced inventory and inventory carrying costs. Competitors couldn't simply focus on imitation of a critical activity. They were forced to focus on the integration of a complex set of activities if they wanted to copy Dell. This, in short, was not easy to do.

Effective coordination and information sharing, then, became a company capability that helped Dell gain a competitive advantage. Integration was the key. Coordinating activities in complex ways defined the processes and parts of a business model that were difficult to imitate. Dell's emphasis on just-in-time delivery, logistics, operations, customer support, and service demanded that the entire organization be integrated. The resultant integration provided a critical source of competitive advantage.

These case examples indicate the importance of integration or coordination for making strategy work. The Wharton surveys also emphasized the contribution of integration to execution. Accordingly, the remainder of this chapter looks at the steps that must be taken to achieve effective coordination and information sharing. Its purpose is to consider those issues that are most central to execution.

What are the critical issues, topics, or steps managers must confront or take to achieve effective integration? What do the previous examples and the opinions of managers surveyed in this research tell us is necessary to help make strategy work? There are four such issues. Three will be handled in this chapter and one in the following chapter. The issues are as follows:

1. How task interdependence affects the choice of methods to achieve effective integration or coordination

2. How to foster information sharing, knowledge transfer, and communication among individuals or organizational units responsible for strategy execution

3. How to clarify responsibility and accountability to ensure that the right tasks get done and are effectively integrated to execute a strategy

4. How to develop incentives to support the dynamism and flexibility of an operating structure geared to effective integration

The first issue, on interdependence, needs coverage because it defines the arena or setting within which integration or coordination takes place. The second and third issues are especially vital to making strategy work, according to managers in both the

Wharton-Gartner and Wharton Executive Education surveys. The fourth issue, dealing with incentives, will be handled in Chapter 6.

INTERDEPENDENCE AND COORDINATION METHODS

The first issue is one that I see popping up repeatedly in strategy-execution efforts. It is the definition of interdependence and the methods of coordination required by different kinds or types of interdependence.

This is an important issue. Managers use inappropriate or wrong integration methods, given the nature of the problem they are addressing. They "under-" or "over-coordinate," both of which can affect costs and execution results.

This issue may seem a bit "under the radar" to some, but mistakes here are real and affect performance. Managers may not use the word "interdependence" in their daily discussions, but they usually respond knowingly when I use the term and discuss its effects on coordination needs. So, let's see what's involved here and what affects execution.

TYPES OF INTERDEPENDENCE

There are three important types of interdependence that can be found in most organizations. I'll discuss them and add examples to show how they relate to organizational tasks and execution needs.[iv]

Pooled Interdependence

This represents a low level of interdependence and need for coordination. Consider the sales organization shown in Figure 5.1. It is a picture of pooled interdependence. Each district manager works in a separate geographical location. The territory could be part of a state, country, or global region, but each is relatively defined, self-contained, and independent. Each sales manager responds to the particular needs of his or her district. There is little need for active, ongoing communication or coordination across districts. This is a case in which "people work alone together." There is a low level of interdependence.

Figure 5.1 Example of Pooled Interdependence

Consider, too, the case of the prototypical conglomerate that, over time, expands and adds new companies to its portfolio. Though part of a "whole" (the corporate entity), each addition is relatively independent. Each does its own thing in different industries or markets. This is another case in which people or companies usually work alone together.

The word "together," of course, suggests some interdependence. If, for example, the bonus of each manager in Figure 5.1 is based, in part, on overall or corporate earnings as well as regional performance, interdependence is clear. One manager may perform outstandingly, but poor performance by the others obviously can detract from the high performer's rewards. Or in the case of the conglomerate, companies performing poorly can negatively affect cash flow and the resources available to the other companies.

Even pooled interdependence suggests, then, that people in an organization are in some ways in the same boat. It usually is a big boat, however, and there is ample room and distance between its passengers, necessitating little direct contact and coordination.

Sequential Interdependence

This is the next type, which is more complex than the pooled variety. Consider the case of vertical integration shown in Figure 5.2. In this example, the flow of work or materials is sequential. Work flows from "S," the supplier, to two end-user divisions. Semifinished goods also flow from End-User Division 1 to Division 2. The movement of product or service is unilateral or unidirectional.

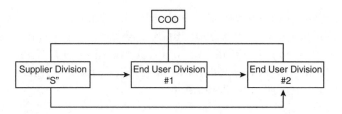

Figure 5.2   Vertical Integration: An Example of Sequential Interdependence

Comparing sequential to pooled interdependence reveals that the cost of failure is higher in the former. In a pooled case, each district office looks and acts like the following:

Each office does its own thing. A problem at A does not directly and immediately affect B or C. Routine communication and coordination across A, B, and C are not vital to ongoing operations.

Sequential interdependence is different and can be represented by the following illustration. Problems at A not only affect A, they also affect B and C directly and immediately. Poor materials from the supplier division have a direct, immediate impact on the end-user divisions shown in Figure 5.2.

In addition, communication and coordination laterally, across A, B, and C, clearly are essential to ensuring smooth flows of work. Managers in all three locations have something at stake under sequential interdependence. The operation of the overall system defined by the sequential chain is vital to each individually. So, communication and coordination laterally affect both the overall system of vertical integration and the parts of that system at work.

The greater complexity of sequential interdependence demands that this form be managed differently than the pooled variety. Methods of coordination and control are different. These differences in method are spelled out later. First, however, let's consider a third type of interdependence.

Reciprocal Interdependence

This is the most complex form and the most difficult to manage. Consider the representation in Figure 5.3. In this case, people in each function deal with people in all the other functions. A, a function, both affects and is affected by B, C, D, and E, other functions and a customer. One function can change the rules or affect much of what is done by the others at virtually any time.

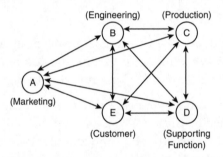

Figure 5.3   A picture of reciprocal interdependence (new product development team).

Coordination and control under reciprocal interdependence are difficult because many things are going on simultaneously. Planning is difficult because members of the network can change their positions or even veto the decisions of others without warning.

Think, for a moment, about the activities of a new product development team (see Figure 5.3). Think of how product development would look if it were approached in a sequential fashion. Someone from marketing, A, contacts a potential customer, E, and asks what she would like. The marketing manager brings the information to engineering, B, where product design must occur. Engineering's response is, "Sorry, there's no way we can design that." Marketing goes back to the customer and asks what else she would take.

When the new request is brought to engineering, the response now is, "You must be kidding!"

By now, the marketing manager is throwing up his hands in frustration. "What can you design?" he finally demands from engineering. But when he brings what's possible to the potential customer, she is not at all interested. Back to the drawing board. And so on—back and forth.

At last, marketing, engineering, and the customer agree on a viable product. They finally can bring the specifications and the product requirements to production (C) or another supporting function (D). Much to their chagrin, however, the production manager says, "Sorry, there's no way I can make something like this. With the pressure on me for volume and low-cost production, this product would kill me. Maybe next time."

Obviously, the production manager has affected engineering, marketing, and the customer. He has negated much of their effort. He is able to veto what others have spent a great deal of time pursuing. Assuming a sequential approach when reciprocal interdependence is the rule can lead to problems, as the new product development case just showed.

The reciprocal case is difficult. Under this form of interdependence, all are equals in the decision process, and any player can affect all the others. Each player is necessary to the solution of a problem, but no one player is sufficient. High levels of cooperation and coordination are needed to make things work. Effective coordination is vital to strategy execution.

COORDINATION PROCESSES AND METHODS

How does the type of interdependence affect the methods or processes used for coordination or integration? Table 5.1 presents some of these methods. The table shows, first, that managing pooled interdependence is relatively easy. Standard operating procedures (SOPs) or rules govern all the independent individuals equally. (All district managers in Figure 5.1 report sales in the same way; all submit quarterly plans.) When problems or unusual cases pop up, the role of hierarchy becomes important—resolving disputes, handling exceptions, and so on. People work alone together but in the same or consistent ways.

Table 5.1   Types of Interdependence and Methods of Achieving Effective Coordination or Integration

Type of Interdependence	Level of Coordination Required	Methods of Achieving Coordination or Integration
Pooled	Low	Rules/SOPs/hierarchy
Sequential	High	Coordination by plan; managing the flow of work and information
		Scheduling/just-in-time inventory controls
		"Transfer" activities such as transfer pricing, terms to facilitate "passing of the baton"
		Having "linking" or transition managers to facilitate the flows of work and information
		Appropriate incentives to motivate the effective flow of work and information
Reciprocal	Very high	Coordination by "mutual adjustment"
		Face-to-face integration, or "managing by living together"
		Removing administrative and geographical barriers to face-to-face interaction
		Fostering communication, processes of agreement, and trust
		Appropriate incentives to work together and make joint decisions

Pooled interdependence does not generate the need for ongoing, active coordination. The SOPs used for control and coordination are consistent for all units, but few, if any, deal with integration across units. Similarly, reliance on hierarchy stresses mainly vertical communication, not lateral forms.

The task confronting managers under pooled interdependence is twofold: (a) ensuring that the SOPs, rules, or routines used for control are appropriate and consistent across all units, and (b) maintaining open communication channels vertically so that exceptions or problems can move up the hierarchy and be handled quickly and effectively. These tasks are basic and common to all organizations, but managers must monitor them carefully to ensure that they are functioning as designed.

Sequential interdependence, as Table 5.1 suggests, raises the cost of sound management. Managing cooperation is more complex, and more time and resources must be devoted to the task. SOPs and hierarchy still play a role, but other, more complex issues surface when focusing on coordination across the value chain, as in the case of vertical integration. Planning and scheduling are critical to smooth, predictable flows of work and materials. Poor planning or scheduling can lead to task interruptions and conflicts, which clearly detract from coordination, communication, and results.

Managing transactions and lateral transitions of work from unit to unit is central to sequential interdependence. Tasks and activities within units are important, but so are the linkages between adjoining work groups. Transfer pricing in the vertical integration example, for instance, is vital to effective linkages. Inappropriate pricing affects not only workflow but perceptions and cooperation as well.

Similarly, the quality of the products, services, or information being transferred affects perceptions and the viability of coordination. Consider the following comments made by a manager in a vertically integrated company:

> *"I'm getting gouged price-wise by my own supplier, which happens to be a sister division in the same company. Nice, isn't it? He sells the good stuff on the outside and sends me the rest, the junk. Why do I have to deal with this?"*

The same issue of quality holds for the transfer of information needed to support a line organization or facilitate decision-making. Poor information or information sharing affects cooperation, coordination, and results.

The managerial task when strategy creates sequential interdependence is primarily one of ensuring the smooth flow of transactions and information laterally across the value chain, as Table 5.1 shows. The focus must be on linking mechanisms—including people—to act as integrators and facilitate the movement of work and information from one unit to the next in the sequential chain.

Appropriate incentives must also be developed to ensure that one division is not motivated to "sell the junk" to a sister division while selling the "good stuff" on the outside.

With reciprocal interdependence, coordination and control are extremely difficult to manage. Under this type, the other forms of interdependence also exist, so many of the previously identified problems are again important. But there are also new obstacles, as Table 5.1 shows, along with new methods of achieving coordination or integration.

The need for coordination and information sharing is very high, as all the members in the network affect and are affected by all the other members. All have something at stake. One person under reciprocal interdependence can negate the work of others, even after significant amounts of time and effort have been expended.

Because of the impact of any one member, coordination greatly relies on face-to-face interaction. Coordination and control are by "mutual adjustment" or, as a manager once expressed it to me, "managing by living together."

In the case of the new product development team introduced earlier, problem definition and solution ideally should be done together, with all team members, even customers, participating simultaneously. All individuals should be "locked up together," with no one leaving until agreement is reached on critical aspects of the new product. Working alone together clearly is ruled out in this case.

But managing by living together is not always easy. Key team players involved in complex tasks related to strategy execution might be spread out geographically or "administratively." They might be all over the company, country, or world, in different functions or divisions, and even at different hierarchical levels. Getting them together and ensuring communication, agreement, and cooperation can be difficult.

Still, reciprocal interdependence demands that the attempt be made. Getting people together via telecommunications technologies (such as teleconferences and interactive video telecommunication sessions) is possible, of course, given advances in technological capabilities. But managers tell me that this alone is not sufficient. They tell me that, under reciprocal interdependence, individuals must meet occasionally face to face. While expensive, managers say that getting commitment to courses of action needed to make strategy work absolutely demands face-to-face interaction. As one vice president of marketing and product development in a recent Wharton executive program stated:

> *"When I need the support of engineering or production, and that support is vital to my plan's success, I want to look directly into the eyes of my colleagues when I ask for help. I'll know if they're serious or lying. I'll see whether their promised support is for real or if they're BSing me or putting me off. Believe me, I'll know."*

Another example of the need for face-to-face interaction comes from Jeffrey Immelt, GE's chairman and CEO, who is trying very hard to assert his own distinctive leadership style after the long reign of Jack Welch. Amidst a host of changes he's instituted at GE, Immelt is spending a great deal of time on the road. Meeting with GE managers, customers, and shareholders face to face, he has stated that "seeing people in person is a big part of how you drive any change process."[v] New strategies, operating plans, and methods of coordination take on new and important meaning when discussed face to face.

These individuals' stance on face-to-face interaction is certainly clear. It also has a ring of logic and practicality to it that can't easily be denied. Enough managers I've known agree with these statements that I feel there must be some truth to them. Face-to-face interaction can add immensely to the effectiveness of coordination and management of change, especially when strategy results in reciprocal interdependence.

Finally, the role of incentives is important. The managerial task is to make sure that the individuals or units bound together under reciprocal interdependence are motivated to work together. Team-based incentives may be needed to prevent individuals from going off and doing their own thing and hurting group performance. The need for joint decisions demands this focus on appropriate, team-performance-based incentives. (Incentives are discussed further in Chapter 6.)

THE GE "WORK OUT"

Does all this make sense? Should managers worry about defining interdependence before designing coordination or integration mechanisms? I think so, obviously. But let me focus on GE for a while and use the well-known example of Jack Welch's "Work Out" to bolster and support my claims." "Work Out" was based on a simple concept—generate ideas about how to improve company performance and then execute those ideas—but it had far-reaching positive results.

I spent a significant amount of time as a "Work Out" consultant for GE's Aerospace Division before it was sold. I enjoyed my "Work Out" experience and felt it was tremendously effective in solving problems and furthering GE's goals. I felt that it worked extremely well as a vehicle to capture ideas for improvement from employees and for implementing or executing those ideas. "Work Out" worked. Why?

A Philosophy of Challenge and Stretch

Welch was always looking for something new to challenge employees. He hated complacency and sitting on one's laurels. He wanted his managers to focus on "stretch" objectives—higher-level goals that forced people to reach higher and higher to achieve them. "Work Out" helped to create this challenge and provide the right incentives for action.

A "Learning Culture"

This, too, was part of Welch's philosophy. He liked to say that "the operative assumption was that someone, somewhere, had a better idea. By sharing knowledge, GE businesses would gain a competitive edge," which would result in better performance.[vi] "Work Out" was premised on this learning culture, based on good ideas and the sharing of important knowledge throughout the company.

The Structure and Process of "Work Out"

Besides the sizable impact of Welch's philosophy, there was the structure and process of "Work Out" itself. Consistent with the present argument, "Work Out" was treated as a case of reciprocal interdependence.

Most "Work Outs" focused on complex problems. To define and solve them, it was necessary to bring together managers and technical people from different functions or operating groups within the Aerospace Division. All these functions or groups were necessary for problem definition and solution. No function or group alone was sufficient to solve the problem. Cooperation and coordination were necessary.

The process of running a "Work Out" demanded that all individuals necessary for problem definition and solution be brought together. "Management by living together" was the norm, as were face-to-face discussions and interactions. Managers couldn't leave or run away when things got hot and disagreements exploded. They had to stay, toe-to-toe and face-to-face, and confront the issues, no matter how stressful or volatile the situation.

"Management by living together" also demanded that no one could leave until an agreement was reached on problem definition and solution. Invariably, an action plan was created, indicating objectives, timelines, and responsibilities for action-plan items. Follow-ups, including additional "Work Out" sessions, ensured that things were accomplished as planned. People were held accountable for defined tasks and simply couldn't shirk their obligations defined by the process.

In essence, "Work Out" was run as an example of decision-making characterized by reciprocal interdependence. The methods of achieving integration or coordination were consistent with this form of interdependence and no doubt contributed to its success. In addition to Welch's philosophy and GE culture, the processes and methods of defining interdependence and coordination needs were important to "Work Out"'s contributions to problem definition and solution and to making strategy work.

An Analytical Process

In sum, an important aspect of integration is the definition and consideration of interdependence. Looking at the issues we've talked about in the last three chapters would suggest the following analytical process:

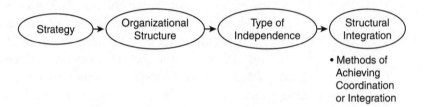

What this shows is that strategy affects structure, which defines interdependence and the units, functions, or people who must work together. Structure and the interdependence defined by it and strategy then determine the methods of coordination or integration necessary to get work done. This figure, in effect, shows what's necessary to execute the strategy shown in the first part of the preceding flow or process diagram.

The same steps and analyses can be undertaken by all managers interested in strategy execution or making strategy work. At the business level, managers first define a clear, focused strategy (see Chapter 3). They then should examine organizational structure, given the demands of strategy (see Chapter 4). Finally, they should define the interdependence created by strategy and structure and develop methods of coordination consistent with the form or type of interdependence noted in this chapter.

Following these prescriptions will force managers to choose appropriate coordination methods. It will help avoid problems of "under-coordination" by matching coordination methods with the task at hand. It will also help avoid problems of "over-coordination," such as setting up committees and other burdensome, time-consuming tasks when they're not needed. Following the preceding prescriptions will result in great strides toward making strategy work.

FACILITATING INFORMATION SHARING, KNOWLEDGE TRANSFER, AND COMMUNICATION

The second major topic of this chapter is also an important one. It is recalled that "poor or inadequate information sharing between individuals or business units responsible for strategy execution" was ranked as one of the largest obstacles to execution by managers responding to surveys in the present research. The panel data collected from managers involved in execution and my own personal experiences add to these opinions: Information sharing, knowledge transfer, and the communication that supports them are vital to making strategy work.

The obvious next question deals with what facilitates or impedes the information sharing, knowledge transfer, and communication necessary for the effective execution of strategy. What affects the "stickiness" of information flows between or among organizational units? To frame the relevant issues, let's begin with a quick look at two companies, McKinsey and Citibank.

CREATING, USING, AND SHARING KNOWLEDGE

McKinsey and Co.

Everyone knows McKinsey and its reputation in consulting. Perhaps fewer people realize the challenges it faces in the creation, dissemination, and use of knowledge.

It is a large company with offices around the world housing thousands of consultants and staff. Organizational size contributes to the complexity of doing business. It also exacerbates the difficulty of the company's two primary tasks: creating and using knowledge.

As a consulting company, McKinsey must stay on top of things. It must create specialized knowledge that keeps it on the leading edge. As a professional service organization, the knowledge is predominantly in its databases and, more importantly, in the minds of its human resources—its specialists and consultants. Creation of centers of competence and development of "T-shaped" consultants with both broad, general knowledge and deep, industry-specific competence has helped the company develop the expertise and knowledge needed to prosper in an increasingly competitive industry.

But creating knowledge is only half the battle. McKinsey must also focus on using the knowledge across its client base and geographical reach. It must be able to share new information to leverage its learning and avoid costly duplications in knowledge creation. Consultants who deal with client and industry problems in North America need to disseminate their knowledge and insights to colleagues in South America or Europe. "Snowball making" is important, but "snowball throwing," with its emphasis on sharing and using information to service clients and make money, is even more important.

McKinsey uses a number of methods, tools, and processes to integrate and use knowledge. Its "Yellow Pages" lists the firm's experts and areas of knowledge to facilitate personal contacts among its consultants. Common databases of core knowledge are made available through an effective IT system. Practice coordinators are used to facilitate access to information and to coordinate the use of expertise throughout the company. Client service teams focus on the integration of knowledge and its application to clients over the longer term, creating a culture with clients' needs at its core. Efforts are made to facilitate consultants talking to other consultants, specialists talking to generalists, and those with technology-based skills (such as IT) talking with individuals pursuing the "art" or "craft" of getting close to customers.

Before extracting some general principles that can help all organizations share information and knowledge, let's briefly look at the case of Citibank.

Citibank

Like McKinsey, Citibank is a large company with global presence. On the institutional side, for example, it deals with and services large multinational corporations (MNCs) worldwide. It is concerned with "following" MNCs across countries or geographical regions to provide an integrated set of products or services. In so doing, it is deeply concerned with the integration of skills and capabilities worldwide and the sharing of information or knowledge across geographical boundaries.

Of course, the company must simultaneously be aware of regional or local impacts or constraints on its global thrust. Differences in banking regulations, culture, and standard operating procedures by country or region exist, and their impact on banking practices must be recognized. To execute strategy worldwide, both global and local views must be included simultaneously. Following and servicing MNCs effectively requires an understanding of their global needs, but it also requires recognition of local or regional constraints on the methods or services employed to meet those needs.

To achieve the necessary coordination and knowledge sharing and give sufficient attention to local and global needs, Citibank uses a number of methods or approaches. Account manager types are employed to focus on large, important MNCs and take care of their business needs worldwide. These client managers disseminate knowledge about MNCs and coordinate with other managers in different parts of the world. Regional or country managers disseminate information about how to carry on business locally within a country or region. A matrix organization couples managers with global and local perspectives and forces them to confront problems and integrate global business needs with local or regional concerns. Global information systems and databases exist, allowing individuals to tap into a wealth of client or regional information.

These descriptions of McKinsey and Citibank of necessity are brief. Yet they provide insight into how organizations can facilitate information sharing, knowledge transfer, and communication across organizational or subunit boundaries when trying to make strategy work.

METHODS, TOOLS, OR PROCESSES FOR INFORMATION SHARING

The preceding examples suggest a number of formal methods that organizations can use to aid information sharing and knowledge transfer. These formal approaches have received attention in the management literature, so I'll only handle them briefly. There also are informal methods of information sharing. These are also very important, but less attention has been paid to them, so I'll go into more detail on this topic in the next section.

IT Systems/Databases

Creating databases and IT systems to access the data clearly can aid information sharing. The McKinsey databases of core knowledge with broad IT support represent one example. For years, ABB has relied on ABACUS, its information system, to keep top managers apprised of happenings in the businesses or geographical regions. Citibank has its IT systems and databases on its largest multinational customers. IBM deploys its IT expertise to achieve savings through the transformation of business processes and the optimization of manufacturing operations. A host of other companies have done similar things.

Before entering the academic world, I worked for Ford Motor Company in a number of capacities, including as a district field manager. I traveled a region and interacted frequently with dealers. At my disposal was a form, FD 1984 (I loved the symbolism!), which was remarkable. On one page, a wealth of information about a dealer was summarized, including benchmark comparisons to other dealers. Big Brother was clearly watching, and the form made that oversight a manageable task. I'm sure that better dealer summaries or databases exist today. Still, at the time, the FD 1984 was a helpful tool that fostered the sharing of important information and highlighted potential problems for remedial action.

Formal Roles and Jobs

Companies hire and train people to coordinate work and communicate across subunits. Project-management organizations, for example, manage and move projects or products. Project managers may or may not have authority over functional and other personnel who work on their projects. They usually, however, have responsibility to coordinate the contributions of diverse functional groups and manage information flows among contributing personnel. They often act as liaisons, linking diverse groups within the organization. McKinsey, Citibank, Boeing, Microsoft, and other companies routinely use product or project managers to achieve effective coordination. The recent talk in Washington, D.C. about creating a position of "Intelligence Czar" is arguing, in effect, for the creation of an integrating role to link and coordinate activities of the many diverse groups currently responsible for intelligence.

In some companies, formal teams or committees are created to facilitate coordination, communication, and information flows. Quality assurance groups, "six sigma" teams, or customer service teams often share this status as integrating units. Customer service teams, for example, usually have members from different functions who bring their points of view and expertise to serving customers. They "own the customer" is a typical beginning to a description of what the team does. Customer service is the higher-level goal, and the team focuses on the process of integrating work across functions or departments to achieve it. The customer service teams at McKinsey are good examples of these formal integrating mechanisms.

The steering committee of managing directors at Shell represents another example of a formal team or committee charged with the responsibility of integration across operating units. Its charge is to facilitate the planning and coordination of independent Shell units, a task it apparently didn't do very well when reporting estimates of oil and gas reserves.

Matrix Structures

A host of organizations I've dealt with have some form of matrix structure. In fact, most large companies, especially global players such as Citibank, Boeing, ABB, and others pursuing coordinated global strategies, rely on this form of structure somewhere for information processing and coordination.

The simplest way to describe the integrative and information-processing workings of a matrix is to use the "matrix diamond," shown in Figure 5.4.[vii] In a global matrix, for example, business managers push products worldwide, while geographical managers make decisions about the best products and use of investment funds within their country or region. Often the two disagree or have different goals or perceptions of how to run a business or a country. Someone must help them reach agreement to allow for the execution of global strategies. This individual must also coordinate valuable information between businesses and regions.

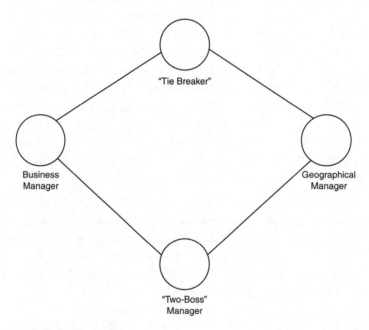

Figure 5.4   The "Matrix Diamond"

Who does this integration and consensus building? The "two-boss" manager is in this dynamic and sometimes stressful position and is absolutely vital to the matrix functioning effectively. This individual must integrate diverse, even conflicting, views. He or she must understand the business manager's problems as well as those within the bailiwick of the country or functional manager. While the job of the two-boss manager was once described to me as "magic worker," a more formal description would simply be integrator and information processor.

If the two-boss manager cannot reduce the conflicts or cannot solve problems to everyone's mutual liking and understanding, the top manager or the "tie breaker" in the matrix diamond steps in, breaks the impasse, and allows work to progress.

The matrix is obviously a complex operating structure. Its goal is lateral communication and coordination, with the co-located two-boss manager integrating business and geographical or business and functional views. It seemingly violates some age-old management principles, such as unity of command, but it does work well, especially when executing strategies in the global arena.

INFORMAL FORCES AND INFORMATION SHARING

Everyone knows something about formal methods of fostering communication and coordination such as those just discussed. Yet managers in our surveys still listed poor information sharing as a huge problem when executing strategy. Why?

Because something else must be happening to affect or negate the formal methods. Because knowing what the methods are (for example, a matrix) and knowing how to make them work are two separate issues. Because managers may or may not be motivated to share information and make strategy work.

In my experiences with strategy execution, I have found that managers know the terminology of information sharing and coordination. Everyone has IT systems and formal databases. Everyone knows what an integrator does. Many managers tell me constantly that their companies have been "matricized" in some way.

Yet problems with information processing and knowledge sharing persist. This is so because there also are informal forces at work that affect the outcomes. Let me share with you what some of these forces or issues are.

Poor Informal Contact

The simplest and most common form of information sharing is probably informal contact, regardless of the formal methods employed. People talk to people to seek information and solve problems. A manufacturing manager in New York or Detroit calls or sends a fax to a counterpart in Tokyo, Mexico City, Sao Paulo, or San Francisco. Delivery dates or scheduling problems are discussed and ironed out. A consultant in Germany calls a colleague in Paris to seek help with a client's particularly bothersome problem. A physician doing research in a major pharmaceutical company in Pennsylvania calls an expert in statistics in Germany to help with an important research question. Informal, direct contact between or among managers is arguably the most common form of everyday communication and coordination. Yet even this simple tactic cannot work without same basic underlying prerequisites for success.

Knowing whom to contact, for example, is basic yet critical. Knowing the people, positions, and responsibilities in other locations is necessary for informal contact to work. This seems basic, and yet consider the following comment from a manager in a Wharton executive program:

> "I really wanted to help (a client company) get a nice loan package for his operations in Brazil. But I must admit I didn't know the person who handles this type of loan there, so I mailed the materials I had to the "Loan Manager" in Sao Paulo. I really don't even know if anyone got the papers or helped the customer."

One remedy is obvious: Publish a directory listing key personnel in different geographical locations, showing their responsibilities and areas of expertise, a la McKinsey.

Go Direct—Not Through Channels

People who can solve problems without getting approvals galore or going through their bosses, their bosses' bosses, and so on, to contact people directly in other offices or parts of the world usually can make informal contact work effectively as a communication and coordination technique. This represents one of the key ideas underlying flat organizations: People can focus directly on a problem without waiting for hierarchical approval. In contrast, the delay of requests as people go through "channels" or undergo numerous checks and approvals often destroys or detracts from the speed and spontaneity of informal, personal contacts.

Create a "Common Language"

As odd as this may sound, people in the same organization may not be on the same page when sharing information or communicating on important issues dealing with strategy execution. They bring different perspectives, technical capabilities, definitions of key terms, or cultural biases that detract from their ability to see and understand divergent points of view. Selective perceptions caused by functional myopia and regional or global differences get in the way of shared ideas and common understanding.

When executing strategy, it is absolutely essential that the strategy be clear, focused, and translated logically into short-term objectives or metrics (see Chapter 3). It is vital, too, that these objectives and measurements be defined consistently to avoid problems of different, competing views of execution outcomes.

Consider a case in which sales performance is measured by revenue, a top-line number, but a function such as manufacturing or an entire division is measured on a bottom-line figure, revenues minus costs. Add to the mix marketing, which is evaluated in part on customer satisfaction. In this case, different metrics almost guarantee different views of strategy execution and reliance on competing performance measures. Sales focuses on volume. It is accused routinely of selling anything and making deals with little concern for costs or the bottom line. Production feels that sales is "giving the shop away." Marketing cares about customers and feels that no one else gives a hoot. Conflicts between or among the functions are a common occurrence. The division manager sees the conflicts as detracting from divisional performance.

The solution? Focus on common, consistent measures of perform-ance. Define or operationalize the measures carefully. Develop some shared objectives. Place constraints on unilateral, independ-ent measures of performance. Make sales responsible for margins, not just volume. Decide whether costs or customer satisfaction is the driving force behind execution decisions. Determine how and when the functions should cooperate to achieve important results and then hold them accountable. This is not a case where people should be working alone together.

The Power Structure and Culture

Methods of information sharing and coordination are often affect-ed by the power or influence structure of the organization as well as its culture. These factors affect what information is transmitted. They affect who is listened to and who isn't. They affect the rela-tive weight attached to coordination attempts and which transfer of "facts" is believed or discarded.

Power and culture are extremely important to many aspects of execution. Accordingly, they will receive additional attention in two later chapters (Chapter 8 and Chapter 9).

ADDITIONAL INFORMAL FACTORS AFFECTING INFORMATION FLOW AND KNOWLEDGE TRANSFER

Let me focus on some additional factors that affect information sharing and knowledge transfer. A Wharton colleague once pub-lished an insightful paper about these factors.[viii] I've built upon his work in my own experiences with strategy execution and can share some of my observations here.

Table 5.2 lists factors that affect information sharing and knowl-edge transfer. These factors reflect aspects of information and organizations, but they also indicate the effects of individuals' motivations on information sharing and knowledge transfer. Some of the factors or issues are new, others touch on things already stated or implied, but all are important, ultimately, to the information sharing and coordination needed to make strategy work.

Table 5.2   Factors Affecting Information Sharing and Knowledge Transfer

---

- Characteristics of the knowledge being transferred:
  - Codified vs. tacit knowledge
  - Proven record of usefulness
- Characteristics of the source of knowledge:
  - Expertise and trustworthiness of source
  - Reliability of source
  - Perceived motivation of source:
- Characteristics of the recipient of knowledge:
  - Lack of motivation (NIH)
  - Lack of absorptive capacity (ability to search for, receive, and evaluate new knowledge depends on the store of existing knowledge)
  - Retentive capacity (ability to use, institutionalize received knowledge):
- Characteristics of the context:
  - Organizational structure
  - Operating structure (existence of coordinative/integrative mechanisms)
  - Incentives
  - Culture

Characteristics of the Knowledge Itself

Codified knowledge can be transferred more easily than tacit knowledge. Writing or following an instruction booklet on "how to assemble a bicycle" is straightforward. "Take part A, insert into part B, and place the entire part into the frame C at location D," and so on. The booklet conveys codified, structured knowledge.

Next, write a set of instructions on "how to ride a bicycle." "First, get on the bike and ride. If you fail, repeat step one."

What else can you say? The knowledge here is "tacit," harder to describe and communicate. It is far less structured than telling people how to put the bike together. Communication in the tacit-knowledge case demands "feel," watching others, practicing, and learning from observing experts. New consultants, for example, learn from experienced consultants. They act as "apprentices" and absorb knowledge over time. They work with their more senior colleagues to learn the "art" of the consulting relationship. Conveyance of tacit knowledge usually requires a hands-on, inter-active approach to information sharing.

Strategy execution and learning are difficult in some organizations because of tacit knowledge. R&D organizations, professional departments or firms (such as legal departments, law firms), con-sulting groups, sales or marketing units, and so on must purpose-ly develop methods or processes to transfer tacit knowledge. This must be taken into account when executing strategy. Teaching consulting skills or how to close a deal often requires observation and hands-on interaction over time. Knowing how to handle group interactions and discussions for new product development usually takes practice and observation of experienced managers at work.

Organizations with large amounts of tacit knowledge to share must be willing to invest in staff and allow the time for interaction, dis-cussion, and emulation that is needed to transfer information effec-tively. R&D organizations and professional departments cannot be rushed in their attempts to share and use important knowledge.

Characteristics of the Source of Information

Is the source trustworthy, reliable? Have I benefited from using this source previously? What is the motivation of the source? Is there a hidden agenda involved? Am I becoming too dependent on a source, thereby increasing its influence over me?

These are a few questions that often arise when considering the source of information. The answers obviously will affect information sharing and knowledge transfer. Answers to the questions usually reflect previous experiences or encounters with different sources of information. They also could reflect the company's culture.

I once knew a company in which no one trusted anything that marketing had to say. The function was seen as always furthering its own agenda, even at high cost to other functions or organizational subunits. A culture of distrust marked the company, affecting information flow and acceptance.

This distrust led to even more serious execution problems. Marketing bore responsibility for new product development, including extensions of or significant modifications to existing products. Marketing had to "sell" production on the new products so that production could develop, test, and modify them. But production incurred a large cost to work on new products: Production lines had to be shut down and the flow of work altered. Efficiency was injured because of the discontinuous production, and prototypes had to be produced and tested, disrupting normal operations.

To get production's cooperation, marketing felt it had to "exaggerate" the benefits of the new product. In fact, it often lied about the product's profit potential or the efficiency benefits that ultimately would accrue to production. Marketing promised the world, if only production would help with such an important task.

When the promises proved to be false and production saw the deviousness behind marketing's hype and exaggeration, when the new product was dropped abruptly, negating production's efforts and sacrifice, the distrust and conflict grew even greater. Marketing as a source of information or knowledge was discredited further. Production saw marketing as untrustworthy and unreliable. Most importantly, the execution of product development strategies received almost irreparable damage, representing a major blow to the company's future competitive position.

The perceived motivation, trustworthiness, and reliability of the source are at question here. So, how does an organization affect this situation? By creating and using effective incentives and controls. Setting up the right objectives for cooperation and communication, and then rewarding the appropriate behavior, will help ensure that the sources providing information are doing the right things for knowledge transfer. This example highlights the importance of effective incentives, a topic covered in detail in the next chapter.

The company should also define product development as a case of reciprocal interdependence, as previously discussed. This would force marketing and production to work together, jointly develop the rules and constraints of new product development, and share the rewards and costs of these innovative ventures.

The point is that marketing as a source of knowledge was suspect at best. Something had to be done to avoid permanent damage to the execution of product development strategies and to avoid competitive disaster in the marketplace.

Characteristics of the Recipient

What is the motivation of the recipient? I have seen managers accused of NIH—rejecting information because it's "not invented here." Clearly, the potential recipients don't trust the source, or they feel that their own way of doing things is better. Such rejection, of course, can be costly, leading to duplication and even less fruitful or effective work. What's needed again are incentives to get the groups working together for a common goal. If the recipients and senders of knowledge have something in common or something important at stake, the occurrence of NIH-related problems will diminish.

The "absorptive capacity" of an organization has a major impact on knowledge transfer.[ix] Absorptive capacity (AC) affects the ability of an organization to recognize new information (such as new science, new technologies), assimilate it, and apply it in some way to achieve organizational goals. AC is the result of learning. The ability to recognize and use new knowledge varies as a function of the accumulated base of existing knowledge in an organization. AC, that is, implies a critical mass of knowledge or investment in knowledge-based capabilities (such as R&D, scientists, engineers, IT systems) before new knowledge can be recognized and used to foster and support strategy. Failure to invest in and accumulate AC results in an inability to see, understand, or use new outside knowledge.

Consider a firm without this accumulated base of expertise. Assume next that another firm develops a new technology of some sort. Can the first firm import the new technology, be "second in" with its use, and use it to achieve competitive advantage? Can it import the new ideas and technology for new products or better-performing old products? Can it follow its competitor's lead, imitate the new technology, and remain competitive in the industry?

Without AC, the firm cannot judge the value or potential uses of the new technology. It doesn't have the scientists or engineers who can do an effective technological evaluation. Consequently, it doesn't act. It falls behind other firms with the requisite AC and loses its ability to execute needed new strategies in its industry. Not only can't a firm without AC innovate or be a first mover, it cannot even be an effective follower. It certainly will lose any competitive advantage it once enjoyed.

The solution is clear: A firm must invest in AC if it wishes to stay abreast of technological trends or disruptions, adapt successfully, innovate, and continue making strategy work.

Different firms in different industries will face different demands on developing AC (for example, high tech vs. low tech), but the basic principle holds for all organizations. Investment in knowledge and accumulation of a critical mass of information are vital to organizational innovation and adaptation. Without this critical mass of accumulated knowledge and capabilities, an organization cannot recognize, understand, or use new, state-of-the-art breakthroughs. It can't easily adapt or change and execute new strategies.

Characteristics of the Context

The context includes organizational structure, whose impact on knowledge transfer has been suggested in Chapter 4 and noted explicitly in this chapter. It simply is important to set up the IT systems and other formal mechanisms for knowledge transfer and information sharing. It's important to use integrators, teams, or matrix structures to achieve effective coordination and communication laterally, across organizational functions and other operating units.

It's also important to know how to make these elements of operating structure work. It's one thing to set up teams or matrix structures for coordination and information sharing. Making them work is often quite another issue. Problems here usually result from one of two sources: (a) technical problems in implementing the operating structure, or (b) problems with incentives, controls, and culture.

As an example of technical problems, consider once more the matrix structure and, specifically, the matrix diamond of Figure 5.4. A common problem with a matrix is not having a "tie breaker," the top role in the matrix. Consequently, conflicts between division and country managers or business and functional managers are not handled or solved immediately. Work comes to a virtual standstill as information moves slowly up two hierarchies. Information sharing suffers immensely. The matrix structure is accused of all sorts of shortcomings. The truth, however, is that it was set up incorrectly. Poor execution guaranteed failure. Technical issues affected performance and knowledge transfer.

The solution? Make sure that a tie-breaker or tie-breaking mechanisms are set up formally when employing the matrix. Addressing this technicality will save the organization a host of operating problems as it attempts to use and share information needed for strategy execution.

The second set of problems—those due to culture or poor incentives and controls—is also important to information sharing and knowledge transfer. Culture, for example, defines a host of things: how a company operates, what it values, how open or "closed" managers are when sharing information, and what's important for individual recognition. Factors such as these clearly can affect the knowledge transfer needed to achieve coordination and execute strategy effectively. A culture of cooperation based on a common, perceived mission will affect execution positively, whereas a culture marked by error avoidance and the need to blame others for poor results clearly will have negative effects on execution outcomes. Again, these aspects of organizational culture or context will be handled in Chapter 8 because of their significance for making strategy work.

Similarly, the incentives and controls that are employed are important factors affecting information sharing and knowledge transfer. Hoping for cooperation and coordination, but rewarding excessive and inappropriate competition, can only injure information sharing and, ultimately, execution efforts. Again, because of the importance of incentives and controls, Chapter 6 deals with the topic in detail.

This section of the chapter has focused on information sharing and knowledge transfer, supporting and reinforcing the previous discussion of interdependence and coordination methods. Communication and information sharing are vital to making strategy work, as managers indicated emphatically by their responses to the Wharton surveys on strategy execution. The various factors discussed in this section affect the "stickiness" of information flows and the usefulness of information to the execution of strategy.

CLARIFYING RESPONSIBILITY AND ACCOUNTABILITY

The third aspect of structural integration, clarifying responsibility and accountability, is also vital to making strategy work.

In the preceding discussions of interdependence, coordination, information sharing, and knowledge transfer, there was a basic but critical assumption that all responsibilities and accountabilities are clear. The presumption was that all individuals know what their roles or jobs are. Managers know with whom they must interact, when, and why and are fully cognizant of others' tasks or duties.

In reality, this clarity of roles is not always the case. Job-related responsibilities are not always clear, and authority is not always unambiguous. Responsibility and accountability often are blurred when people from different functions or divisions come together, often from different hierarchical levels in the organization. This is especially true in matrix-like structures where both lateral and hierarchical influences can easily cloud the responsibility and accountability picture.

Confusion often results from multiple points of responsibility or when many managers share responsibility. I recall a case at GM when, having learned of some problems with truck transaxels, I asked who was responsible for the quality of the component. I was told, "Around here, we're all responsible for quality. We all worry about it." A further check indeed revealed a number of groups or functions in different organizations and at different hierarchical levels that were responsible for quality, including engineering, quality assurance, plant managers, and production supervisors.

No problem, right? Quality appears to be covered adequately. Yet what happens when those responsible for quality are found in different places or have different perceptions or measures of quality? What can happen when things go drastically wrong with quality? What I found was that when everyone is responsible, then no one is responsible. When things went wrong, accountability was also elusive, as managers told me that "someone else really was responsible," not them.

This situation really isn't rare. In fact, it is fairly common, especially in organizations trying to adapt to widespread or rapid change. Roles and responsibilities transform quickly as managers try to cope with change. When many individuals and skills are brought to bear on a problem, the overarching accountability or responsibility often becomes muddled over time. Hence, everyone's responsible; everyone must worry about the problem. Yet the problem is never solved when everyone is responsible and no one is accountable.

The pervasive or widespread occurrence of this type of responsibility-related problem clearly was reflected in the research discussed in Chapter 1. It is recalled that unclear responsibility and/or accountability for execution decisions or actions was ranked in the top tier of execution problems by managers in both of the Wharton surveys. The data are strong and compelling. Managers who routinely confront execution issues point to this problem as one sorely in need of remediation.

Unclear responsibility and accountability in an execution plan or process can hurt efforts directed toward strategy execution or making strategy work. This clearly is not a trivial issue. It is worthy of management's attention at all levels of the organization.

RESPONSIBILITY PLOTTING AND ROLE NEGOTIATION

What can be done to confront these problems? One really good technique still is the process of responsibility plotting and role negotiation.[x] This process can help identify interdependence and assign responsibility and accountability for tasks or decisions instrumental to strategy execution. This technique has been used successfully by managers at all levels of an organization. Several steps are involved in the process.

1. The first step is to identify a goal or outcome that is related to strategy or strategy execution and is important to the company but that is not being achieved in a satisfactory manner.

   In Figure 5.5, based on an actual case I worked on a few years ago in a medium-size company in Texas, the goal or desired outcome was "new product development." The company's pipeline in this case had dried up, no new products were forthcoming, and the company was losing market share and its competitive advantage. (It had been a market leader for years.) Why new product development had taken such a hit was one topic to be discussed at the company's annual strategy retreat. What to do about rectifying the dismal situation was another, equally important strategic question for the meeting.

Strategic Goal: New Product Development

Major Tasks, Activities, or Decisions to Achieve Goal	Key Positions/People				
	CEO	V.P. Marketing	V.P. Engineering	V.P. Manufacturing	V.P. Finance
1. Do Market Research		"R"			
2. Decision on New Product					
3. Build Prototype					"C"
4. Market Test					
5. Decision on Mass Production					
6. Product Introduction					
7.					
8. Etc.					

R = Responsible for Decison or Action A = Final Say/Accountability for Decision or Action	I = Must be informed after a decision or action C = Must be consulted prior to a decision or action ? = Don't know

Figure 5.5 A Responsibility Matrix

2. The second step in responsibility plotting is to list the major tasks, activities, or decisions that are instrumental to achieving the desired goal or outcome. The people who are important to the goal or outcome and who might be called upon to perform key tasks and activities are also noted.

   Figure 5.5 shows some, but not all, of the key tasks, activities, decisions, and people (functions) involved in new product development in the company being studied, solely in the interest of space. Still, the main idea should be clear: List the key decision-makers and the tasks or activities that must be accomplished to develop new products or extensions of an existing product line.

3. The third step is to define different types or degrees of responsibility. The types must be relevant but simple and few enough to ensure manageability. The codes for types or degrees of responsibility or authority in Figure 5.5 are as follows: R, for those having some responsibility for a task, activity, or decision; A, for the person(s) who is ultimately accountable and who must answer for a decision, activity, or task; C, for those who must be consulted prior to making a decision; I, for those who must be informed after a decision; and ?, when you don't know whether this role is involved or what the extent of its involvement should be.

4. The fourth step is for all managers participating in the process to fill in the matrix by assigning what they feel are the appropriate responsibility codes for the individuals listed, below their function (name, title) and next to the relevant task, activity, or decision. In Figure 5.5, for example, the marketing function or person is seen as having some responsibility for the market research necessary for product development. Similarly, the VP of finance must be consulted prior to committing funds to building a prototype of any new product.

   The matrix should be filled out individually (privately) at first to avoid excessive groupthink or arguing too early in the process. Also, it is imperative to tap into all participants' opinions to add a richness and diversity of thought to the next steps.

5. The fifth step is to assign participants to a group and combine all participants' responses on just one matrix. In the company case I'm referring to in this example, the responses of individuals in each group were put on one matrix. They were all over the place, indicating strong disagreement about who was responsible for what in the new product development process. This disagreement obviously speaks loads about the underlying problems or obstacles that existed. Differences in perceptions about who is responsible or accountable clearly must have contributed to problems of communications and decision-making in the company's product development process.

6. The sixth step has each group present its single matrix to all participants to highlight disagreements, not only on each group's combined matrix but across the groups as well. Discussion then focuses on why such differences in perception exist and how those differences or conflicts relate to problems with new product development (or whatever the desired goal or outcome listed).

A word of warning is appropriate here. It is important for the leader or facilitator to control the discussion and the heated debates that often occur during this step. In the company presently being referenced, the CEO had A's for most tasks, activities, or discussions. People (after some hesitation) opened up and hurled criticisms of micromanagement at him. They provided examples of how his interference was screwing up new product development and other important outcomes for the company. Tempers occasionally flared, and breaks were needed to calm things down. But all ended well, as the following steps will show.

7. The seventh step is to have the groups then separate themselves, with each group coming up with one ideal matrix. Based on the discussions, heated arguments, and apparent agreements in step six, each group creates a single matrix, indicating its ideal solution to the assignment of responsibilities and accountabilities for activities related to new product development. Each group, in turn, then presents its matrix to all the participants, and similarities and differences across groups can be addressed and debated.

8. The eighth step is to create one responsibility matrix from the different group presentations. This is done publicly, with the facilitator's goal being one of reaching agreement on the assigned responsibilities and accountabilities for new product development. Successful completion of this step results in one matrix, one unified approach to product development. With this finalized, agreed-upon output, the work of the responsibility and role negotiation process is complete.

9. In the company from which this example was drawn, managers added an additional, ninth, step: publication of a *Guide to New Product Development*. This manual or handbook became a source book, laying out what should be done, by whom, and when for new product development, as well as who was responsible at every step along the way.

   Subsequent to the guide's development, actual new product development increased significantly, strengthening the company's competitive position. Its strategy of differentiation once again was being executed with favorable results. "The proof of the pudding is in the eating," and the proof of any process is in its results. Happily, the process in the company worked.

In sum, it is important to clarify roles and responsibilities related to desired strategic outcomes. Without this clarification and an unambiguous assignment of responsibility for critical tasks, decisions, or actions, strategy execution cannot happen. This will cause major problems, as managers participating in the Wharton surveys told us loudly and clearly.

Unclear responsibility and accountability for execution decisions and actions can kill an otherwise well–thought-out process of execution. Managers interested in making strategy work simply cannot allow this situation to occur. Responsibility for execution decisions and actions must be clearly assigned and understood.

SUMMARY

Three major conclusions or key takeaways were suggested in this chapter. Each is an important aspect of structural integration, and each is critical to making strategy work.

1. It is necessary to define interdependence before choosing or investing in coordination methods. The three types of interdependence—pooled, sequential, and reciprocal—demand different methods or processes of achieving the integration necessary for strategy execution.

Adding this chapter on integration to the previous chapters on strategy and organizational structure suggests a process that all managers can follow when designing methods for coordination or integration:

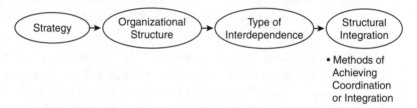

Strategy affects structure, which determines the type of interdependence involved and the methods needed to achieve effective coordination and information flows. Following this process will help define the coordination methods that are important to making strategy work.

2. Information sharing, knowledge transfer, and effective communication are vital to execution. Poor or inadequate information sharing, in fact, was rated as a major obstacle to strategy execution by managers in the Wharton surveys. This chapter considered many of the formal and informal factors that affect communication and knowledge transfer among those responsible for making strategy work. Managers have an array of formal methods or processes at their disposal, including use of databases, IT processes, formal roles, and matrix structures.

A focus on the formal, however, is not sufficient. Informal methods or processes can aid or inhibit the functioning of formal methods to achieve information sharing and knowledge transfer. Using informal contacts, direct communication, and a "common language" (clear, agreed-upon metrics and goals) facilitates communication. The characteristics of knowledge senders and users, the type of information transferred, and the context within which information sharing occurs all conspire to facilitate or block the communication needed to make strategy work.

3. Finally, for execution to work, all responsibilities and accountabilities for key decisions and actions must be clear or unambiguous. They must be understood by all managers involved in the execution process. Without clear responsibility and accountability, effective coordination and cooperation simply will not occur. Clarifying responsibility and accountability, then, is vital to execution success.

   One way to confront the problem is via the use of responsibility plotting and role-negotiation techniques. This chapter presented an actual example by looking at the strategic need for new product development and how responsibility plotting can help meet the demands of this need. The steps for responsibility plotting and role negotiation were spelled out in this chapter, along with their underlying logic and utility.

Managers who focus on the three major issues presented in this chapter will generate structure and integration methods that are supportive of strategy execution. Another issue, mentioned but not covered in depth in this chapter, is the importance of incentives and controls for operating structure and for making strategy work. Consequently, this is the topic of the next chapter, as we continue to look at ways to execute strategy successfully.

ENDNOTES

i.   "Boeing is Merging Businesses Dealing with Space, Military." *The Wall Street Journal,* July 11, 2002.

ii. "At Shell, Strategy and Structure Fueled Troubles," *The Wall Street Journal,* March 12, 2004.

iii. Michael Porter, "What is Strategy?" *Harvard Business Review,* November-December, 1996.

iv. The forms of interdependence defined in this chapter were originally discussed by James D. Thompson in *Organizations in Action,* McGraw-Hill, 1967. They clearly are still useful for a full understanding of interdependence and the need for appropriate coordination mechanisms or processes.

v.   "GE Chief is Charting His Own Strategy," *The Wall Street Journal,* September 28, 2003.

vi. For a good discussion of "Work Out" and other programs under Jack Welch at GE, see Amir Hartman, *Ruthless Execution,* Financial Times/Prentice Hall, 2004, pp. 53–69.

vii. For a full discussion of the matrix diamond and matrix structure, see the following: Jay R. Galbraith, *Designing Complex Organizations,* Addison-Wesley, 1972; L.G. Hrebiniak and William Joyce, *Implementing Strategy,* Macmillan, 1984; S. Davis and Paul Lawrence, *Matrix,* Addison-Wesley, 1978.

viii. Gabriel Szulanski, "Exploring Internal Stickiness: Impediments to the Transfer of Best Practice Within the Firm, *Strategic Management Journal,* Vol. 17, 1996.

ix. W.M. Cohen and D.A. Levinthal, "Absorptive Capacity: A New Perspective on Learning and Innovation," *Administrative Science Quarterly,* Vol. 35, 1990.

x.   Previous work defining and discussing responsibility plotting and the process of role negotiation can be found in the following: L.G. Hrebiniak and W.F. Joyce, *Implementing Strategy,* Macmillan, 1984; Jay Galbraith, *Designing Complex Organizations,* Addison-Wesley, 1973.

6

Incentives and Controls: Supporting and Reinforcing Execution

Introduction

The last element of the execution model presented in Chapter 2 is incentive and controls. Both affect strategy execution. Incentives motivate behavior toward ends or actions consistent with desired execution outcomes. Controls provide feedback about performance, reinforce execution methods, provide a "corrective" mechanism, and allow for organizational learning and adaptation.

Managers in the Wharton-Gartner and Wharton Executive Education surveys did not note incentives and controls as a major problem area for execution in their companies. However, the open-ended responses and panel discussions noted in Chapter 1 identified a few problems in this area, most notably with controls.

This chapter will focus on the main issues or problems identified in the surveys and how they relate to making strategy work.

ROLE OF INCENTIVES AND CONTROLS

Incentives and controls are last in the logical flow of execution decisions and actions because they must be. Creating sound strategy, structure, integration mechanisms, methods of knowledge transfer, and short-term objectives is necessary for execution. These steps are not sufficient, however. It is also necessary to ensure that people are motivated and committed to making strategy work. Similarly, it is necessary for an organization to be able to change and adapt if feedback reveals problems with execution decisions, actions, or methods.

Execution will fail if no one has skin in the game. Execution will suffer if people are rewarded for doing the wrong things: behavior and actions that are inconsistent with or detrimental to desired execution outcomes. It's that simple: Incentives must support key aspects of the execution process. Increasingly, companies are showing CEOs the door or changing their incentive schemes because key strategic objectives and execution outcomes are not being met.[i]

Controls are also vital to execution success. They allow managers to evaluate execution efforts and make necessary changes. Control systems or methods "round out" the execution process by (a) providing feedback or information about performance against execution objectives, (b) reinforcing execution methods and decisions, (c) providing a corrective mechanism to keep the execution process on track, and (d) allowing for organizational learning to facilitate change and organizational adaptation. These four elements define "controls" in the present approach to making strategy work.

The focus in this chapter is on incentives and controls and how they affect execution. Let's begin with a discussion of incentives.

INCENTIVES AND EXECUTION

Much has been written about incentives and individuals' motivation to perform. Different fields of study, including psychology and management, have saturated us with countless ideas about the links among work, motivation, and effort on the job. Attempts at summarizing this vast literature would be an impossible task, and this discussion won't attempt it. Instead, it will focus on a few critical incentives-related issues. Let's first introduce a basic point about motivation and incentives that was provided by managers actively involved in the execution process.

A BASIC RULE: DON'T *DEMOTIVATE* PEOPLE

The essential underlying reality in most organizations is that individuals want to perform well. Managers are motivated to seek and attain positive results. They have a high need for achievement, which motivates them to set challenging objectives and work hard toward their attainment.[ii] There are exceptions to every rule, of course. Still, virtually all the managers I've known have this drive to succeed, this need for achievement. Organizations usually recruit good people who are motivated to do well.

The basic rule, then, when developing and using incentives is as follows: *Don't demotivate people.* Don't kill, penalize, or handicap the golden goose, the high achiever. Most managers want to perform. Help them do so.

Incentives fuel and guide this basic motivation. They don't cause or create it. Good managers want to achieve. The role of incentives is to support this basic motivation and push it in a direction to facilitate strategy execution.

Execution suffers primarily because of two interrelated problems. First, incentives don't support the right things. The basic, underlying motivation of managers is pushed in the wrong direction, working against successful execution. High achievers respond to incentives; it's vital that the incentives support desired execution-related behaviors and outcomes.

Second, poor incentives demotivate people, even individuals with a high need for achievement. The first problem just mentioned builds upon a strong motivation but deflects it in the wrong direction. The second problem results in an adverse effect on motivation. The wrong incentives turn people off and seriously injure their motivation and drive for excellence.

These problems are basic and important. They should be kept in mind as we discuss incentives and controls and their effects on execution.

GOOD INCENTIVES

Let's build on these basic points and start by stressing that there are many different incentives, but some are better than others.

Generally, good incentives are positive and come in two packages: utilitarian and psychological. The former includes things of extrinsic value (salary, bonus, promotion), while the second is more intrinsic or personal (autonomy, enjoying work, psychological identification with a job or its outcomes). Many rewards, of course, smack of both, as when someone receives a pat on the back or other recognition for work well done, which certainly also bodes well for the prospect of a healthy pay raise or promotion in the future.

Everyone knows about the importance of utilitarian rewards. The view of Nucor's CEO that "motivation is green" needs no interpretation. The statement by Robert Wood Johnson at J&J, "Make your top managers rich, and they will make you richer," is perfectly clear in its meaning. So, too, are the statements of a manager in a program at Wharton to the effect that "money is critical, both in its own right and as a way to keep score."

The last point does suggest the psychological side of incentives. "Keeping score" suggests relative position versus peers or colleagues. Pay raises and promotions tell people how they're doing or what their value is to the organization, which clearly implies perceptions of self worth, influence, and achievement.

For our purposes, these managers are suggesting that good incentives are important to strategy execution. What defines "good"? Here are some opinions and ideas reinforced in the surveys or by my own experiences with execution.

Good incentives are tied to strategic objectives or short-term objectives that are derived from strategy. For effective execution, strategic objectives must be reinforced and rewarded, especially at higher organizational levels. At all levels, incentives must support short-term objectives that are related logically to longer-term strategic ends (see Chapter 3).

More and more CEOs, for example, are taking (or being forced to take) incentive deals that focus on company performance and shareholder value. Jeffrey Immelt of GE will pass on stock options and restricted stock in favor of "performance share units." These will become stock only if performance goals related to shareholder value and cash flow are met. Paul Anderson of Duke Energy accepted a contract that pays him exclusively with stock, a move that focuses on growth in shareholder value. Other examples of tying incentives to strategic performance can be seen daily in the business press.

The popularity of programs such as the Balanced Scorecard also suggests that efforts are being made to ensure that short-term measures of performance are consistent with desired strategic outcomes. These approaches stress that short-term objectives and incentives are related to the execution of important long-term, strategic objectives. "Strategic thinking" involves the integration of long- and short-term needs, and incentives play an important role in this integration task.

Good objectives are measurable. Managers involved in execution emphasize that they want to know if they've accomplished something of value. This feedback or feeling of worth is consistent with a high need for achievement. Objectives, then, must be measurable. Execution objectives related to strategy that are not measurable convey no sense of accomplishment. They also lead to different interpretations as to what is actually being accomplished. Clear, agreed-upon metrics are critical to reinforcing the right execution-related performance.

Short-term metrics also must be important and relevant to strategic success. I was working with a CEO of a small Internet services company. His biggest execution problems, he said, included translating company strategy into short-term, measurable objectives. The strategy focused on differentiation in a competitive, hostile marketplace. Components of differentiation included technical and customer service aspects. His problem? Developing measurable outcomes that both internal staff and customers could agree on and get excited about. Technical people tended to focus on "nerd-like" performance indicators that customers didn't understand. Customers, in contrast, wanted results that clearly tied into real-world outcomes, such as lower costs and programs to help them with their customers.

The two points of view had to be reconciled. First, consistent with the previous section's discussion, strategy had to be translated into short-term metrics. Second, those metrics had to be measurable, relevant, and important to both customers and technical people alike. If what excites and motivates technical people turns off customers, there clearly will be a problem with strategy execution. After a great deal of work, the problems of relevancy, importance, and measurability were solved and short-term measures supported the company strategy.

Good objectives facilitate accountability. Accountability is really a control issue and will be discussed again later in this chapter, but the last point about measurability demands that it be mentioned here.

Managers in failed or faltering execution programs usually complain that accountability for performance against objectives is weak or nonexistent. Their advice? Make sure that objectives measure something of value and then hold managers accountable for performance against these metrics.

Execution suffers heavily if performance measures aren't used as the basis of managerial responsibility and accountability. Measurability and accountability are vital aspects paving the path to execution success, as the following suggests:

Measurable Objectives $\longrightarrow$ Accountability for Performance Against Objectives $\longrightarrow$ Execution Success

Without accountability, people can never feel that they really have skin in the game. Without clear accountability, the motivational aspects of incentives are basically thwarted or destroyed. Without a focus on accountability and its reinforcement of desired objectives, execution plans suffer because people don't know who's doing what, when, and why, leading to a lack of focus in execution efforts.

Good objectives are never "all or nothing," black or white, or reflective of other such binary distinctions. They refer instead to degree of accomplishment along some continuum of performance.

I worked for Ford Motor Company years ago as a district field manager in marketing. I had clear sales objectives in cars and light and medium trucks. Every ten days, I was judged on whether or not I had made my objectives. The answer was black or white, yes or no. There was no "rounding"—99.5 percent was a failure, while 100 percent was a success. Even if 99 percent resulted in a trouncing of Chevrolet (one of the important strategic goals), I didn't "make it." I had failed at execution.

The effect of this all-or-nothing approach on motivation is probably obvious. I made sure I always made my objectives. I "lowballed" during planning to ensure having objectives I could easily attain. When the answer to questions about successful performance is yes or no, one tries to ensure success by shooting low, not high. When dire consequences befall those "not making it," the emphasis on lowballing is even stronger, negatively affecting motivation, execution, and the attainment of important strategic and short-term objectives.

Good objectives are not binary, black or white. They reflect degree of performance against some continuous standard. Consider the following simple graphic:

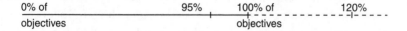

If someone achieves 95 percent of his objectives, is he a failure (black vs. white)? Not necessarily. Other factors must come into play. If I at Ford achieved 95 percent, but my counterpart from Chevrolet in the same region achieved only 75 percent, allowing me to gain market share, should I be forced to bear the title of failure? Granted, I shouldn't receive the same reward as a colleague who achieves 120 percent of important objectives and also beats Chevrolet; she clearly has outperformed me. Still, treating anything less than 100 percent consistently as a failure and not going beyond some simplistic black-white, good-bad judgment will surely lead to game-playing, lowballing, and the massaging and manipulation of data. To use objectives and incentives in such a simplistic way invites reactions inconsistent with execution success.

REWARD THE RIGHT THINGS

Again, the opinions of managers involved in execution and my own experiences weigh heavily here. If strategic plans posit the importance of something, but incentives reward quite something else, then clearly execution will suffer. It's foolish to hope for one thing while rewarding another. Effective execution demands that this foolishness be corrected. Incentives must support decisions or behaviors consistent with an organization's execution plan.

The stories about cost controls at Wal-Mart are legion and legendary. Managers sharing hotel rooms to save money. Associates being asked to bring home pens and notepaper from conferences they attend. Wal-Mart buyers calling suppliers collect. Shrinkage incentives directed toward employees, in effect motivating them *not* to steal.

Whether every one of the many stories coming out of Wal-Mart over the years is true is not the issue here. The real issue underlying them, whether fact or folklore, is that people at Wal-Mart believe that frugality is pervasive and good. Cost controls are desirable. All company associates must worry about cost. The strategy demands an emphasis on low cost, which is the right thing to incentivize and reinforce. Actions indeed speak louder than words. It is important, then, to recognize and reward the right actions.

Reward performance against agreed upon objectives. The main point here is to avoid surprises. Objectives related to desired execution outcomes must be developed and clarified up front, and performance appraisal must focus on these agreed-upon measures. The links between rewards and performance then can be forged consistently and unequivocally.

What shouldn't happen is an arbitrary choice of performance measures after the fact. Good leaders do not foster arbitrariness. A sales manager responsible for increased sales volume and market share believes he has performed well, only to be chided for lower margins. A head of engineering focuses on improving the quality of a product, thereby increasing customer satisfaction, but is warned about cost increases in his department and the future dire consequences if costs don't go down.

The relative importance of competing objectives must be established up front in the execution process; measures to evaluate performance cannot be chosen arbitrarily after the fact. If it's important for the sales manager to worry simultaneously about market share *and* margins, then say so up front when execution-related objectives are being negotiated. Lay out the desired relationship between sales volume and margins. If costs provide a necessary constraint on quality improvement or customer satisfaction, clarify this fact for the head of engineering up front, before action plans are executed to achieve departmental objectives.

Managers are telling us something basic here: Avoid surprises and the arbitrary changing of performance criteria after the fact. There is nothing worse than celebrating success against certain metrics, only to be told that performance against other, previously unspecified objectives is sorely lacking.

One last point: Organizations always get what they "pay for." Managers can hope for certain behaviors or outcomes. If the organization actually rewards different behaviors or outcomes, however, what's hoped for or desired will not materialize. Execution success relies heavily on this straightforward fact of organizational life: Organizations always get what they actually reward, pay for, or reinforce, even if it is occasionally unintentional or unanticipated.

The underlying takeaway in all these examples is simply that organizations must reward the right things. Rewarding the wrong things, even if done unintentionally, will hurt the execution process. Thorndike's age-old law of effect always holds true: Behavior that is reinforced tends to be repeated.[iii] Leaders of execution programs and processes must keep this fact and others discussed in this section squarely in mind.

CONTROLS: FEEDBACK, LEARNING, AND ADAPTATION

The discussion of incentives has repeatedly suggested the importance of controls, which should not be surprising. Incentives and controls are interdependent, flip sides of the same coin. After setting objectives and providing incentives for execution, controls come into play.

THE CONTROL PROCESS

As Figure 6.1 shows, controls provide feedback about performance, reinforce execution methods, provide a "corrective" mechanism, and facilitate organizational learning and adaptation.

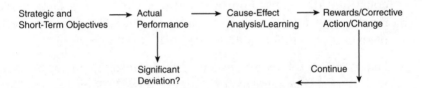

Figure 6.1 The Control Process

Control always begins with a comparison of actual and desired performance, as Figure 6.1 indicates. If there is a significant deviation between the two, it must be analyzed or studied. Cause-effect clarity is the goal; the question is, what caused the deviation? Was it due to an organization's missteps? The unanticipated actions of competitors? The existence of inadequate capabilities or poor incentives? Emphasis clearly is on learning, as managers try to dissect the problem and understand the logical reasons underlying the significant aberration in performance. After learning has occurred, steps then can be taken to provide feedback or correct the situation, leading to change and organizational adaptation.

This picture of the control process is accurate but deceptively simple. The truth is that it contains some significant pitfalls for the execution process. Leadership and sound management are absolutely essential to the avoidance of these pitfalls or problems.

Oticon

Consider the case of Oticon, a Danish manufacturer of hearing aids. In the early 1990s, Lars Kolind, president and CEO, decided that he was sick and tired of organizational specialization and his organizational structure. He wanted to get away from excessive hierarchy and a departmental or functional structure that presumably was creating problems. He made a very bold move. While people at first thought that Kolind was kidding, they realized he was not, and many wound up supporting what he did.[iv]

What he did was set up a new structure—the "spaghetti organization." The traditional organizational structure was out. A new, fluid structure was in, based on the notion of a fungible pool of human resources or capabilities, people who could choose their own jobs and projects. Job assignment was voluntary. There was little or no formal management control as was the case in the past. There was a management group that reviewed the progress of chosen projects, but it wielded no control over spending and staffing.

Other changes were interesting, to say the least. Additional aspects of the new organization were "one thousand birch trees" and an elimination of all paper. People moved from project to project, dragging their own trees, desks, and files with them. Projects demanded movement and physical co-location. This movement was seen as beneficial because, among other things, it resulted in informal interaction and chats among people as they moved and encountered each other on stairs (only desks and files used the elevators!).

There was an objective of the new organizational structure and process. It was a 30 percent improvement in competitiveness in 3 years, giving the name "Project 330" to the execution of the "spaghetti organization" and its related moves. Many people were excited by their new, loose, formless organization.

Results, however, were far from happy. Net sales in the full year following the changes did increase by 5 percent, but other measures of performance didn't fare too well. Production costs increased significantly, R&D expenses increased almost 90 percent, and selling expenses increased about 15 percent in the same period. The company suffered a net loss. It also had market effectiveness problems, as a new, black (competitors' products were skin colored), behind-the-ear (not in-the-ear) hearing aid failed to make competitive inroads in the market. The company basically experienced a weakening of demand for some of its products.

What went wrong with the experiment at Oticon? There were many problems, but let's focus on its logic, the development of key objectives, and other aspects of control suggested by Figure 6.1. Kolind was sick and tired of specialization and organizational structure, but why? Oticon was experiencing performance problems. Were specialization and a departmental structure part of the problem, negatively affecting performance? This cause-effect relationship and its probable impact on performance were never established, only implied by Kolind's actions.

The key objective—and key input to the control process—was a 30 percent increase in "competitiveness" in three years. But what is competitiveness, and how was it measured? Poor objectives, including those that are ambiguous, not measurable, or subject to varying interpretations, will challenge the control process early when comparing actual and desired performance (see Figure 6.1). In addition, the relevance of the performance objectives can also be questioned without prior explanation of Oticon's past performance problems.

Finally, what caused Oticon's poor performance after the changes? Can clear cause-effect inferences be drawn from Oticon's experiment that would lead to organizational learning and changes in the future? Indeed, had sufficient learning occurred in the past to justify Project 330, the setting of remedial objectives, and an execution plan based on the "spaghetti organization" and other organizational changes previously mentioned?

The Oticon case suggests important problems related to control execution and organizational performance. Before examining them in greater detail, let's look at two contrasting cases.

Circuit City

In contrast to the loose "spaghetti organization" of Oticon, Circuit City relies on a more structured model of control and execution. Its organization relies heavily on consistent and disciplined performance and a control process that supports its operations.

Circuit City's strategy focused early on becoming a large-scale, big-ticket consumer sales company, emphasizing low cost, large product selection, and good service to customers. It also wanted to add consistency in stores across a wide geographical range. Management wanted the company, though large, to run smoothly, with each store doing the same things, almost running automatically despite differences in geographical location. Strategy, then, drove consistency and discipline, which affected the control process depicted in Figure 6.1.

Objectives by store reflected the strategy based on price, selection, and customer satisfaction. Store managers had some discretion for their operations, but they were held responsible for store performance and staying within the bounds of Circuit City's methods. Responsibility was clear and constrained by the goals of the corporation. Managers were accountable for their performance.

Actual store performance was compared to goals, and the company's emphasis on consistency and routines ensured that any deviations were analyzed and corrected quickly and expeditiously. Their consistent business model and approach to retailing allowed the company to understand reasons for good or poor performance, which facilitated learning and organizational adaptation over time in a very competitive market.

Whereas Oticon was loose and virtually formless, with little consistency and discipline, Circuit City was the opposite, a model of controlled growth and consistency of operations. Evaluating and understanding performance aberrations clearly was more difficult for Oticon than a company such as Circuit City, with its adherence to routines and controlled operations.

The Quick-printing Industry

Some interesting research in the quick-printing or copying industry sheds additional light on the importance of management and controls.[iv] One finding is particularly revealing and significant.

It seems that "mavericks" or entrepreneurs who were part of a quick-printing or copy company, but who leave the corporate fold to venture off on their own, perform much more poorly than stores that stay attached to the corporation. These mavericks learn the business and the operating routines while a franchisee of the company, but they seemingly forget and change their methods when becoming an independent, and this hurts their performance. The business or technology hasn't changed, and quick printing is hardly rocket science, so what's going on? What explains these results?

The simple answer is management control. When part of the corporation as franchisees, top management enforces important routines and discipline over them. Management ensures that the company's way of doing business is followed. Objectives are clear, methods of operation are spelled out, and any deviations from acceptable procedures are quickly corrected by top management.

It is management and the controls they impose, then, that make a difference. Top management's ensuring discipline and the following of routines or standard operating procedures positively affected franchisees' performance. Mavericks who went off on their own and rejected the pressure of routines and proven business methods in favor of their own methods and approaches did not fare as well as franchisees who stayed.

In the quick-printing business, then, management makes a difference (a finding we all can happily relate to!). The imposition and use of standard procedures and the discipline and consistency they impose clearly make a difference in performance. The emphasis on a control system based on clear objectives, proven routines, and a disciplined, consistent approach to management across locations in a relatively stable industry is reminiscent of Circuit City's methods, but it is far removed from Oticon's model of a formless and loosely controlled business.

Let's now try to extract some general principles of control from the preceding examples and relate them to the process shown in Figure 6.1. Combining these cases with the experiences of practicing managers reported in Chapter 1's research, the goal is to understand control, including "do's" and "don'ts" and what works and what doesn't. Let's look at some guidelines for good controls.

DEVELOP AND USE GOOD OBJECTIVES

Poor objectives can hurt the control process and immediately doom execution efforts. If objectives aren't measurable, the comparison of actual and desired performance that marks the early stages of the control model in Figure 6.1 is problematic and extremely subjective or arbitrary at best. If objectives don't relate logically to strategy or strategic problems that need fixing, the objectives aren't relevant or worth pursuing.

Good strategic and short-term objectives rely on sound planning. The objectives must relate logically to the definition of strategic needs and short-term problems that need attention. Objectives at the operating level at both Circuit City and in the quick-printing industry were closely tied to strategy and critical needs, but the same cannot be said about Oticon.

Good objectives stress the right things. With poor objectives, the wrong things may be reinforced. Relatedly, with poor objectives, the link between performance metrics and incentives is unforged and unclear. Oticon did have a forced-ranking performance apprais-al system, with most people getting raises and a few receiving none, but the link between stated company objectives and performance appraisal was not clear. This link was apparently forged much bet-ter in Circuit City and in firms in the quick-printing or copy indus-try, where management controls and performance appraisals emphasized consistency, discipline, and rewarding the right things.

Poor objectives hurt controls. Without clear, relevant, measurable objectives, the control process, which relies on a comparison of actual and desired performance, simply cannot begin to function. Significant deviations from goals cannot be identified. Learning and organizational adaptation are simply not possible.

REWARD THE DOERS, THE PERFORMERS

For execution to work, it is absolutely critical that the organiza-tion reward the doers, the performers.

Incentives must motivate performance toward desired outcomes. Hoping for one thing but rewarding another is confusing and wrong. So is the neglect of solid performance. The execution process will suffer if the doers aren't recognized and rewarded. It is critical that the organization celebrate success and reward those who helped achieve it.

This simple fact alone can make or break the control process and execution attempts. The model of execution presented in Chapter 2 discusses a number of important decisions or actions that are vital to execution success. Individuals become committed to mak-ing strategy work, and incentives ensure that they have skin in the game.

What's absolutely critical next is that the organization celebrates success. Those who perform must be recognized. Their behavior and its results must be reinforced. It is absolutely essential that the doers be rewarded as part of the feedback mechanism noted in Figure 6.1.

Managers have emphasized this point to me time and time again, suggesting that as basic as it is, it is violated often enough to become an execution problem. Their point reinforces the basic argument being made presently: Reward the performers. Give positive feedback to those responsible for execution success and making strategy work.

FACE THE BRUTAL FACTS HONESTLY

Jim Collins stresses that the "great" companies in his sample always confronted brutal facts openly and honestly.[v] I couldn't agree more with this aspect of control. The managers in my surveys, like those in Collins', talked openly and convincingly about the need to conduct autopsies when things went wrong. Autopsies are consistent with the analysis of significant deviations and the need for learning and feedback, important aspects of the control model of Figure 6.1.

A major strength of GE that I observed time and time again, especially during "Work Out" sessions, was the ability to confront poor performance openly. "Work Outs" were often loud, rambunctious affairs, but the underlying principle driving the discussion was always the same—find out what's causing a problem and eliminate it. Focus on learning and understanding, which can occur only if people confront the brutal facts and dissect a problem.

The sad fact is that many managers really don't want to hear the truth or confront the brutal facts openly, even though this is exactly what will help their companies the most. An industry analyst recently told me that many companies he deals with never accept the brutal reality that they are performing horribly at certain execution tasks, even though these weaknesses may sow the seeds of poor performance, even destruction of the company. These companies want analysts to ignore the bad news, including poor performance vis-á-vis competitors, and report only the good news, even if it means compromising credibility. This may be a special case that combines brutal honesty, ethics, and stock price or market valuation. Still, the avoidance of brutal reality in control systems can only lead to poor execution and performance problems. Conducting autopsies is certainly no fun, but it clearly is an essential ingredient in making strategy work.

Autopsies, of course, won't result in learning and organizational change if people perceive that their main purpose is "finding some idiots to blame for poor performance and please the gods," as one manager aptly expressed it. Execution demands that leaders and followers focus on the issues, confront problems with honesty and a healthy curiosity, and be committed to learning and change. Emphasis must be on embracing error and understanding it, not just on finding, conveniently, someone to blame or fire.

Facing the brutal facts honestly and learning from them are integral aspects of a disciplined, change-oriented culture. This discipline has characterized companies such as Wal-Mart, Southwest Airlines, GE, Crown Holdings, Circuit City, and the firms in the quick-printing or copy industry previously referenced, but not the companies examined by my industry analyst friend. Ignoring the real facts can only hurt strategy execution.

REWARD COOPERATION

This is becoming an increasingly important issue, one that follows logically from a previous point about the need to reward the doers. The fact is that organizations reward individual performance much more than cooperative achievement, and this can hurt execution.

The world of strategy execution is becoming increasing complex, and it is often the case that task interdependence is high. Individuals' efforts in different functional areas must be combined and coordinated to achieve positive outcomes. Cooperative efforts are needed to achieve integrated results, consistent with the discussion of reciprocal interdependence in Chapter 5. Individual efforts are important, of course, but it is the coordination of those efforts and the cooperation across diverse functions or units that occasionally are vital to execution success.

The problem surfaces when incentives recognize and reward only individual performance and neglect or ignore task interdependence and cooperation.[vi]

Incentives and rewards tell people what's important. They motivate certain behaviors but not others. If the controls and feedback of Figure 6.1 foster only individual recognition, the cooperative behavior demanded by increasingly complex and highly task-interdependent execution processes will suffer. As two managers once pointed out when talking to me about the failure of execution programs in their companies that demanded a high level of functional integration and teamwork:

> "Stars get ahead around here, not constellations."

> "The execution plan stressed the need for cooperation and coordination. But incentives and performance appraisals recognized only individual performance. The message was very clear about what really counts."

The solution is obvious but rarely simple. The need is to reinforce cooperative behavior. If execution demands highly interdependent activities and the integration of tasks or individuals in diverse functions for success, then group-based incentives may be needed. All individuals on a SWAT team charged with an important task, for example, should be held responsible for the team's output. All should see the same incentives and receive the same performance appraisal upon task completion, an important control element. Not recognizing the need for cooperation and joint effort when interdependence is high can only hurt execution and its outcomes.

CLARIFY RESPONSIBILITY AND ACCOUNTABILITY

The discussion of individual and group-based performance, incentives, and feedback presupposes an important point, namely that responsibility and accountability are clear. This issue was discussed earlier in this chapter and in Chapter 5, but it certainly is important to reinforce when talking about controls.

The control process shown in Figure 6.1 cannot work if responsibility and accountability are muddled or confused. Objectives belong to individuals and, occasionally, teams or units. Without this ownership and accountability for the objectives, feedback cannot be effective, rewards cannot be assigned unequivocally, and a thrust for change cannot work. Assignment of responsibility clearly is much more problematic in a "spaghetti organization" than in a more disciplined organization, which affects performance in significant ways.

It is important, then, to clarify responsibility and accountability for the execution process to work. This is an important element of sound management and control that must be attended to. Accordingly, managers responsible for leading execution are referred to Chapter 5 and its discussion of role negotiation and the responsibility matrix.

CONTROLS REQUIRE TIMELY AND VALID INFORMATION

The control process of Figure 6.1 suggests the importance of good information. Planning and objective-setting demand industry and competitor analysis, as well as an assessment of organizational capabilities, and this information must be circulated and be well understood. Deviations between actual and desired performance suggest the collection and dissemination of data. Feedback loops and evaluation of performance rely on sound information.

Good information must be timely and valid. For controls to work, up-to-date information about performance must be valid or correct. Changes in strategy, objectives, or incentives depend on feedback, as do organizational learning and adaptation.

A company entering a totally new market, such as China or Japan, needs good feedback about customer reactions to its products or services. It also needs to know competitors' reactions to the incursion into their market. Are they retaliating? How? Where? Are they attacking elsewhere, such as in Europe, because attention is focused on China or Japan and Europe may be vulnerable? Is the new emphasis on the Far East taking the company's eye off the ball in other markets?

The company's information must also be timely. Old or stale information precludes a timely, effective response to competitors' actions or customer complaints. So, the company entering a new market needs timely, up-to-date information to support strategic actions.

Both timeliness and validity of information, then, are needed. This makes sense for control and the quality of feedback on which to base future strategic decisions. However, there is a catch here, a potential problem, namely the following: *Timeliness and validity of information are negatively correlated.*

Increasing the validity of information by gathering more data from different sources usually consumes more time. A desire for validity and thoroughness, then, can actually hurt timeliness. In contrast, an overly strong emphasis on timeliness runs the risk of generating too hasty and invalid information. Timeliness and validity are not perfectly correlated, but they are negatively related.

Achieving the right balance between timely and valid information is a major challenge facing management, but it's one they must confront. Poor decisions here will affect the quality of information and the feedback that organizations need to ensure successful adaptation to changing or fluid market conditions and to execute strategy effectively. This is an important control-related task needing management's attention.

Make sure, too, that the information is used. Assuming the feedback about performance is good, the next questions are who gets it and can they act on it? Execution relies on good information. Execution also demands, however, that the right people receive the critical information and that they can act on it to make changes, as Figure 6.1 indicates. Without these additional considerations, good information and the control systems that rely on it are virtually useless.

I once did some work with the Social Security Administration in Washington, D.C. Administration personnel and I were looking at, among other things, the relative costs of an office-based vs. regional-based structure in the Office of Hearings and Appeals. My requests for cost data to test some structural hypotheses were met with a series of responses or reactions:

1. I was told that the requested data probably didn't exist.
2. If the data indeed did exist, I probably couldn't get access to them.
3. If I received access, I'd probably find the format of the data not to my liking.
4. If the information was not to my liking, I'd have to use it anyway. After all, this is what the administration has. Take it or leave it.

To make a long story short, I finally got access to the data and could even modify files somewhat. And, actually, they were very good, helpful data, shedding a great deal of light on costs and how they might relate to organizational structure. I was impressed with the information the organization had routinely collected.

I was also shocked, however. I was the first person to retrieve and use these valuable data in years. No one was using this valuable resource. Control systems rely on feedback, information to fuel organizational change and adaptation. But if no one sees or uses the information, then clearly controls aren't working. Change and adaptation aren't being supported.

This situation is possible in a government agency that faces no market competition, is supported by tax dollars, and has always been "profitable" by government accounting standards. The same cannot be said about an organization in a highly competitive market, where agility and responsiveness to customer needs and competitors' actions are absolutely essential to survival. Not using solid information in the latter case can only lead to execution nightmares and competitive disadvantage.

LEADERSHIP, CONTROLS, AND EXECUTION

Control processes and methods routinely test managers' leadership capabilities. Leadership plays a central role in the control process of Figure 6.1. The problem occurs when managers aren't up to the leadership task.

"Do as I say, not as I do."

This is a frequently voiced control-related problem. The charge is that managers ask for one thing but then act as if something else is more important.

One company I worked with wanted increased product development and innovation as part of a new strategy and approach to the market. Innovation, of course, requires experimentation before new ideas or solutions are discovered, tested, and tried successfully. This company's culture, however, was marked by conservatism and risk avoidance, which created an interesting dilemma.

On one hand, managers preached the value of innovation. On the other, their actions worked against the reality of what's needed for innovation. The manufacturing VP, for example, echoed the top management team's stated emphasis on new product development. However, he "discouraged" his subordinates from stopping and reworking production lines to develop and test new product prototypes. Work stoppages are expensive, after all. They hurt scale and scope economies. Needless to say, their leader's actions caused confusion among subordinates about priorities and execution needs.

In another case, a large government agency had developed a program to achieve client satisfaction. The strategy ostensibly placed clients at the core of a social services network, with their needs as the prime generator of other actions and support services.

As a result of increased service to clients, however, professional contact hours and administrative support time increased markedly, causing a significant jump in expense and support activities. Higher authorities in the government bureaucracy soon noted the increased costs with alarm. Feedback on the performance of all the agency's units and programs soon included a heavy emphasis on the need for cost controls.

Client-related efforts, though effective, predictably became secondary to cost reduction. Agency leaders asked for a client focus but acted in a totally different way. The message was clear: Client satisfaction is desirable but only if costs don't increase. It was painfully clear to everyone that: *Actions do indeed speak louder than words.*

Managers, then, must lead by example. What they do is scrutinized by subordinates, regardless of organizational level. What leaders do becomes the benchmark or example for followers to emulate, resulting in controls on behavior or action.

Rework Performance Appraisals

Many traditional performance appraisal methods are terrible. They often destroy teamwork, pit individuals against each other, and promote mediocrity. They destroy risk taking, change, and innovation, often encouraging people to play it safe or maintain the status quo.

These negative outcomes are never intentional, but they often are very real, as I've often been reminded. Companies don't want to cause problems with performance appraisal. Indeed, they try very hard to be objective, even scientific, in their approaches. Still, problems with poor performance appraisals persist, hurting execution.

Performance appraisal and the feedback it gives are critical aspects of the control process of Figure 6.1. As just stated, however, the effects are often negative. The use of forced rankings, for example, is often divisive at best. Forced elimination of "deadwood" creates distrust and injures cooperation. New hires are scrutinized carefully; it's not wise, after all, to hire really good people who increase the probability of your being forced eventually, but most assuredly, into the deadwood category. Risk taking is shunned, as it increases the likelihood of mistakes and poor performance, dangerous outcomes given the nature of the rankings. Innovation suffers if people won't take risks for fear of making mistakes and being forced out of the organization.

An important role of leadership is to mitigate or eliminate these negative effects of poor performance appraisal methods. Even if the company approach, such as forced rankings, is basically problematic, good managers can help overcome the negatives and focus on positive techniques that support execution. What can they do?

1. **They can negotiate objectives for use in performance appraisal.** Insightful leaders don't rely solely on the company's forced ranking or similar systems. They negotiate objectives, the performance against which will determine, in whole or part, the position of the subordinate on the rankings. Use of the agreed-upon objectives tempers or ameliorates the negative impact of the forced-ranking method.

2. **They avoid all-or-nothing objectives at all costs.** The reasons for this were listed previously. Basically, good leaders recognize that nothing good comes from the use of all-or-nothing, black vs. white, performance metrics. They know the price to pay includes lowballing or lying, as well as underachievement or constrained performance. They avoid all-or-nothing appraisals.

3. **They demand brutal honesty from subordinates when it comes to analyzing performance and explaining aberrations from the execution plan.** Their main emphasis is on learning, however, not fixing blame or finding scapegoats for poor performance. Brutal honesty facilitates learning and the fine-tuning of execution efforts.

4. **They reward the performers.** They let everyone know what's valued and what counts. They define clearly the parameters of success. They recognize those who contribute to successful execution outcomes. Good managers celebrate success and the people who achieve it.

Managers are important for the success of the control process shown in Figure 6.1. It's important that they lead by example, create a climate of discipline and honesty, and mitigate the negative effects of formal control mechanisms such as performance appraisal methods. This leadership role is vital to execution success.

THE STRATEGY REVIEW: INTEGRATING PLANNING, EXECUTION, AND CONTROL

The consideration of controls completes discussion of the execution model presented in Chapter 2. This provides an excellent opportunity to look back and summarize the main points for execution success considered thus far. The tool or approach we can use for the summary and integration is critical in its own right for successful execution and, consequently, is deserving of attention, namely, the strategy review.

The strategy review is an intensive analysis of strategy, execution, and performance. It allows corporate to test the worth of business plans and execution methods. It's useful for corporate reviews of business strategy and performance. It's also useful within businesses, allowing management to test and evaluate the contribution of functional or product-line strategies to important strategic and short-term outcomes.

The review is not meant to be a mind-numbing "numbers" exercise whose outcome is lots of paperwork and data. It isn't a "gotcha" session in which some people catch others' exaggerations or fabrications and make them look bad. It is intended to be a dynamic, creative, interactive session that focuses on real results and improvement of organizational performance. Its intention is to foster strategic thinking and a better feel for the conditions that lead to competitive advantage and organizational success.

A good strategy review is invaluable. It provides a framework that can be used for integrating planning and execution. It highlights the incentive and control issues discussed in this chapter. It provides an opportunity for communication, the analysis of strategy and execution methods, and testing the reality or feasibility of plans or methods in the real world. It also identifies "holes" or problem areas in an organization's plans or execution methods, allowing for change, adaptation, and corrective actions to improve future plans and execution processes.

Every organization must fashion its own strategy review process. It's not a luxury but a necessity. It's that important. A good review fosters debate and the confrontation of conflict. It facilitates learning. It allows leaders to test their people and develop good managers. It facilitates the integration of strategy across organizational levels. It supports execution.

The strategy review was considered briefly in Chapter 3. Figure 6.2 shows a slightly expanded version of the review and the critical six steps involved. Delineation of the steps isn't meant to suggest some mechanistic, "lock-step" approach or some overly formal view of strategy and execution. It is merely intended to ensure the identification and consideration of important aspects of the strategy review. Organizations certainly should craft their own reviews based on what they feel is most critical and illustrative, given their competitive situations. Let's follow the steps and see how planning and execution decisions come together and make sense.

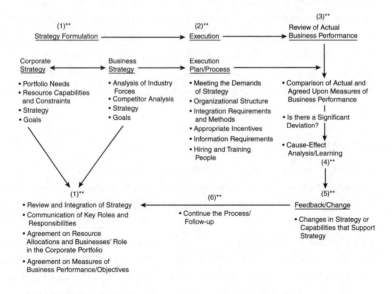

** Steps 1-6 are noted in parentheses. See the text for discussion of the steps

Figure 6.2   The Strategy Review: Planning, Execution, and Controls

STEP 1: STRATEGY FORMULATION

Chapter 3 noted the importance of strategy at both corporate and business levels. Logically, then, the strategy review begins with sound planning (step 1). The review in Figure 6.2 focuses on integrating corporate and business plans. However, the same process as previously noted can be employed at the business level, integrating business strategy with functional or departmental plans.

Corporate Strategy

The corporate level must articulate a strategy as part of the review. In a multibusiness organization, it must create a portfolio model to guide investments and the acquisition or elimination of companies. The description of the portfolio serves as a device to communicate to a business the nature and logic of the portfolio mix and the business' place in it. Corporate needs to develop clear diversification criteria if diversification and portfolio expansion are intended as a corporate strategy.

Corporate planners also need to decide what resources or capabilities are best housed at the corporate level to serve as centralized functions or units to achieve economies of scale and scope or to provide critical support services to the different business units. Investments in technical- or R&D-oriented centers of excellence are part of corporate's consideration of centralization or decentralization of scarce resources or competencies.

Business Strategy

Strategic analysis at the business level must include an in-depth consideration of industry forces.[vii] The focus of industry analysis is on an organization's positioning within the industry and how it tries to differentiate itself from other key players. Analysis is done to determine the power of suppliers and customers and how relative power affects operations. The business must accurately assess the number of substitutes for its products and services, as there is a positive correlation between numbers of substitutes and competitive rivalry within the industry. The existence of entry barriers must be analyzed, including how to build them to protect competitive advantage. Industry forces affect the intensity of competition in the industry, which, in turn, negatively affects profitability, underscoring the importance of this aspect of strategic analysis.

Analysis of competitors and competitive rivalry in the industry is also essential for business strategy formulation. Who are the main competitors? What are their capabilities or competencies? Which ones are the greatest threats to our domain of strategic activity? What are their current strategies, and how will they compete in the future? Will they retaliate, and how, if we try a new strategic move? These are but a few of the questions that must be answered in a sound competitor analysis.

A business also must conduct an internal review of its resources and capabilities. Whether the company has the requisite capabilities to meet the demands of its strategy is the basic issue being considered. A low-cost strategy, for example, requires capital investments that lead to standardization of production and the achievement of scale economies. It also may require investments in information technology and the development of incentive plans to support the low-cost position. Yet another critical question is, are the right people on board with the requisite training to execute the strategy? Capabilities and human resource needs change over time. Even the "right" people might occasionally have the wrong capabilities or an incomplete set of skills, necessitating remedial action to ensure effective performance.

Integration of Plans

Corporate and business strategy and the goals they produce are important in their own right. Even more important, however, is the integration of those plans, shown as part of step 1 in the strategy review. This integration was discussed in Chapter 3, and the key elements are listed in Figure 6.2 for consideration.

A first critical step in the integration process is the corporate review of a business's strategy and plans. This is a forum for discussion, communication, and understanding, not merely a dry presentation of numbers and statistics. Businesses aren't on trial here. The purpose is to confront, honestly and openly, the key elements and assumptions of business strategy and how the corporate level can actively support the business' plans. Emphasis is on a qualitative discussion of factors affecting strategy, not on the size and bulk of planning documents.

The review should ideally be an in-depth exercise in creativity, including the discussion of different future scenarios of competitive conditions and company actions. The review is not something to get over with quickly by avoiding key issues or questions. The tough issues or questions, in fact, should be at the heart of the review process, representing the "meat" of business strategy formulation and the relationship between corporate and business plans.

The importance of these points is reinforced by Larry Bossidy and Ram Charan in their book on execution.[viii] Bossidy's experiences at GE under Jack Welch come through loudly and clearly. The strategy review at GE was a positive force for the articulation and communication of strategy, a process also stressed by Bossidy at Allied Signal. My own experiences as a "Work Out" consultant in GE's Aerospace Division also support the importance and usefulness of a results-oriented strategy review. Similar reviews in companies such as Becton-Dickenson, Crown Holdings, and others lend credence to the integrative and informative aspect of a good review rather than its use as a regurgitive or coercive event.

The roles and responsibilities of businesses in the corporate portfolio must be hashed out next between corporate and business planners. Agreement on resource allocations across businesses must also be reached and understood as part of the discussion of roles and responsibilities.

The cash cow at the business level, for example, performs an important function for the execution of corporate strategy. It provides an internal source of funds for corporate distribution. How the funds will be distributed, along with the criteria for distribution, to "stars," new growth companies, or "question marks," must be clearly delineated, understood, and bought into at the business level.

An important outcome of step 1 in Figure 6.2 is agreement on business objectives or the measures of performance that will be used to monitor and gauge business success. Based on the discussion of corporate and business strategies, performance metrics are set up consistent with the role of different businesses in the corporate portfolio. These metrics should vary by role or responsibility, with cash generators being held accountable for different performance measures (low cost, cost reductions) than growth companies or stars (market shares, margins).

STEP 2: THE EXECUTION PLAN

Once business strategy is set and integrated with corporate strategy, the business can focus on its execution plan or process, as shown in step 2 in Figure 6.2.

The execution process pays attention to the execution decisions, actions, or issues discussed to this point in the book. As Figure 6.2 indicates, this would include consideration of the following issues:

- **The "demands" of strategy.** To execute a strategy successfully, the right resources or capabilities are critical. Different strategies demand the development of different capabilities. Without these capabilities, successful performance cannot be attained.

- **Organizational structure.** Strategy affects the choice of structure. Low-cost strategies, for example, usually demand an emphasis on centralization or process specialization in a quest for efficiencies or economies of scale and scope. Complex global strategies often demand the use of matrix or "simultaneous" structures emphasizing two different points of view (such as worldwide business vs. country needs).

- **Integration requirements.** Execution cannot be successful without consideration of interdependence across units and the requisite methods needed for coordination, knowledge transfer, and information sharing. A clear delineation of responsibility and accountability is also necessary for successful integration and achievement of unity of effort.

- **Appropriate incentives.** The early part of this chapter focused on good incentives and their role in execution. Execution often suffers because managers don't develop and use incentives that logically support execution decisions and options.

- **Other execution issues.** An organization may focus on yet additional issues necessary for effective execution in its industry or on its competitive landscape. These might include information requirements or IT capabilities; hiring of the right people for certain execution tasks; training and development programs, including top-management executive development programs; and an introduction of a management-by-objectives program to integrate strategic and short-term objectives. Again, the purpose presently is not to be all-inclusive, but simply to provide examples of execution issues that appear in a strategy review.

Whatever the assessment of execution needs may be, the organization must create a *formal execution plan* as part of its business strategy or business plan.

All too often, execution is assumed. Leaders "hand off the ball" to subordinates, and execution and follow-through are taken for granted. This should not be the case.

Step 2 in Figure 6.2 demands that more formal attention be devoted to execution. "Formal" doesn't mean the creation of thick notebooks, scads of words and numbers, and needless bureaucracy. It simply means that execution must be recognized as a valid part of the business plan.

Execution plans must be developed, indicating tasks, time frames, and the people responsible for task completion. "Work Out" worked at GE because the process focused on execution tasks, people, accountability, and ensuring that the important jobs were done in a timely fashion. The same emphasis on execution is needed in every company's strategy review. Attention must be paid to execution issues and obstacles, as the survey data from managers and the model in Chapter 2 argue for emphatically. Nothing less will do if execution is to be successful.

STEP 3: INITIATING THE CONTROL PROCESS

Step 3 in Figure 6.2 begins the process of control. Comparison of actual and agreed-upon measures of business performance is the first step in the control process. These measures could be derived from strategy and the quest for competitive advantage, or they might represent metrics that come from the execution plan. Whatever their origin, actual performance against the objectives initiates the control step.

The main issue is to determine whether there are significant deviations from the desired performance measures. This includes positive as well as negative deviations. If a business is aiming for a 5 percent increase in market share in some part of the world, but achieves no increase or a small, insignificant change, this deviation is very likely significant and in need of attention. However, if the company achieves a 15 percent increase, this also is significant and deserving of additional management scrutiny.

Leaders who only focus on negative aberrations increase the probability of creating a culture of risk aversion or error avoidance, which can seriously impede execution and organizational performance. This aspect of culture is important and is discussed in greater detail in Chapter 8.

STEP 4: CAUSE-EFFECT ANALYSIS AND ORGANIZATIONAL LEARNING

Step 4 is vital to organizational learning and adaptation. It represents a critical aspect of the strategy review.

If significant deviations in performance were identified in step 3, cause-effect analysis is absolutely essential. How can the deviation in business performance be explained? What can the organization learn from the noted aberrations in performance? This is not an easy step. It can backslide into a finger-pointing blame session. It can create defensiveness and close-mindedness that absolutely destroy curiosity and the ability to learn. Effective leadership is clearly needed to prevent this injurious backslide and keep the review positive, on track, and focused on learning.

Determining cause-effect clarity is difficult, often demanding intensive analysis of data, actions, and the factors that affect or determine performance. A culture or reward structure that supports risk aversion or blaming others won't generate the necessary analysis. Such a climate guarantees an inability to learn and adapt. Individuals simply won't let objective data get in the way of their biased or defensive opinions, which is deadly for learning and change.

Again, leadership is critical. Leaders must confront the brutal facts and explain poor performance. Autopsies are required, but in the spirit of learning and inquisitiveness, not the need to blame or injure others. Creating a climate conducive to learning is essential. Leaders must ask tough questions, and subordinates must respond in kind, with data and opinions that explain performance. Creating such a culture is where managers earn their keep. Again, this issue is revisited in Chapter 8 on managing culture.

STEP 5: FEEDBACK AND CHANGE

If learning has occurred in step 4 and managers understand what caused the significant deviations in performance, then feedback, changes, or corrective actions are possible, as step 5 in Figure 6.2 shows.

Feedback may include rewards or recognition for great performance. It may demand changes in strategy or execution methods based on the brutal analysis of data in the previous step. Business leaders are responsible and accountable for their unit's performance, and feedback is directed toward options and methods to improve it.

Emphasis in step 5 is, of necessity, on preparing for organizational change. The results of the learning process of step 4 must be implemented. Additional capabilities may be required and obtained. Incentives may need modification. Additional coordination or integration methods may need to be introduced and perfected. Business strategy might need to be tweaked to achieve better results for a particular product in a given market or part of the world.

The problem is that managing change, while critical, is also very difficult. Because of its centrality and difficulty, the next chapter picks up where step 5 in Figure 6.2 leaves off and considers the enormous task of managing change effectively.

STEP 6: FOLLOW UP AND CONTINUE THE PROCESS

The strategy review does not end with step 5. Indeed, step 5 provides the inputs for a whole new process. Figure 6.2 suggests that continuous attention to key variables is essential for ongoing execution success.

In my "Work Out" experiences with GE, for example, step 6 always defined follow-up activities. If changes were being implemented, additional discussions with key people or additional group meetings were planned routinely. If managers were responsible for new actions or activities, time and attention had to be devoted to determine whether desired changes were actually being executed.

Follow-up is critical to the strategy review and good execution. Left to their own devices, people may leave a strategy review and go back home, hoping that demands will simply go away and life can go back to normal. Inaction is a decision of sorts, the hoped-for result often being an avoidance of change and return to a comfortable status quo.

This cannot happen. The review process of Figure 6.2 requires attention to feedback and change requirements. Learning and change "prime the pump," leading to additional needs, objectives, or fine-tuning of strategy that regenerates and invigorates the review process.

A VP of marketing and planning for a medium-size company recently developed a strategy review process for his company. His remarks to me clearly summarized the value of the exercise:

> *"The review has helped us immensely. It forced us to develop an execution plan and approach. It emphasized meaningful metrics of performance. It fostered learning and an understanding of what affects performance. Most important of all, it forced people to communicate. Communication between corporate and business staff and across functional areas improved immensely, which really is amazing for this company."*

This, then, is the strategy review and how it relates to effective controls, the support of strategy execution efforts, and making strategy work. This chapter also concludes the analysis of components laid out in the basic execution model or overview of Chapter 2.

Our work is far from complete, however. Important contextual factors affecting execution must now be considered in depth, including managing change, culture, and power or influence. The next chapter picks up where the discussion of the strategy review left off, namely with the process of managing change, a vitally important issue for execution.

SUMMARY

There are a number of key conclusions or takeaways suggested in the current chapter. They are as follows:

- Incentives motivate behavior toward ends consistent with desired strategy execution outcomes. Controls provide feedback about performance, reinforce execution methods, provide corrective mechanisms, and facilitate organizational learning and change. Both incentives and controls are important to making strategy work.

- There are some basic aspects of "good" incentives and basic rules for using incentives wisely in the strategy execution process:

  - One such basic rule is that incentives shouldn't demotivate individuals. Most managers are motivated, with a high need for achievement. The last thing incentives should do is injure this need and deflect behavior away from desired execution outcomes.

  - A related fact is that incentives fuel and guide motivation. They don't create it. The role of incentives is to support motivation and guide behavior in the right direction.

- Good incentives are tied to strategic objectives or short-term objectives that are derived from strategy. Incentives, then, foster strategy execution at all levels of an organization.

- Good incentives reward the right things. It's foolish to hope for certain execution outcomes and then reward other outcomes or behaviors.

- A final point to keep in mind about incentives is that "organizations always get what they pay for." Individuals respond to incentives and give the organization exactly what it is rewarding, even if the results are inconsistent with strategy execution. Rewarding the wrong things, even if done unintentionally, always hurts the execution process.

■ Controls provide feedback about performance, reinforce execution methods, provide a corrective mechanism for an organization, and facilitate learning and change, as Figure 6.1 above clearly indicates. For controls to work effectively and support execution, there are rules or guidelines that must be followed.

- For execution to work, it is absolutely essential that organizations reward the doers, the performers. Only then will appropriate execution-related behaviors be reinforced and guaranteed.

- It is absolutely necessary that the control process face the brutal facts openly and honestly when execution-related performance is poor. It is imperative to conduct autopsies for organizational learning to occur. Without the analysis of facts and the learning it leads to, organizational change or adaptation is jeopardized.

- The control process cannot work if responsibility and accountability for execution-related tasks are unclear. It is necessary, then, to clarify responsibility and accountability for controls to work and strategy execution to be successful.

- Controls need timely and valid information in order to work effectively. A balance between timeliness and validity of information must be achieved, a major problem confronting managers given that these two aspects of good information are inversely correlated.

- The role of leadership in the control process is central and pervasive. Problems occur when leaders aren't up to the leadership tasks vital to controls and execution.

  - Setting an example for subordinates that is consistent with execution-related objectives and behaviors is an absolute must. "Do as I say, not as I do" is a policy that will destroy the control process and hurt execution results. Actions, indeed, do speak louder than words.

  - Good leaders also know how to use performance appraisals effectively. Leaders, for example, must avoid the use of all-or-nothing objectives. They must demand brutal honesty from subordinates. And they must recognize and reward the performers, the doers who contribute to execution success.

- Finally, this chapter has stressed the necessity of conducting a strategy review. Such a review process is critical to supporting the planning and control process and making strategy work. The strategy review is not a luxury or an option; every organization must fashion its own strategy review to execute strategy effectively. A good review fosters discussion, clarifies corporate and business strategy, helps set execution-related objectives, allows leaders to test and understand their people, and facilitates learning and organizational change. It is important to the success of strategy execution efforts.

Discussion of the strategy review ends where the next chapter begins, namely with the important task of managing change. Attention can now turn to this critical aspect of making strategy work.

ENDNOTES

i.   "More Companies Showing CEOs the Door," *Philadelphia Inquirer*, December 24, 2003; "Here Comes Politically Correct Pay," *The Wall Street Journal*, April 12, 2004; "Putting a Ceiling on Pay," *The Wall Street Journal*, April 12, 2004; "The Boss' Pay," *The Wall Street Journal*, April 12, 2004.

ii. Discussion of the need for achievement first began with David McClelland, who also talked about the need for power and the need for affiliation. See: *The Achievement Motive*, Appleton—Century—Crofts, 1953; also see his *The Achieving Society*, Van Nostrand Reinhold, 1961.

iii. Edward Thorndike, *The Elements of Psychology*, A. G. Seiler, 1905.

iv. The changes at Oticon drew worldwide attention. Googling Oticon "organizational structure," "spaghetti organization," etc. revealed hundreds of references to the Oticon experiment. These included academic articles, popular press coverage, and case studies done by the Harvard Business School and other leading universities. The prevailing conclusion of this work is that the changes, while interesting and different, were poorly justified and did not lead to very favorable results for the company. The "looseness" of the new organization simply conflicted with the need for focus, direction, discipline, and control demanded by strategy execution and superordinate goals. Autonomy and discretion are wonderful; too much autonomy and discretion can lead to confusion, anarchy, and a lack of strategic and operating focus.

v.   A. M. Knott, "The Dynamic Value of Hierarchy," *Management Science*, 47(3), 2001.

vi. Jim Collins, *Good to Great*, Harper Business, 2001.

vii. See L. G. Hrebiniak's *The We-Force in Management*, Lexington Books, 1994. This book focuses on interdependence and the other conditions that affect coordination and cooperation in organizations.

viii. Michael Porter's *Competitive Strategy*, Macmillan, 1980, provides a well-known and complete discussion of industry forces and their relation to competitive advantage and profitability.

ix. Larry Bossidy and Ram Charan, *Execution*, Crown Business, 2002.

7

Managing Change

Introduction

Successful execution requires the effective management of change. Indeed, execution is often synonymous with change, as key actions and steps are taken or modified to make strategy work.

Analysis to this point has often referenced or implied the importance of change for strategy execution. It is now time to talk explicitly about the critical importance of managing change. The inability to manage change effectively can destroy or seriously hamper otherwise valid and complete execution plans.

MANAGING CHANGE: A CONTINUING CHALLENGE

The topic of managing change has received a huge amount of attention. The literature in psychology, sociology, and management has contributed volumes on the subject. The popular press has added its share of articles on the issue. Metaphorical treatments of change combining fact and fiction have grown in number and captured readers' imagination, such as Spencer Johnson's wildly popular work on coping with change.[i]

Despite all this attention, managing change is still an ongoing execution issue. The inability to manage change is mentioned consistently as an ongoing execution problem.

Both the Wharton-Gartner and Wharton Executive Education surveys list the inability to manage change as the number one strategy-execution problem. The data collected in the panel discussions and open-ended questionnaire responses further support the findings about the critical centrality and importance of change management for the execution of strategy. Moreover, the issue of managing change is virtually always in the news. Consider, for example, the following change-related problems with mergers and acquisitions:

- Sanofi-Synthelabo's hostile takeover of Aventis had barely been announced when the attention turned to the massive changes in R&D and other functions that would be necessary to execute the acquisition. Changes in methods and operations often breed resistance, especially when scientists or other high-level professional employees are involved.

- Peugeot Citroën in 2003 became one of the most profitable car companies outside Japan because, management argued, they avoided the massive changes associated with major acquisitions and strategic alliances.

- Chrysler-Daimler Benz, in contrast, is still reeling from changes in structure and operations years after their celebrated union. Culture clashes, differences in compensation, and divergent approaches to product development have been challenging the change-management process and making life difficult for the merged company.

- Early discussions of an acquisition of Disney by Comcast had touched on the possible changes in governance, organizational structure, and operations that would be indicated if Comcast's attempt at backward vertical integration proved successful. Disney shareholders' and management's strong resistance to Comcast's overtures killed the acquisition efforts in April 2004. Still, overcoming the problems suggested during merger talks and by the no-confidence vote for

Michael Eisner and other Disney directors in the 2004 share-holders' meeting will only add to the change-related problems Disney must face in the future.

Or consider the following pitfalls inherent in trying to change strategy in a major way:

- Sun Microsystems' strategy of differentiation worked famously until the technology of standard chips and software caught up and provided a ton of competition from lower-cost producers. Scott McNealy, Sun's CEO, conceded that Sun would have to change and become a lower-cost, lower-price company. This change, however, has proved to be difficult, as it conflicts with Sun's cachet, traditional business model, and company culture.

- Hewlett-Packard, too, seems to be stuck in the middle of strategic change in 2004, as it is caught between the differentiating service offerings of IBM and the low-cost strategy of Dell. Changing this position clearly will not be easy.

- The difficulties that competitors face in trying to imitate the complex activity systems that define the strategy of companies such as Southwest Airlines, Dell, and Wal-Mart have been noted in previous discussions. Imitation in these cases involves massive change, suggesting the difficulty of execution efforts.

- Even strategic success can breed change-related problems. Google is a good case in point. Its success is well known. Its brainy, full-spirited culture and business approach fueled remarkable growth. But soon after Google filed for an initial public offering, the company found out that money can change everything.

The IPO process with its instant wealth creation often changes a company's culture and creates conflict and internal divisions.[ii] Managers and professional employees who don't become as rich as the founders or select top executives often feel resentful. They can become depressed, even angry, that others are benefiting from their hard work. They may "drop out," physically or mentally, hurting company performance. Just how many change-related problems

Google will actually face after the IPO is consummated is uncertain. Still, the point can be made that, amazingly, even strategic success can create and nurture severe change-related hurdles.

There are, of course, many other examples. But the ones provided, coupled with the continued prevalence of change-related issues in the popular press, raise interesting questions. If the topic of change management has been researched and discussed so often and extensively, why is it still such a big problem? Why is managing change always a potentially disruptive issue, despite the learning and insights that apparently have accumulated over time?

There are, I believe, two answers to these questions, at least when the issue is strategy execution and its associated changes. First, managing strategic change is terribly complex and difficult. The number of interdependent factors and obstacles that affect execution clearly increases the complexity facing leaders of change efforts. Second, the emphasis in strategy-execution programs or processes has not focused enough on certain aspects of change management that directly affect execution results. Let's pursue these points further.

STEPS IN MANAGING CHANGE

There are six basic or generic steps, issues, or decisions in the management of change:

1. **Size and content of change.** The first step is to decide on the focus of change efforts. What is it that needs changing? How big is the problem or threat facing the organization, and how should the organization respond?

2. **Time available for change.** How much time does management have to execute the change? Does the organization enjoy the luxury of time, or must it act quickly?

3. **Tactics in the change/execution process.** How should the change be executed? Should it proceed in "bits and pieces" or all at once? Should it be implemented slowly and methodically or quickly, to get it done in one fell swoop?

4. **Responsibility or accountability.** Who is responsible or accountable for elements or aspects of the change process? Are responsibility and accountability clear to all involved in change?

5. **Overcoming resistance to change.** It is vital to overcome resistance to change or new execution efforts. Overt and especially covert resistance can kill or injure change efforts and execution in a big way.

6. **Monitoring the change.** Are the changes working? How tightly or loosely should the change process be monitored? What methods for tracking change should be employed? Monitoring results and progress and tweaking or modifying the change process are important to achievement of desired execution results.

All six issues are important and central to sound change management. Overcoming resistance to change is vital and will be discussed in Chapter 8. Clarifying responsibility and accountability is also extremely important. This issue has already been discussed in Chapter 5 in the discussion of coordination and integration, and in Chapter 6 where the requirements for effective controls and the steps in an effective strategy review were spelled out. The need to monitor and track changes was also an important part of the discussion of controls and the strategy review in Chapter 6.

The present position is that far more attention must be paid to the first three issues. The size of a strategic threat or opportunity and the time available for change interact in ways that heavily impact the third issue, how the change process is managed. How the process is managed, in turn, presents both potential costs and benefits to an organization. Put another way, the present argument is that:

The relationship between (a) the size of a change and (b) the time available for change determines (c) how the change is executed, the costs and benefits of change, and the prognosis for success.

These aspects of change and strategy execution are important and in need of attention. Knowing how the size and "speed" of change affect the execution of change and the costs and benefits of different approaches to change is absolutely essential to change management and sound execution.

A MODEL OF CHANGE AND EXECUTION

Building on the previous points, let's construct a model of change and execution that is useful to managers concerned with making strategy work.

COMPONENTS OF THE MODEL

Size of a Problem

The content of change efforts must be chosen carefully. Priorities must be set. Strategic change initiatives must be important and few. There is a real danger in doing too many things at once, a point emphasized later in the chapter.

The content of change must obviously reflect and react to the size of a strategic threat or opportunity facing an organization. Size matters when it describes problems that top management must cope with when managing change. The size of a problem or opportunity is instrumental in marshalling resources and developing commitment to the change process. The bigger the problem, the more complex the content needed to confront it, and the harder it is to manage change effectively.

Time Available for Change

The time element, too, must be considered carefully. The effects of shorter time horizons include increasing the number of changes or change components that must be considered simultaneously. Generally, the shorter the time horizon, the greater the complexity of the change process, as more and more critical factors must be taken into account at once.

Velocity of Change

When many change issues must be considered in a short period of time, the "velocity of change" is high. Generally, the higher the velocity, the greater the costs or problems associated with the change process. High velocity, though occasionally necessary and often exciting, is usually associated with low success in managing change.

RELATING CHANGE TO EXECUTION PROBLEMS

The combination of these components creates a rough but useful model of the change process (see Figure 7.1).[iii] The model, in turn, will help define execution-related problems that emanate from the process of change.

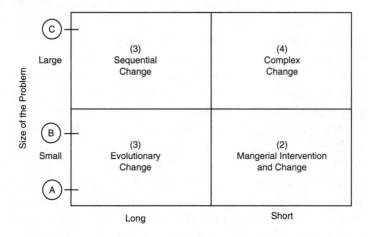

Figure 7.1 A Model of Change and Execution

The x-axis in Figure 7.1 exhibits a time dimension or the Time Available for Execution. Again, this is an important issue for leaders of change, as time defines the velocity of change and the potential problems that result from "speed." The time variable is separated into "long" and "short" time frames to simplify the discussion.

The y-axis in Figure 7.1 focuses on the size of the threats or opportunities confronting an organization. It is simply labeled as Size of the Problem. As previously mentioned, larger problems demand more resources and managerial attention (change "content") than smaller problems. Large problems can complicate the process of change and affect change efforts and their outcomes. Similar to the time dimension, the size of the problem is also expressed in binary terms as "large" or "small."[iv]

Situation A: Many Small Changes

Let's focus first on a common, everyday situation in organizations—a myriad of small problems in need of managerial attention or change. This is situation A in Figure 7.1.

This situation is known to all managers. Rules and standard operating procedures (SOPs) exist in every organization. They usually tell people how to handle small problems or changes that crop up routinely on a daily basis. The quick-printing industry example referenced in the previous chapter provided insights into the importance of management controls (hierarchy) and SOPs for the handling of routine problems or changes.[v] Management earns its keep by responding to problems and developing or changing routines and SOPs that effectively cope with and solve the emerging problems. This information is then passed on to all offices or businesses within the organization to ensure that the same effective SOPs are used routinely throughout the company. However, sometimes even the rules and SOPs don't exactly cover a problem, and managers must exercise discretion to handle it. This, of course, is why we have managers.

Managers throughout the organization, then, are handling problems, many of which are similar or identical. As a district field manager at Ford, I followed the SOPs. I routinely handled dealers' requests, sometimes "bending the rules" or doing dealers favors to expedite sales or solve problems. These usually weren't major issues, so I just handled things the best way I could.

There always was a potential problem brewing, however. Other field managers were handling things their way. Others were responding to the same problems in their zones or regions in different ways. Suboptimization surely existed, as multiple approaches to problem solving were being employed, not the best approach. Because the problems were small, the costs of this suboptimization were low and went unnoticed by higher ups in the company.

Occasionally, however, a problem got larger. It grew a bit in severity, demanding hierarchical attention (situation B in Figure 7.1). The problem still was not huge or strategic, but it loomed larger and demanded additional attention.

A dealer in one region, for example, might feel that a field manager's decisions or solutions to problems routinely favored another dealership in some way. Or a large dealership with facilities in multiple regions might believe that the inconsistency of company methods or field managers' actions across regions (for example, when "bulking" cars, handling credit issues, or deciding on new car allocations) was creating financial problems or uneven treatment of dealers.

The bottom line was that occasionally someone complained. A dealer would go over the field manager's head and complain to someone at the district or regional office. A person higher up in the organization was now involved is a growing problem, clearly with the intention of not letting the problem get larger or out of hand.

This individual would routinely call all field managers and other relevant personnel together. He would define the problem and then ask all of the gathered personnel, "How have you been handling this problem or issue?" The various managers would reply, and something extremely interesting often occurred. When the managers heard the different approaches to handling the problem, there often were comments such as:

> "I've been doing xxxxx this way for years. When did we start doing it *that* way?"

> "When did this happen? When did we begin handling this problem like that? Did the company change its policy?"

These comments are striking because they reveal that the organization had changed over time. Ways of doing things had evolved in different directions. Evolutionary change had occurred (box 1 in Figure 7.1). The evolutionary changes weren't purposeful or planned by the organization. Different people handled the same problems differently. Suboptimization was occurring but was insignificant. No one even noticed until small, routine problems became slightly larger and more salient issues in need of attention.

Evolutionary change happens in all organizations. It is routine and rarely noticed until small, minute problems become larger and loom as significant issues if action isn't taken. The time frame for evolutionary change is long because different decisions can be made or different actions taken ad infinitum, as long as no one calls attention to the problem or demands a unified, consistent approach to problem solving. If and when the latter does occur, the time frame to confront the problem is substantially reduced and action is taken. What types of action?

Typically, when a problem gets larger and moves from A to B in Figure 7.1, the approach to problem solving changes. The movement is to box 2. A regional manager sets up a committee or task force of field managers, tells them that multiple ways of solving the problem are no longer tolerable, and asks them for their recommendations as to the best approach for all managers to follow in the future.

This is an example of a managerial intervention and change, as Figure 7.1 indicates. Someone defines the problem, shortens the time available for change or execution, and demands a solution to the problem.

Responsibility for the change is usually that of an individual or group charged with finding a solution to the problem. When the job is done, life goes back to normal, with managers routinely responding differently to many small problems and issues. There is an equilibrium of sorts until a new, bigger problem arises, demanding a new managerial intervention in a shortened time horizon. Most organizations face this type of situation routinely, as problems "spring up" and need quick resolution.

Situation C: A Large Strategic Problem

This situation in Figure 7.1 is much more serious. A major strategic problem looms, demanding significant change.

A competitor's strategy creates a new business model, potentially rendering ours obsolete and demanding a significant change in strategy, as in the cases of Sun Microsystems or HP previously mentioned. Or a competitor's new product threatens our blockbuster product, demanding action on our part. The direct challenge to Sanofi's prescription drug, Plavix, and the potential loss of exclusivity and profits on the drug are currently major problems for Sanofi to cope with, even as they are preparing for a takeover of Aventis. Here are two major issues—a problem and an opportunity—that demand managerial attention and significant changes. Making the acquisition of Aventis work will especially challenge Sanofi's ability to execute its diversification strategy and to manage a largescale change.

Figure 7.1 suggests that the handling of large strategic problems is a function of top management's perception or assessment of the time available for strategy execution. The execution horizon is the driving force behind the choice of change methods.

SEQUENTIAL CHANGE

If managers believe that the time available for execution is long, Figure 7.1 indicates that sequential change is employed. What's a long vs. short time frame depends, in part, on economic factors, industry forces, and competitive conditions. To General Motors or Ford Motor Company, a long time horizon may be five-plus years because of capital and investment requirements. In contrast, I once reviewed a business plan for Leslie Fay, a designer and manufacturer of women's clothing in New York. In the plan, as I recall, long term was six to nine months, or two-plus "seasons" in the clothing market. As one manager put it at the time, "If we miss two or more seasons, we're really in deep trouble. The fashion business doesn't allow many major mistakes." Clearly, industry and competitive conditions come into play when considering the time dimension.

However it's done, top management decides on the time horizon for execution. If the decision is that there is ample time to execute a strategy, a sequential process can be followed. A sequential intervention means that the organization reduces a large change into smaller, more manageable pieces or proportions. It handles each piece or aspect of the change process before moving on to the next.

Under sequential change, what we see is a chain of activities or steps, with movement to the next step determined by analysis or outputs at a prior step in the process, as shown in this simple graphic:

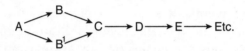

To solve a strategic problem and initiate the change process, market research, industry analysis, or interviews with customers determine that a particular type of product or service or competitive strategy could work in a defined market segment (A). Two prototypes (B and B^1) of a product or service are developed and field tested in a sample market, and product performance and customer reactions are observed. Modifications are made, resulting in a new product or service (C), which is tested further. A decision is made, and the product is placed in mass production (D), with the company ultimately expanding distribution to yet additional market segments (E).

Or, employing the model of execution of Chapter 2, a change in corporate strategy may necessitate a change in structure or even a change in business strategy for a unit in the corporate portfolio. A revised business strategy could precipitate possible changes in business structure or the coordination mechanisms employed to achieve effective integration and unity of effort. Incentives, then, would at minimum have to be examined to see if they adequately support the new strategic and short-term objectives of the company. These are examples of a sequential logic and approach to change. Large problems are reduced to smaller, more manageable proportions, and the analysis focuses on one element of the process before moving on to the next.

"One element" in the change process could include a small number of items or issues being considered simultaneously. In a previous example, two product prototypes were considered (B and B^1) at the same time. The two together make up a single step in the sequential change process. Each element in the sequential change process may contain a small number of issues that are considered concurrently, the emphasis being on "small," as is explained later in the chapter.

Another way of looking at sequential change is to see it as a series of smaller "managerial interventions" (see Figure 7.1). Large changes, that is, are reduced to smaller changes that individuals or groups focus on and solve as part of the sequential chain of activities or steps just noted. Box 3 in Figure 7.1 in many cases is simply a series of smaller changes derived from box 2, with the accumulated steps taking place over a longer time period.

Bank of America (BOA) announced recently that it would follow a slow, sequential change process after completing its acquisition of Fleet Boston in April 2004.[vi] While many changes clearly are in store, including some sizeable job cuts, BOA vowed that it wouldn't execute large, major changes quickly. Rather, it said it will study big problems carefully and focus on handling them in a sequential change process to avoid making big mistakes. BOA's announcement is basically suggesting that there may be some benefits to a sequential change process as compared to faster and more complex methods of managing change.

Benefits of Sequential Change

This process of change has some obvious benefits. It is methodical and paced. It represents a type of planned or rational change, as each step is engaged only after the prior step is satisfactorily completed.

The step-by-step process allows managers to celebrate success and reduce resistance to change. Naysayers and doubters can be shown the results of market research and the initial positive reactions of customers to a new product. The success of the first stages in the change process can be used to win over doubters who were originally against the entire change initiative. The initial success allows an approach that says to the doubter or resistor, "You felt that the proposed new product would never work or sell. Yet initial reactions are positive and successful. Will you come on board and support the new product initiative, now that you've seen the early results?"

The celebration of success also supports the strategy-execution process. Positive results affect buy-in and ownership in a positive way. A "pat on the back" can be given to those achieving positive interim results, which reinforces their motivation and commitment to the planned change.

Sequential interventions allow for clear cause-effect analysis. The effects of an incremental change in the serial process can be more readily observed than the effects of many simultaneous changes. Coordination and learning are thus easier to achieve in this more controlled version of change management.

A sequential process also allows for incremental investments of time and money. Everything need not be invested and put at risk all at once. Small portions of an investment can be done with minimal risk, lowering the overall risk profile and uncertainty for the organization. There is no need to "bet the entire house" on a new venture. Under a sequential change process, management is betting on smaller pieces and only after achieving some measure of prior success.

Kraft and General Foods

A good example of a successful sequential change process is provided by Philip Morris's purchase of Kraft. Philip Morris already owned General Foods, and the acquisition of Kraft was seen as a good step—a related diversification—to increase market share and power in the competitive food industry. There was a high degree of strategic fit between the two companies. General Foods and Kraft each had well-known branded products with little overlap in product lines, and their combination was seen as only adding to the combined company's competitive advantage. For our purposes, how Kraft and General Foods were melded into one company or how integration was achieved suggests a sequential approach to managing change.[vii]

A committee was set up immediately to determine how best to integrate. A quick, one-month study suggested some immediate actions. Striking while the iron was hot helped remove uncertainty about the merger. The merged company was quickly renamed as KGF (Kraft General Foods). Emphasis was on "quick synergies" and symbolic changes to show the value of integration. These quick changes and synergies included the following:

- **Changes in structure.** The frozen foods groups in both companies became one unit. A single international division was created. Responsibility and accountability for key operating issues were clarified immediately to avoid conflicts and to ensure that the combined business continued to function without problems for customers. The chain of command and reporting relationships were set up immediately and clearly, avoiding confusion.
- **Cost reductions and consolidations.** Quick synergies included leveraging centralized purchasing in the combined company; eliminating duplications in international staff; reducing overhead in marketing, finance, and HR; centralizing quality assurance; and consolidating manufacturing and distribution.

Most managers in the new company could see and understand the logic of these first moves. Most could see the "low-hanging fruit," the relatively easy synergies that could be picked quickly, showing some immediate success. The hard part, however, was still to come.

Good planning: thinking it through. Many mergers and acquisitions are rushed, leading to overly complex change and the problems that accompany it. KGF didn't rush. It took some time to plan changes that could be managed sequentially, over time.

Task forces were set up to plan and execute these incremental changes. Uniform accounting systems and standards were seen as vital. However, the company decided to take a four-to-five year time horizon to phase in the changes. Mistakes from rapid deployment could seriously upset customers, so a step-by-step approach was deemed to be logical.

A corporate task force considered the issue of centralization and decentralization of structure. The role of corporate versus business or operating roles was considered carefully, avoiding rapid changes that could be disastrous. At the same time, a technology task force carefully considered changes in R&D, raising issues about the location of basic versus applied research and product development. Again, it was felt that the stakes in R&D were too high to rush into "solutions" that would only create more problems.

Task forces were set up to look at still other longer-term issues, such as merging into three distribution channels (refrigerated, frozen, and dry grocery) or perhaps even two (dry versus refrigerated goods). This change, if implemented, would involve a major change in the sales forces, which in early stages of the merger still included separate General Foods and Kraft personnel. Merging salespeople could affect customers and distribution markedly. Sales-force integration would also require changes in invoicing, inventory management, and accounting methods and standards, so rushing into new arrangements hastily was not seen as an option.

There are many other examples, but the point is that certain large and potentially impactful changes stemming from the acquisition were considered carefully and executed sequentially. It definitely is wise occasionally not to rush and to take a planned, incremental approach to managing change. Doing things fast is not always good. Doing too many things at once in the change process can actually create more problems than it solves, a point considered in detail shortly.

Of course, it must be recognized that there is a potential downside to sequential change. The benefits just mentioned are hardly guaranteed. There are potential costs that must be considered by the leaders of strategic change.

Problems with Sequential Change

Sequential Interventions Take Time

The elements of the change process are spread out over months, even years. One danger is that people lose sight of the ultimate goals of the change process. The desired execution outcomes lose their salience or significance because short-term issues dominate managerial work. Leaders of change must constantly reinforce execution efforts, remind individuals of the ultimate outcome being pursued, and keep people focused on the change process. A few critics of the Kraft merger argued that some of the changes could have been executed more expeditiously, a criticism related to the present point. Top management was careful, however, to publicize and reinforce the changes suggested by the task forces in order to keep employees current on the progress of the merger. Sequential interventions demand this type of continued attention to detail.

The long execution horizon presents an additional problem for leaders of sequential change. Simply, other factors come into play. Exogenous forces change. Competitors' actions or plans change, consumers become more price conscious, or government antitrust decisions hold implications for a company's own strategic scenarios. The sequential change process must always be adapting to these external shocks.

An organization's internal capabilities may also change over time. Critical human resources may leave the organization. Developments in R&D or in IT systems may necessitate alteration of a sequential execution plan to account for the new developments. As with exogenous changes, managers must be attuned to internal changes and account for their impact on a sequential intervention with a long execution horizon.

Transitions Must Be Managed

In a sequential change process, the passing of the baton must be managed carefully. The sequential picture, A→B→C, seems simple and inherently logical. Work done in marketing on customer needs is passed routinely to engineering for product design. The transition from one group to another is obviously necessary and espoused by key players in both functional groups.

A word of caution is in order, however. Chapter 5 noted significant problems with knowledge transfer and information sharing in organizations. People in engineering may not trust marketing's research methodologies. An NIH ("not invented here") syndrome may lead to the rejection or modification of transmitted information. Engineering and marketing's cooperation may be affected by a climate or culture of distrust based on previous bad experiences between the two functions.

In brief, the logical and obvious transitions between groups, functions, or organizations under sequential change processes must occasionally be managed actively and carefully. Transition managers may be required to carry information and the explanations of data development from unit to unit. An engineering person may act as a liaison to marketing, perhaps even be part of marketing's deliberations. The goal of this two-function participant is to facilitate information flow and acceptance of data by the two groups.

Other mechanisms to facilitate transitions under sequential interventions may be needed. Transfer pricing under conditions of vertical integration is one such obvious mechanism. Formal project- or product-management systems are yet another. The point is that the required transitions cannot be left to chance. They need the active attention of managers as they cope with sequential strategic change.

Sequential Interventions May Be Boring

This is a point that has arisen more than a few times in my change-related work. Managers may see sequential change processes as less than exciting. They see the logic of serial changes that feed one into another. They espouse the benefits of planned or rational change. Still, the logical, sequential process is seen at times as mundane, an exercise in project management more than an exciting challenge in managing strategic change.

The leader's job here is obvious but not always easy. Use of intermittent feedback or rewards, the celebration of interim successes, partial strategy reviews of goals and performance, and other such activities are necessary to keep key personnel's eyes on the ball. Important industry or competitive changes could go unnoticed because of this boredom or malaise, and leaders of sequential interventions must work to ensure that appropriate attention is continuously paid to important execution outcomes.

The costs and benefits of managing large, strategic changes in a sequential fashion are noted in Table 7.1.

Table 7.1 Costs and Benefits of Sequential and Complex Changes

	Sequential Change	Complex Change
Benefits	■ Planned, rational change. ■ Methodical and paced. ■ Opportunity to celebrate success and reduce resistance to change. ■ Clear cause-effect analysis, allowing for organizational control and learning. ■ Incremental investments can be made.	■ High "speed"; large problems are confronted quickly. ■ Complex change is exciting, seldom boring. ■ Creation of *esprit de corps*.
Costs/Problems	■ Sequential interventions take time. ■ Exogenous forces and organizational capabilities change. ■ Transitions must be managed. ■ The change process may be "boring."	■ Coordination and control are difficult. ■ Cause-effect clarity is low. ■ Learning suffers. ■ Certain performance criteria must be relaxed, and managers cannot be held accountable for them.

COMPLEX CHANGE

If the leaders of large-scale, strategic changes feel that the time available for execution is short, complex change is the result (box 4 in Figure 7.1).

In 1997, C. Michael Armstrong was named CEO of AT&T's struggling empire. Over the next few years, he made some major acquisitions and changes in the lumbering organization. In 1998, he announced plans to buy cable giant TCI, preparing to offer telephone services via cable. In 1999, AT&T outbid Comcast for MediaOne. In 2000, he split AT&T into three separate companies.

While making all these changes, Armstrong asserts that he was also dealing with WorldCom, Inc. and other competitors that were fraudulently jacking up their numbers—higher projected revenues and lower costs than AT&T—and making AT&T look bad in the eyes of Wall Street analysts.[vii] The added pressures by competitors and analysts forced Armstrong to speed up execution of his strategy, thereby detracting from the time he had to make things work. In his opinion, the sheer size of AT&T's strategic endeavors, coupled with WorldCom's action and Wall Street's pressures, coalesced to cause AT&T to falter and fail in attempts at strategic change.

Armstrong's description of his change-related problems puts AT&T squarely in the complex change category in Figure 7.1. Many large changes had to be handled in a short period of time, creating major difficulties. Indeed, Robert Gensler, manager of T. Rowe Price's Media and Telecommunications Fund, argues that Armstrong's "tragic mistake" was trying to change everything at once in too short a time period.[viii] Armstrong tried to juggle many things, but sometimes it's just too hard to do it all. Such is the nature of complex change; doing it all at once is a challenge to the best of managers.

With complex change, the strategic problem facing the organization is large. Many aspects or elements of change are needed to respond to and cope with the problem. And given the short time for execution, they all must be handled or done simultaneously. This, then, is a defining characteristic of complex change: Everything important is going on at once during the intervention. The short time frame demands the simultaneous consideration of key change variables in order to beat the time constraint.

There arguably are some benefits of employing a complex change. Large problems are confronted faster. This approach increases the speed of response to change, which may be touted as an advantage. Things are attacked and attended to quickly rather than being drawn out.

Complex changes can also be exciting. They certainly seldom are boring. Managers at all levels of the company roll up their sleeves and pitch in, all at once, to confront and solve a major strategic problem. This pervasive, overriding approach often breeds a camaraderie of sorts, an *esprit de corps*, as C-level managers "toil in the soil" with middle managers, get their collective hands dirty, and solve the organization's vulnerability before a large strategic threat.

Speed and camaraderie are seemingly both attained when confronting change. This sounds wonderful, a positive testament to the virtues of complex interventions involving big problems and many individuals or functional units simultaneously.

If this sounds too good to be true, it's because it usually *is* too good to be true. The seemingly positive aspects of complex change notwithstanding, this change process teems with problems. It flirts with disaster. It creates a number of issues that virtually guarantee the failure of change and poor execution outcomes. Indeed, let's make the following assertion:

> *Complex change should be avoided. Unless it's absolutely inevitable, a complex intervention should rarely be used purposely and willingly. Complex change courts disaster and, more often than not, guarantees the poor execution of strategic change.*

To managers who say they enjoy complex change, these indeed are fighting words. Obviously, this strong statement needs justification. How can I or anyone raise such emphatic storm warnings about complex change? To answer the question, let's consider some of the problems that are routinely encountered with this approach. Examples can then be used to highlight the problems in actual change situations.

Problems with Complex Change

There are at least four major problems that characterize complex change. The overall difficulty of this change process is exacerbated by the fact that all four problems are always present. These, then, are not separate, intermittent problems; they are constant elements of the change that, together, increase the difficulty of change management and jeopardize execution outcomes.

1. **Coordination and control are difficult.** Under complex change, it is difficult to set up effective coordination mechanisms and controls. Too much is going on at once. Different individuals or units are responding to change-related problems in real time, at once, and this simultaneous treatment of multiple problems in multiple areas or geographical settings defies easy coordination.

   A ranking manager in the National Hurricane Center in Miami not too long ago attended a Wharton executive program. He suggested that his organization routinely faced huge problems of coordination and control during major hurricanes (a big problem!). When a huge storm hits, people are working everywhere to save lives (first) and property (second). Different organizations and resources are marshaled into action (the Red Cross, National Guard, State Police, Army Reserve, emergency medical personnel, local hospitals, and so on). They all respond to the problem, handling things as they occur and change, usually according to their organization's own rules and standard operating procedures.

   So much activity in so many different organizations, all with their own methods and hierarchical arrangements, provides a nightmare for coordination and control. A command center is set up. However, the many decentralized activities that are occurring in the teeth of a vicious storm that rarely acts in a predictable manner make establishment of centralized controls extremely difficult at best. That organizations such as the National Hurricane Center can perform at all under such adverse conditions is remarkable.

   The same problems of coordination and control exist in any organization facing a major strategic problem and the need to tackle it on many fronts simultaneously. A major competitive threat or external discontinuity (for example, a major innovation or technological "revolution") may demand a change in strategy, pricing, distribution, incentives, marketing plans, and manufacturing schedules. If all must be done simultaneously, within a short execution horizon, one can easily see the problems of control and coordination that can arise in such a situation.

2. **Cause-effect analysis is difficult, if not impossible.** Assume a company is in the throes of a complex change. By definition, time is of the essence, and many things are going on at once. If one were to "package" and depict the change process, it might look like the following:

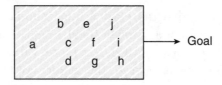

What we see is an organizational "black box" of sorts with many activities, tasks, or change programs (a–j) going on at the same time, the intention being to solve a problem or achieve some goals as quickly as possible.

Assume next that the change process fails miserably. The goal isn't attained, and the organization suffers major, but hopefully not irreparable, damage. Clearly, an autopsy is in order, and the reasons underlying the failed change must be identified and understood.

The problem is that a clear cause-effect model cannot be drawn. It is nearly impossible to explain with great certainty exactly what happened. It is difficult to explain what went wrong.

Did single elements in the "black box" of tasks, activities, and programs affect goal attainment independently of the others, as the following suggests?

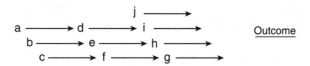

Did a through j, that is, have separate, independent effects on the outcome, as the preceding picture shows? Or were there interactive effects? Did a subset or various subsets of the ten tasks, activities, or programs interact with each other to negatively affect the outcome, as the following suggests?

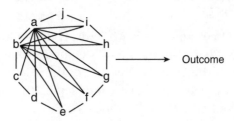

Considering that there are a huge number of possible binary combinations of a through j and a host of other combinations or permutations of three or more variables in interaction, explaining what caused the failure is virtually impossible. What explains the outcome when so many things are going on simultaneously? Nothing does, at least not easily and transparently. Cause and effect remain uncertain and unclear.

3. **Learning suffers.** The result of an unclear model of cause and effect leads logically and inexorably to yet another problem: Learning cannot occur.

   A failed major change is serious. Many resources were dedicated to the complex change, including a great deal of management's time, efforts, and commitment. At minimum, the organization wants to learn from its mistakes and prevent the reoccurrence of such a huge change-related failure in the future.

   The problem is that it can't learn. The unclear cause-effect relationship when many tasks or activities are being attended to simultaneously prevents learning. Given the difficulty of determining the independent and interactive effects of a through j on change outcomes in the previous example, what would the organization do differently in the future? What corrections in the set of tasks and activities that were handled concurrently in the complex change would be made? Which tasks or activities would be eliminated or reinforced?

There are no simple answers to these questions. Learning is not an easy option when failure results under complex change. Top management surely will try to make some educated guesses as to what needs fixing, but this represents an exercise in judgment at best.

4. **Relax the performance criteria against which people are held accountable.** The only way to make a complex change work is to reduce its complexity. The need is to focus on a small subset of simultaneous tasks, activities, or programs and not hold individuals accountable for performance in other areas. In other words, set priorities, focus on key performance outcomes, and let other performance measures slide.

Why is this cure listed as a problem of complex change? Because organizations usually aren't willing to relax or eliminate the performance criteria against which people are held accountable. They insist that managers continue to do it all. They won't let managers focus on some aspects of change and let others slip or go to Hades. They'll usually ask the overworked and embattled managers involved with complex change to:

"Do the best you can."

Being asked to "do the best you can" is usually the kiss of death. Without relaxing the number of measures that managers are responsible and accountable for, the complex change won't work. The change will be seen as a failure, and the managers involved will often be tainted by it and seen as failures by the organization.

Asking subordinates to do everything well is basically inconsistent with sound performance management. Amir Hartman's study of successful business leaders and "ruthless" execution found, simply, that these individuals do the following:[ix]

■ Focus on a few select performance measures when managing, including when managing change. They take great care not to dilute the need for focus with too many competing measures that can detract attention from critical goals and change needs.

■ Believe that a broad set of measures slows down execution and severely complicates the management of change.

Consistent with this assertion, Hartman is arguing, in effect, that setting and using too many targets, forcing managers to focus on all of them simultaneously, and refusing to back off and relax the performance criteria against which managers are evaluated and held accountable can only lead to a nightmare for the organization trying to cope with complex change. Clearly, a focus is needed on a smaller number of critical change objectives.

Let's consider a few actual examples to bring the preceding points to life and show the negative consequences of complex change.

The National Hurricane Center

This organization succeeds because it sets priorities and relaxes less important performance criteria.

Faced with a hurricane and the complex coordination problems previously mentioned, the center focuses on its primary goal: saving lives. Saving property is a distant secondary goal, and little else matters.

Imagine if other performance criteria weren't relaxed. Picture a situation in which managers were held accountable for "sandbag utilization per life saved" or some other such hypothetical measure. Imagine the anxiety or angst of managers and workers toiling during a major storm if they knew they would be held accountable for the efficient use of sand and sandbags!

Is this an unrealistic example? Perhaps not, if one considers other real-world examples depicting similar issues.

General Motors: A Case of Quality Improvement

I once observed a case of needed quality improvement involving transaxles at GM. Quality problems had surfaced, and the company wanted to do something about them.

The first major problem was that early analysis uncovered a host of individuals or units responsible for quality of the affected component. Ultimate accountability, however, was unclear. This was a case of "when everyone is responsible, then no one is responsible." The situation was eventually cleared up, and individuals were assigned the responsibility of tackling the quality problem.

One individual (whose identity is not in my notes but whose plan was given to me by James Powers of Corporate Strategic Planning) had a novel approach to the problem. He and his unit would focus solely on certain, clearly defined quality parameters and solve the problem. The company would have to agree to relax or eliminate other, less important performance indicators against which he or his unit was usually evaluated. One example is overtime expense. Whereas overtime expense is usually a measure that plant managers or department heads would be held accountable for, the plan in question would have had upper managers disregard overtime expense and similar metrics while the main focus was on quality improvement.

Higher-ups in GM in their infinite wisdom rejected the proposed plan. They realized the difficulty, of course, of focusing on a complex issue such as quality improvement while also being held accountable for a host of other performance measures. Still, their advice was, "Do it all; do the best you can," under the trying circumstances.

The manager and his people, however, remained adamant: They refused to do it all. They would solve the quality problem but only according to their plan of action, which required the relaxation or elimination of many normal or routine measures of performance. This stubbornness was clearly risky, as it presented an ultimatum to higher management. Still, the manager persisted, arguing that his approach was the only way to tackle and solve the complex problem at hand. To try and "do the best you can" and meet a large number of performance objectives simultaneously would surely culminate in failure or unhappy results.

The company finally relented. They accepted the plan with its focus on the key quality issue and relaxation of secondary measures of performance. The plan worked, and the quality improvements were achieved in a relatively short period of time, much to the credit of those in charge of execution.

GE: The "Stars" vs. The Second Team

Another example comes from my experiences as a "Work Out" consultant in GE Aerospace.

I was working closely with an extremely capable and committed manager on a very difficult project. The situation clearly was a complex change. The problem being solved was huge, and the time frame was short. The manager (I'll call him Bob) and his charges, a cross-functional team, had reacted cautiously and somewhat reluctantly when first asked to tackle the problem. They knew the low probabilities attached to the successful outcome of the complex situation that was presented to them. Still, being good "company men," they agreed to the task. They agreed to do the best they could with a tough assignment.

Progress on the complex change was haltingly slow. A focus on one area was met with new problems or unanticipated shocks in another. Despite the hard work, hours spent, and total commitment of the change team, positive results were scarce and short lived.

One day, after an especially frustrating and unsuccessful attempt at making a dent in an important technical component of the overall change, Bob asked if I'd meet him for a drink after work. He'd like, he said, to talk over a few things pertaining to the project. I suspected, ominously, that something was up, and was I ever right.

Bob announced, after a drink and the exchange of general pleasantries, that he was leaving GE. This shocked me, as he clearly was seen as a star with a bright future in the company. He was accepting a great new job in a higher position with better pay, so the move was a positive step in his career. Yet he did add something that was, at the time, very disconcerting.

Bob mentioned that the complex project he was laboring on was getting him down. Hard work was getting him and his team nowhere. Too much was going on at once to allow a good handle on the problem, and the prognosis for success really looked bleak.

He also said that he worried immensely about the prospect of failure in a company such as GE that really focused on getting results.

In fact, he envisioned a scenario he didn't like. He and other top-notch people ("stars," the "first team") had been assigned a huge problem to solve. The task was difficult and complex, but again, they were encouraged to do their best. Now it began to look like they could not succeed with the task. Bob then explained what he really feared would happen.

He feared failure, of course, as he was definitely a high achiever. He also feared that the "first team" would be tarnished in the eyes of many. He said he saw it happen before, at GE and elsewhere.

The first team, the stars, falters and fails. Everyone will say it was an impossible task to begin with, so failure or at least major problems were not unexpected. The first team's efforts are acknowledged, but the bulk of the original problem still exists.

The company then redefines the problem. It reduces its difficulty and even breaks it down into smaller chunks. A "second team" is assigned the new task, and they usually fare much better than the first team could with a much more difficult and complex task. The second team succeeds where the first team couldn't.

Bob's fear, based on his perception of the situation, was that his status within the company could be tainted. As silly as it sounds, he said, he felt that what is perceived becomes what is real. If he and his first-team colleagues were perceived as failures, this indeed could become part of the company folklore or insidious reality over time. This, he offered, could affect his career advancement in some way.

Was Bob paranoid or just wrong? Perhaps both, but this case is not totally far fetched. Companies do hurl individuals into the fray of complex changes, and performance suffers for all the reasons just noted. Does the performance mishap—or possibly multiple mishaps—affect the perception of an individual's value to the organization? It certainly is possible, and probably very likely, in a competitive climate that stresses results and consistent performance. In a company such as GE, results count greatly. Failure to produce them, even when constrained by the difficulties of a complex change, could easily be seen over time as managerial failure.

The intention here is to emphasize that examples abound to show that complex change is difficult and problematic. It often fails because of the following four reasons (listed in Table 7.1):

- Coordination and control are extremely difficult to achieve when many changes are happening simultaneously.

- The cause-effect analysis that is vital to explaining significant deviations in performance is virtually impossible.

- The organization cannot easily learn from its mistakes.

- Organizations are unwilling or reluctant to reduce the number of performance criteria against which individuals are held accountable, which can guarantee poor performance.

The last requirement—that organizations focus on as few critical performance or execution outcomes as possible—is absolutely vital to making complex change work. The more tasks, activities, or change programs that must be attended to simultaneously, the greater the velocity of change, the pressure on individuals, and the probability of failure or major change-related problems.

Faced with large strategic problems, an organization should rely on sequential change, despite its unexciting nature. If complex change is inevitable, then the warnings and issues presented on the vagaries and difficulties of complex change must be acknowledged and addressed by management in as effective a way as possible. At minimum, top management must reduce the number of performance criteria against which individuals are held accountable to give the change a chance and increase the probability of success.

OTHER FACTORS AFFECTING CHANGE

There are, of course, other factors that affect the success of change attempts that are needed to make strategy work. This chapter has focused on how the nature of a change—defined by its size and the time available for execution—affects how the change is managed and the prognosis for success. These issues, it was argued, are usually not discussed well in the massive literature on change and, thus, are in need of attention.

Again, however, our task is not yet complete. Managing change and execution successfully demands that attention be paid to two additional issues: (a) managing culture and cultural change, and (b) understanding power or influence in organizations. Both affect execution success and whether strategy works. Both affect the process of change, as an organization copes with competitive conditions and challenges over time.

The next chapter picks up where this one leaves off. Chapter 8 deals with managing culture and cultural change, including how to overcome resistance to change. Chapter 9 then considers the role and impact of power and influence on the strategy-execution process and its outcomes.

SUMMARY

There are a number of key points about managing change that are important to the success of execution. They are as follows:

- Managing change is important for strategy execution. Execution often implies change in key factors such as strategy, structure, coordination mechanisms, short-term measures of performance, incentives, and controls. How change is implemented often means success or failure of strategy-execution efforts.

- Managing change is still a major execution problem, as the data reported in the present research strongly suggest. In fact, both the Wharton-Gartner and Wharton Executive Education surveys listed the inability to manage change as the single biggest obstacle to effective strategy execution. The problem is due in large part to the complexity of the steps required to manage change effectively. These include:

  - Assessing accurately the size and content of a strategic change

  - Determining the time available for the execution of change

  - Determining the steps or tactics to be employed in managing the change

- Clarifying responsibility and accountability in the change process
- The need to overcome resistance to change
- Setting up controls to monitor the results of change management

- This chapter has focused on the first three issues, as these have not been systematically considered in the literature on change management. Specifically, the impact of the relationship between (a) the size of a change problem and (b) the time available for execution on (c) how a change is executed is explored. Four approaches to change—evolutionary, managerial, sequential, and complex—are analyzed in depth, along with their costs and benefits for an organization.

- A major conclusion of this analysis is that complex change is difficult and dangerous, often resulting in poor change management and failed execution. Complex change occurs when the strategic problem facing an organization is large and the time frame for execution is short, resulting in many change-related tasks or activities being attended to simultaneously. This simultaneous treatment of many difficult change issues is characterized by four major problems:

1. Coordination and control are difficult to achieve when many tasks, activities, and change-related programs are being attended to simultaneously.
2. Cause-effect analysis explaining significant deviations in performance is virtually impossible.
3. Organizational learning is jeopardized because of the lack of cause and effect clarity.
4. Organizations are not willing to reduce the performance requirements for which managers are accountable, which virtually guarantees poor outcomes under complex change.

- When the strategic problems facing an organization loom large, sequential change is preferred. It is logical to break the large change into smaller, more manageable pieces or elements and manage change sequentially, focusing on each element only when the previous one is completed satisfactorily. There is a downside to sequential change—it takes time, unanticipated factors can impinge on the process over time, and it is unexciting—but it is an effective way to handle large changes rationally and methodically.

■ Other factors affect the success of change management, including culture and overcoming resistance to change. These are considered in Chapter 8, the next chapter that deals with effective execution and management of change.

ENDNOTES

i.   Spencer Johnson, *Who Moved My Cheese*, Putnam, 2001.

ii.   "Google Founders Face Wealth, Resentment and a Changed Culture," *The Wall Street Journal*, May 18, 2004.

iii. An early, "barebones" version of this model and its components without an in-depth discussion of execution-related issues and problems can be found in L.G. Hrebiniak and William Joyce's *Implementing Strategy*, Macmillan, 1984.

iv.   Use of binary variables for continuous variables such as time and size of change may not represent an ideal way to operationalize these factors. Still, for the purposes of this discussion, use of binary distinctions such as "long" and "short" time frames is useful and valid for describing the effects of variables such as size and speed of change on execution outcomes.

v.   A.M. Knott, "The Dynamic View of Hierarchy," *Management Science*, Vol. 47, No. 3, 2001.

vi.   "Shareholders OK Merger for Creating No. 3 Bank," *Philadelphia Inquirer*, March 18, 2004; "Bank of America Vows Slow Post-Merger Change," *Philadelphia Inquirer*, April 2, 2004.

vii. This merger and its results – changes in structure, cost reductions, changes in and consolidations of responsibilities, etc. – have received a great deal of attention. Googling the merger revealed hundreds of references, discussions, and case studies that go much beyond the present analysis, which is concerned primarily with sequential change processes. In addition, I owe a huge debt of gratitude to two managers from an executive program who worked for Kraft or General Foods and who knew the industry well. I have their notes, but did not record their names. If these managers should see this, I would ask that they send me their names so that a future printing might recognize their contributions.

viii. "Former Chief Tries to Redeem the Calls He Made at AT&T," *The Wall Street Journal*, May 26, 2004.

ix.   Ibid.

x.   Amur Hartman, *Ruthless Execution*, Prentice-Hall/Pearson Education, 2004.

8

Managing Culture and Culture Change

Introduction

Managing culture is important to strategy execution. A solid alignment of culture and execution methods fosters execution success, while a misalignment creates horrendous problems.

James Burke, a past CEO of Johnson & Johnson, was emphatic and succinct when he explained his company's outstanding performance and ability to handle crises by stating that, "Our culture is really it." Culture makes a big positive difference in execution.

In contrast, a "corporate culture of concealment" was blamed by Mitsubishi Fuso Truck and Bus president Wilfried Porth when explaining his company's cover-up of defects in its products.[i] Similarly, a House subcommittee was told that Enron's culture was "arrogant" and "intimidating," discouraging employees from blowing the whistle on shady deals that were going on within the trading company.[ii] Culture clearly affects behavior.

Recent research supports assertions about the effects of culture. One in-depth research project found that a company culture geared to high standards and a strong emphasis on results produced outstanding performance at both Campbell Soup and Home Depot.[iii] Another well-known study found that a culture of discipline was instrumental in producing positive execution results at Circuit City, Nucor, Walgreens, and other companies.[iv] Cultures that support risk taking have been associated with such outcomes as innovation, cooperation, and product development in yet other analyses of the impact of culture.[v]

Additional support for the importance of culture comes from the present research. The ability to manage change effectively was ranked in both the Wharton-Gartner and Wharton Executive Education surveys as the single most important requisite for execution success. Interviews and panel discussions with managers emphasized the importance of culture when managing change. In fact, to many of the managers interviewed, the ability to manage change really means the ability to "manage cultural change." This discussion of managing culture, then, is really a logical extension and integral aspect of managing change, a critical requirement for execution success.

Culture is pervasive and important. It affects and reflects methods of strategy execution. Culture is enduring and difficult to change. Yet, occasionally, culture change is necessary. Leaders in charge of strategy execution simply must understand what culture is and how to change it. There is no other option if the goal is to make strategy work.

A major problem is that managers often don't know how to change culture effectively. They understand fully that culture affects execution, but their attempts at culture change fall short. The purpose of this chapter is to show how to change culture, when necessary, to achieve execution success.

WHAT IS CULTURE?

There are many aspects of culture, which makes it a complex phenomenon. At the societal level, it refers to the development of intellectual and moral faculties via education and learning, the enlightenment and excellence of taste acquired by aesthetic and intellectual training, the tastes and behavior of a group or class of people, and a stage of advancement of a civilization, among other things.[vi] These aspects of culture, while interesting, are not extremely helpful to leaders of organizational change and strategy execution.

What is more interesting and to the point is organizational culture. This normally includes the norms and values of an organization, including the vision shared by organizational members. Culture usually has a behavioral component, defining the "way an organization does things," including decision-making, how it competes, how much risk it tolerates, the emphasis it places on ethics or fairness in its transactions, and how people treat or evaluate one another's actions and contributions to the organization. Culture also refers sometimes to the outcomes of these behaviors, including organizational creativity or innovation.

For our purposes, let's use the following simple model of culture and behavior:

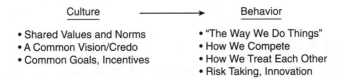

Culture	$\longrightarrow$	Behavior
• Shared Values and Norms		• "The Way We Do Things"
• A Common Vision/Credo		• How We Compete
• Common Goals, Incentives		• How We Treat Each Other
		• Risk Taking, Innovation

Culture refers to the shared values, vision, or "credo" that creates a propensity for individuals in an organization to act in certain ways. Goals and incentives reflect and reinforce this propensity to act, and the result of this cultural bias is reflected in actual behavior. While admittedly very simple, this model suggests some important characteristics of culture and behavior in organizations that affect execution.

CULTURE IS IMPORTANT FOR EXECUTION

It is necessary to talk only briefly to someone from J&J about the importance and contribution of its "credo" over the years to understand this assertion about the importance of culture. Critical decisions and their consequences are constantly held up against the "credo" by J&J's management to help them assess the relative worth of strategic decisions and execution methods. The "credo" is a live and pervasive aspect of J&J's culture that affects behavior.

In my experience, culture is so important in some companies—for example, Microsoft, Nucor, and GE—that new hires must virtually pass muster on an informal "cultural due diligence" before they are hired. Someone who recently interviewed at Microsoft told me that people he spoke to cared little about his academic background and professional accomplishments. They were concerned much more with his ability to meld with the team he might be joining.

More and more companies are conducting formal cultural due diligence before entering mergers or executing acquisitions. Southwest Airlines spent two full months analyzing the cultural compatibility of Morris Air before acquiring it. In contrast, insufficient early cultural due diligence probably is adding to the woes of DaimlerChrysler as it tries to work out the kinks in its merger. An emphasis on cultural due diligence is becoming increasingly prevalent and important because of culture's impact on execution.

CULTURE IS NOT HOMOGENEOUS

While some aspects of organizational culture may be pervasive and homogeneous throughout an organization, other aspects are more heterogeneous.

Organizations, as with a country or a society, have subcultures. Manufacturing personnel have different goals, values, perceptions, or time frames for decision-making than the scientists in R&D. Marketing people see the competitive world differently than individuals in operations or engineering. While culture refers to values, incentives, or behavioral guidelines that people share, subcultures sometimes define differences in these same characteristics within the organization. To simplify the present discussion, reference will be made primarily to organizational culture unless an explicit example of subcultural differences on execution is introduced.

CULTURE AFFECTS PERFORMANCE

For our purposes, this is a critical aspect of organizational culture. Culture affects performance. The simple model just introduced can be changed to look like the following:

Culture ⟶ Behavior ⟶ Organizational Performance

Culture elicits and reinforces certain behaviors within organizations. These behaviors, in turn, affect organizational performance in vital ways. If this weren't true, culture would hold little interest for managers involved in execution efforts. Because it is true, it is necessary to pursue this point further to ensure a better understanding of the role of culture in making strategy work. Consider just a few examples of the effects of culture on performance:

- Corporate culture clashes are a leading cause of merger failures. A 10-year study of 340 major acquisitions by Mercer Management Consulting, Inc. suggests strongly the negative impact of culture clashes on performance outcomes and the execution of diversification strategies.[vii]

- Ciba-Geigy, prior to its merger with Sandoz to form Novartis, attempted major changes in culture because of poor performance. Swiss signatory requirements, emphasis on social status and positions, and appraisal systems that ignored performance in favor of official titles and position were aspects of company culture that hurt performance in an increasingly competitive and changing industry. A change in organizational culture and ways of conducting business was deemed necessary to improve execution and performance.

- Josef Ackermann's streamlining of management structures in 2002 at Deutsche Bank and the introduction of Anglo-Saxon methods of doing business while eliminating old German ways were done to improve performance. He and others felt that the bank's shedding of some aspects of its German past and cultural constraints was absolutely essential to its achieving global growth.

■ At the 2004 Disney shareholders' meeting, Roy Disney argued that only a return to the old, revered Disney culture of family values and creativity could reverse the performance malaise that has characterized Disney for the last five to ten years of Michael Eisner's reign as CEO and chairman. Performance clearly reflects company culture, and the current culture in Mr. Disney's eyes is dysfunctional, negatively affecting performance. The company's 71 percent jump in net income in the quarter ending March 31, 2004, over the year-earlier net weakens Mr. Disney's arguments against Eisner, using the same culture-performance connection.[viii] So, stay tuned, as they say, to see if Eisner can hang on until and after September 2006, when his present contract expires.

■ The high-stakes clash and struggle between Bristol-Myers and the much smaller (and by now famous) ImClone is an extreme example of how culture clash can affect strategy execution. Companies such as Bristol-Myers operate uncomfortably in a biotech universe populated by small companies, extreme risk taking, inadequate research methods, and perhaps even poor conduct of trials necessary for the introduction of new drugs. The FDA's refusal to review the drug Erbitrex, a joint-venture product of Bristol and ImClone, due to deficiencies in clinical testing data and other problems posed a serious performance lapse that negatively affected the stock of both companies.[ix]

■ An effect of culture of a different sort is interesting and worthy of attention. When Advanced Micro Devices Inc. (AMD) held a meeting in late 2003 for an important chip announcement, some big PC companies were noticeable by their absence. AMD's chief executive, Hector Ruiz, said that the companies didn't attend because Intel "intimidated" them, and fearing retribution, they opted out of the meeting. According to Ruiz, they didn't want "to risk angering Intel by becoming 'too visible' in supporting AMD," a rival chip maker.[x] Intel's culture, he felt, is prone to retaliation, which can affect the behavior of other companies. Whether true or not, the case defines an interesting perception of company culture and how it can affect the actions of others.

- Finally, the storied culture at Southwest Airlines that emphasizes a "family" atmosphere, core values built on doing things well, and advancement via performance, not only motivates workers, it also has contributed to the company's success as one of the most profitable U.S. airlines. Culture has affected Southwest's performance. It will be interesting to see if recent rumors of cultural strain, including labor unrest, affect this enviable performance record.

Many other examples can be noted, but it is clear that culture affects performance. Culture and culture clashes certainly affect the execution of strategy.

ORGANIZATIONAL PERFORMANCE AFFECTS CULTURE

This is a significant point that is not always obvious in discussions of culture. Much more attention has been paid to the effects of culture on performance than the obverse, the effects of performance on culture.

The logic underlying the assertion that performance affects culture is straightforward and compelling, and it is based on previous discussions of feedback and controls in Chapter 6 and managing change in Chapter 7. If organizational performance is poor, cause-effect analysis is undertaken to explain the negative deviation. This analysis usually results in decisions about what must be changed to improve performance. But changes in critical variables aimed at improving performance—such as changes in incentives, people, capabilities, or organizational structure—can affect culture. These changes and the modifications in behavior they produce can shape the "ways an organization does things." They can affect core values and norms in which organizational attributes are seen as important or significant.

The reverse impact of behavior on culture change is suggested by Edward Zander's comments when he took over as CEO of Motorola. Zander bemoaned the lack of "urgency" in the company. Having lost market share and leadership positions in important parts of the business, especially cell phones, Zander asserted that complacency can no longer be tolerated.

So, how does one change such a situation? According to Zander, ". . . we've got to get people who want to win and get a sense of urgency."[xi] The suggestion is that placing aggressive new people in key positions and letting them loose to do their thing will change a culture of complacency. New behavior will affect culture.

Zander also referred to a technological subculture that stressed, "build it and they [customers] will come." In this view, technology drives and defines customer needs. A more logical and desirable approach, according to Zander, is to build a subculture that reacts to what customers want and need. Let customers' demands and market performance dictate what Motorola does technologically and product-wise, not vice versa. Responding to customers (a new behavior) can create a culture or subculture that values customer service and recognition of customer needs more than a technological imperative.

In effect, the simple model previously shown is again being modified slightly to add a feedback loop:

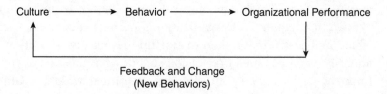

Culture ──────▶ Behavior ──────▶ Organizational Performance

Feedback and Change
(New Behaviors)

The point suggested by this model is simple but important: Culture both affects organizational performance and is affected by organizational performance. Culture is not a one-way street. Culture is both an independent, causal factor and a dependent variable that indeed can change, however slowly or reluctantly.

Let's now take the argument one step further to explain culture change. Let's try to integrate the effects of culture and what affects culture and culture change into one useful model. The effects of culture on strategy execution and the effects of execution on culture can then be seen more clearly, allowing leaders of culture change to deal more effectively with execution-related issues.

A MODEL OF CULTURE AND CULTURAL CHANGE

Figure 8.1 depicts a model of culture and culture change. The top part of the model (steps 1–4) shows the effects of culture. More importantly, the bottom part (steps 5–8) shows how to change culture, which is the main point of interest at the present time.

THE TOP LINE: THE EFFECTS OF CULTURE

The top line in Figure 8.1—steps 1 through 4—shows the effects of culture on behavior and organizational performance.

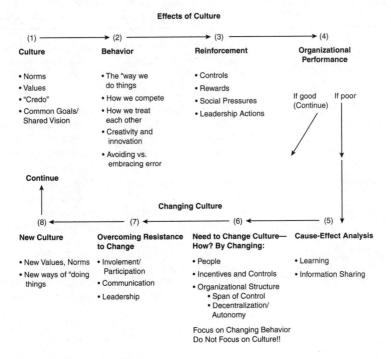

Figure 8.1 Managing Culture Change

Step 1: Culture

Again, culture comprises the main values, norms, "credos," or belief systems of an organization. It defines and creates a propensity to act in certain ways. This step assumes that there is an organizational culture in place.

Step 2: Behavior

Culture affects individual and organizational behavior, the "way we do things." Behaviors include how companies compete, how people treat each other, the extent of risk taking, and desired outcomes such as creativity and innovation. For example, culture can affect the degree to which organizations avoid or embrace error, the effects of which can impact heavily how an organization operates and executes plans on a daily basis. Table 8.1 lists some examples of different behaviors, performance outcomes, and managerial "mindsets" in organizations that avoid and embrace error.[xii]

Table 8.1 Effects of Avoiding vs. Embracing Error in Organizations

	Avoiding Error	Embracing Error
Controls	Top-down, repressive or constraining; emphasis on "being right" at all times	Emphasis on self-control; emphasis on getting the facts
When a mistake or problem is alleged	Deny the problem or play it down; if cannot deny problem, emphasis on blaming someone else	Admit the error; determine and analyze the causes so as to prevent recurrence; conduct "autopsies"
Individual needs being met	Survival; defensibility of actions against threats or accusations of others is critical	Higher-level need satisfaction due to growth, learning, and acceptance of challenge
Setting of Objectives and performance standards	Top-down, unilateral; little participation or negotiations; "all-or-nothing standards"	Participative process; effective discussion and confrontation of conflict; goals and performance standards are not "all-or-nothing" or "black and white"

	Avoiding Error	**Embracing Error**
Attitude toward change	Resistance to change is high	Embraces change as unavoidable, necessary, and beneficial
Interpersonal orientation	Guarded; low trust; alienation	Open; high levels of trust; emphasis on cooperation and joint efforts
Innovation and creativity.	Low	High

The point of Table 8.1 is to show that culture affects behavior in big ways, some of which may occasionally be negative. In extreme cases of risk avoidance, culture creates an emphasis on blame, survival, and low trust. It hurts organizational learning and fosters high resistance to change. Error avoidance is disastrous for creativity, innovation, and successful organizational adaptation.

In contrast, organizational cultures that embrace errors treat mistakes as necessary components of risk taking. They focus on conducting "autopsies" and facing the brutal facts. They also embrace change as unavoidable and beneficial for the achievement of organizational goals, including those related to execution. Clearly, culture can exert positive and negative effects on behavior in organizations, potentially affecting execution outcomes.

Step 3: Reinforcement of Behavior

As Chapter 6 stressed, incentives and controls guide and reinforce behavior. The reward structure tells individuals what's important. It reinforces behavior that is consistent with organizational goals and culture. Leadership actions likewise signal what behaviors and outcomes are valued by the organization. The sum total of activities in step 3 in Figure 8.1 is to reinforce desired behavior and aspects of culture, creating a form of peer pressure and hierarchical influence on doing the right things.

Step 4: Organizational Performance

Culture affects performance. If performance is good, there is a positive alignment of culture, goals, behavior, and reinforcement methods. All is in sync. Good performance lends credibility to the top line in Figure 8.1. The effects of culture are positive, and all is right with the world. Poor performance, however, poses a problem. Poor performance indicates that something isn't working. It is necessary to discern what the underlying problems are, which takes us to step 5 in Figure 8.1.

Step 5: Cause-effect Analysis

Step 5 provides an important transition between the top line in Figure 8.1 (Effects of Culture) and the bottom line (Changing Culture), so it is mentioned in the discussion of both topics. Consistent again with the discussion of controls in Chapter 6 and change in Chapter 7, significant deviations in performance, positive or negative, must be explained. This example focuses for discussion purposes on poor performance only, meaning significant negative deviations from desired goals or outcomes. What is needed is a complete cause-effect analysis to explain the negative performance. This is a necessary prerequisite for organizational change. Without cause-effect clarity, learning and organizational change are simply not possible.

Assume for a moment that cause-effect analysis indicates that major changes are needed. New competitive or industry forces exist, technological innovations have rendered current methods virtually obsolete, and new strategies and ways of doing business are necessary. Assume, too, that top management decides that cultural change is needed to facilitate and support the massive changes in strategy and operations that are required. The question, then, is how does one change organizational culture to support execution of the new strategy?

THE BOTTOM LINE: CHANGING CULTURE

The bottom line in Figure 8.1 deals with culture change. The process of change begins in step 5, with the cause-effect analysis just discussed. The results of this analysis, including the underlying problems negatively affecting performance and the logic behind the contemplated changes, must be fully understood and communicated adequately. Cause-effect analysis tells us what went wrong and why. But this knowledge or learning is useless unless it gets to the right people, individuals who can act on the information. This information, then, must be transferred and communicated effectively.

The first step in changing culture, then, is communication and information sharing. The reasons and logic underlying the need for change must be complete, unambiguous, and compelling. The data supporting and justifying change must reach the right people.

Refer momentarily to the discussion of complex change in Chapter 7. When the causes of poor performance cannot be determined because of the many forces or factors under complex change that are going on simultaneously, learning cannot occur. Cause-effect analysis sheds little or no light on the causes of poor performance.

It follows logically that under these conditions, communication and information sharing about the need for change cannot occur. The reasons and logic for change are not complete, unambiguous, or compelling. Cause-effect analysis yields no clear results. The first step in changing culture, then, cannot be achieved. Effective communication and information sharing cannot occur.

This is why step 5—cause-effect analysis—is so important for culture change. Without it and the communication of findings that result from this analysis, culture change is on a shaky footing. It is doomed from the outset.

For purposes of discussion, assume that the cause-effect analysis is complete, clear, and compelling. Assume, too, that the results of this analysis and the need for change have been communicated clearly and completely to the right people. The culture change process can then move on to step 6 in Figure 8.1.

Step 6: Changing Culture

This is a critical step. It suggests that, to change culture, it is not wise or effective to focus directly on culture. To change culture, that is, don't focus on culture itself or the underlying defining aspects of culture: values, norms, and "credos." Don't try to change attitudes, hoping for a change in behavior. Focus instead on behavior.

The logic here is twofold. First, it is virtually impossible to appeal to people to change their beliefs, values, or attitudes. Requests of managers for more open-mindedness in decision-making or more tolerance of subordinates' mistakes or risk taking sounds nice, but they usually have no impact whatsoever on managers' underlying beliefs, values, and attitudes or execution-related behavior. Managers will say that they'll try to do things differently, but such a promise usually bears little fruit. Behavior doesn't change easily in the face of requests to do so.

Second, it is important to recall that culture both affects behavior and performance *and* is affected and reinforced by behavior and performance. Culture and its effects are not a one-way street. Culture affects behavior, but behaviors also affect and reinforce culture. It is possible, then, to posit the following relationship:

Behavior ⟶ Culture

Changing behavior, that is, can challenge cultural norms and, ultimately, change them. Culture is a dependent variable, affected by behavior, as well as a causal variable, affecting behavior.

In light of these points, how does one change behavior and, ultimately, culture? The answer is by changing people, incentives, controls, and organizational structure, as Figure 8.1 suggests.

Hiring new people often results in bringing fresh ideas, capabilities, and new ways of doing things into an organization. Transferring incumbents of jobs to other positions and replacing them with fresh blood can do much to affect changes in culture and the norms supporting it. This seems to be Zander's approach at Motorola. The fastest and most effective way to eliminate complacency is to bring in people with a sense of urgency. Trying to appeal to complacent people to change alone won't work. Bringing in fresh blood from inside and outside the organization can change things faster.

The CIA has been under fire of late because of its intelligence shortcomings. George Tenet has stepped down. Critics of the intelligence community point to an increasingly ineffective, bureaucratic approach to execution of the agency's work.[xiii]

There are two tasks that an intelligence organization must perform. It must (a) collect data or information and then (b) analyze that information, looking for coherent patterns or emerging facts. According to the critics, the collection of intelligence data is being done well; it's the shortage of qualified analysts that's causing the problem. Bureaucrats have been replacing qualified analysts, and execution of the analytical side of intelligence work has suffered. The remedy? Bring in new blood. Bring in analysts who know how to discern patterns in information or intelligence data. Search for and hire people with the right capabilities. Doing so will transform the CIA's culture away from the bureaucratic morass it's in and back into the analytical juggernaut it used to be.

Collins' argument about getting "the right people on the bus" also suggests the impact of people on behavior, execution, and culture change.[xiv] Hiring the right people, individuals with certain desired characteristics—skills, aggressiveness, achievement-orientation, dogged determination, and so on—can affect execution and culture.

Changing incentives and controls likewise can affect culture change. Rewarding people for performance or competitive success goes a long way in changing a culture in which rewards had been based on seniority, official titles, or the legal "signatory requirements" of a culture, as previously mentioned in the Ciba Geigy case. Incentives guide behavior in new directions and add value to the pursuit of new ways of doing things. Likewise, controls reward the new, desired behaviors and outcomes, reinforcing their importance and creating new norms and values about the appropriate ways to act and compete.

The right incentives and controls can even effect change in the "wrong" people. Managers may exhibit complacency in execution simply because that's what the organization rewards and reinforces, even if unknowingly. Changing incentives and controls may bring out the right behaviors in at least some portion of a group of "wrong" or complacent managers. Combining new people with new incentives and controls is clearly an aggressive way to change behavior, execution methods, and culture.

Changes in organizational structure also can affect behavior and lead to cultural change. Flattening organizations, for example, usually leads to larger spans of control, by definition. Larger spans, in turn, mean that individuals must exercise autonomy and discretionary decision-making in a more decentralized structure. Relying on a superior is possible when spans of control are small. When spans are large, reliance on hierarchy to solve problems virtually disappears as an option. Individuals must take the bull by the horns and make decisions, as they are unable to easily pass on their problems and concerns to a higher hierarchical position.

One can easily argue that exercising autonomy in a flatter, decentralized structure surely affects culture. The need for autonomy becomes a core cultural value. The exercise of discretion and autonomous decision-making becomes valued, and individuals come to resent any incursions on or detractions from their managerial freedom and self-control. Structural change indeed can bring about cultural change.

> When changing culture, it is far wiser and more effective to focus on changing people, incentives, controls, and organizational structure. These changes affect behavior that, in turn, brings about changes in culture.

AT&T Case

This book began with an early example of changes in the Consumer Products Division of AT&T. Let's expand the example here under Step 6, the topic of culture change.

When Randy Tobias took over the division, he knew he would have to instill a new culture and spirit into the organization. He would have to change some core values and norms. To accomplish something new and totally foreign—successful performance in a new, highly competitive landscape—culture change was absolutely essential. It wasn't something nice to do or a luxury; cultural change was vital and necessary.

The first attempts at culture change mirrored those of many companies, before and since the events being discussed. The focus was on appeals to change, telling key managers that their mindsets would have to be different to compete successfully. Appeals were made to think differently (think "strategically") and form a new cultural thrust that centered on competition and new, value-added measures of performance.

Emphasis early on was also placed on teamwork and building a cohesive top-management team to handle the challenging new competitive thrusts. Again, this is consistent with the actions of many companies as they hold retreats, raft white water, climb rocks, have paint-gun battles, and so on, all in the name of team building.

The simple fact is that these early attempts at cultural change are often virtually useless and ineffective. Appeals for teamwork and cultural change sound great. Teambuilding activities are fun, and they might have some positive effects in the short term. The problem is that when all is said and done, when the teambuilding exercises are over, managers return to the same organization, the same structure, the old incentives and controls, and processes that characterize the same old decision-making and power structure. In a brief period of time, everything is back to "normal," with the familiar, same-old ways of doing things. The old culture is intact. Nothing has changed.

It may indeed be that some things actually deteriorate. I remember vividly the comments of one manager who, upon getting "back to normal" after a period of off-site teambuilding, remarked on the value of his experiences:

> "I always felt that my boss was close-minded and intolerant. After spending a week with him and others becoming sensitized to critical areas of teamwork and cultural change, I now am positively sure of it. He'll never change, and this is frustrating."

If appeals to teamwork and admonitions about culture change go unheeded, what does one do to affect culture? Again, the answer is seen in Figure 8.1.

Effective Leaders Change Incentives and Controls

If a new competitive industry is looming, managers can change incentives to reward competitive success. Put more pay at risk. Tie rewards to performance. Cease rewarding seniority or, as Tobias once put it, stop rewarding people solely for "getting older."

Forging a link between performance and rewards will change behavior. It will also increase the value of the new behaviors because they are instrumental in achieving positive feedback and desired rewards. The reinforcement of competitive behavior will lead to a new culture, a new set of values or beliefs about performance and the right ways to conduct business.

To his credit, Tobias tried to institute new programs, a new emphasis on performance, and new incentives and controls. Frankly, however, his bids for change were made difficult by an unyielding AT&T bureaucracy that strongly worked against the change efforts. His plans and ideas in retrospect were right on but were difficult to execute because of the larger confining corporate culture. AT&T at the time was a rigid company whose culture didn't easily tolerate change. Its size and unwieldy organizational structure worked solidly against new methods of communication and incentives favoring performance over seniority or position. New ideas often ran into stonewalls of opposition. Attempts at change by Tobias and others faced a dim prognosis for success. Doing the right things doesn't always work.

Effective Leaders Change People

Some people simply won't like a change in incentives, controls, or structure. They'll resist wholeheartedly, desiring a return to the old comfortable incentive methods and ways of doing business. Faced with this situation, managers may opt out. They leave the organization or take jobs elsewhere in the same company where incentives and controls are not tied to actual performance.

But happily and more importantly, in these situations new people come in. Individuals attracted by jobs with clear linkages between performance and rewards enter the organization or change jobs within it. Typically, they are managers with a high need for achievement lured by the prospect of accomplishment, positive feedback, and control over the conditions that affect their rewards.

New people with positive mindsets about the links between performance and rewards provide grist for the cultural mill. They help create a new culture. Bringing in managers with the requisite skills and motivation to compete brings about a needed cultural change.

In brief, savvy managers I've known have changed culture, not by appealing to managers' beliefs, attitudes, and values but by fostering changes in behavior. Behavioral change in response to new incentives and controls can effect culture change. Bringing in new people with fresh ideas and new capabilities lays the foundation for culture change.

Structural Change at Sears and Wal-Mart

Changing structure, too, can bring about culture change. Examples of how structural change can affect behavior and culture can be seen in two cases: Sears and Wal-Mart.

I recall a situation at Sears in which top management was concerned about undue corporate influence on decisions made at the store level. Corporate staff and regional managers were seen as having too much say over local decisions about product lines, merchandising methods, and competitive strategy at its many, geographically dispersed stores. The immediate issue was how to minimize centralized interference in operations that had to become increasingly decentralized due to competitive conditions. The longer-term, strategic issue was how to create a culture of autonomy, action, and a desire for local control at the store level to foster quicker local reactions to competitive trends and consumer tastes.

To create the desired store culture, Sears could have appealed to corporate and regional managers to butt out of store operations, keep a low profile, and let store managers control the bulk of local decisions. An appeal could have been made simultaneously to store managers to exercise autonomy and take charge of their operations. But management at the time was smart enough to know that such admonitions simply wouldn't work. Old habits die hard. A culture based for years on the values of centralized control wouldn't easily succumb to simple requests to do things differently.

What Sears did made sense. They eliminated or consolidated many of the regional management positions. They, in effect, increased the span of control of the remaining regional managers, thereby making it difficult for them to interfere in or tightly control local decisions. The store managers, in turn, were forced to exercise their discretion and autonomy and make decisions for their stores. A culture in which centralized controls were the way they did things for years was directly challenged by behaviors that clearly would lead to different methods of management.

The attempt to change operations and, ultimately, to infuse a new culture based on locally dominated decision-making worked well in some stores. Other stores fared less well, primarily because store managers didn't have the knowledge, capabilities, or confidence to assume a general management role. We also know that the new structure and methods weren't sufficient to cope with the many changes and challenges that eventually confronted the retail industry, giving rise to Wal-Mart as the ultimate discount retailer. Still, the example has merit in that it shows how changes in structure can affect culture more directly and effectively than simply appealing to people to change their values and accepted ways of doing business.

Similar structural changes were tried at Wal-Mart, but with greater success. Sam Walton certainly knew the value of certain centralized functions or operations, but he also felt that local autonomy at the store level was critical to Wal-Mart's success. He saw the need to create a culture based on local autonomy, accountability for decisions and actions, and a reward structure that recognized superior performance. He also wanted employees ("associates") to feel like part of the Wal-Mart family. He wanted them to take part in the celebration of company success and to see how their pay and promotions were inextricably tied to that success.

To execute this plan to create operations that would foster a culture of local control, autonomy, decentralization, and the worth of "associates," Walton pushed many decisions down to the store level. Stores became profit centers. Large departments were treated as "stores within stores," and they also were profit centers under the control of local management. Managers were granted large amounts of autonomy, but they were held responsible for performance. Incentives were tied to performance objectives, and rewards were based on results against those objectives. Stories about associates moving up the organization or retiring, having amassed small fortunes, created a folklore and culture that led to Wal-Mart's amazing performance and current position as largest company in the world.

Of course, there may be a downside to Wal-Mart's size, power, and success, but this is a topic for another day. For our purposes, the point of the preceding examples is to show, consistent with the model of Figure 8.1, that when changing organizational culture:

- It is not wise or beneficial to focus directly on culture. Appeals to individuals to change deeply embedded values, norms, or accepted ways of doing things hardly ever work, despite the admonitions to do so.

- Attempts at cultural change that emphasize teamwork and challenging "games" (white-water rafting, rock climbing, and so on) are fun, but they rarely work. They'll never affect culture change if other critical organizational variables or characteristics do not also change.

- To achieve cultural change, it is necessary to focus on critical individual and organizational variables or characteristics, namely people, incentives, controls, and structure. The goal is to alter behavior and perceptions of what's important and rewarded, knowing that these alterations can result in changes in organizational culture.

■ This approach to culture change can work because culture both affects behavior and is affected by behavior. Culture exerts its effects (it's an "independent" variable), but it is also affected by people, incentives, controls, and structure (it's also a "dependent" variable). Culture can change in response to other changes.

Step 7: Overcoming Resistance to Change

Even if steps 1 through 6 in Figure 8.1 are executed flawlessly, there still may be a problem. A few key managers may resist the culture change or the new execution methods—modifications in incentives, people, controls, and structure—that are directed toward culture change. It may be necessary, then, to reduce resistance to change, which is step 7 in Figure 8.1.

Much has been written about resistance to change. The underlying logic in most of these treatments seems to be that, when managing change and trying to overcome resistance to it, it is essential to focus on the positive and avoid the negative aspects of change.

The active involvement or participation of key players in the planning and execution of change, for example, can reduce resistance. Most individuals resist changes or new execution programs that are foisted upon them. They resist new methods that are "surprises" or that they had no hand in developing. Some participation, discussion, and involvement in changes that affect culture usually have a positive effect.

It also is important to define the benefits of an intended execution plan and the proposed changes, cultural or otherwise. The benefits of change must be advertised, along with the new values and drivers of excellence. If culture change is expected to add new and exciting elements of work, this fact must be clear. New incentives tied to performance, increased autonomy in a new, decentralized structure, and opportunities to learn, grow, and advance are examples of positive aspects of new execution methods and culture change that can be emphasized to reduce resistance to change.

A related point is that it is important to advertise the preservation of the best aspects of the old culture when managing change. These include such elements or characteristics as an entrepreneurial climate, informality among colleagues, and a client orientation. Preserving what's good and familiar during times of change can reduce resistance to the new methods or situation being proposed.

Changes in culture or execution methods may have some negative effects. Even here, the "negatives" can be turned into "positives" of sorts. Certain jobs may be eliminated or altered (a "negative"), but assuring that displaced employees will have the first crack at training for the new jobs is a "positive." Or outplacement services for displaced managers within the company can be set up to help them find new jobs, in the same division or at other divisions or locations (a "positive"). Or, while there may be a reduction in the number of technical or administrative jobs (a "negative"), the reductions will be accomplished by natural attrition and projected retirements (a "positive").

Culture change may create uncertainty and perhaps even fear about job security issues, new responsibilities, and different ways of doing things. Accentuating the positives of the change is important to reducing resistance to it.

DaimlerChrysler tried to focus on the positives when, in the earliest stages of its merger, it announced that, in a merger of growth, layoffs would not occur. Growth would actually create new opportunities, it argued, which represents an exciting and positive aspect of the merger. The company clearly was trying to calm fears, reduce uncertainty, and paint a positive picture of the benefits of the merger, aspects or conditions that are important to companies undergoing major change.

Of course, if DaimlerChrysler or any other company cannot deliver on a positive promise, problems can actually be exacerbated. If layoffs cannot be avoided due to severe redundancies, the original promise will come back to haunt top management as it attempts to execute the diversification strategy. Obviously, careful planning and consideration of all options are needed *before* any promises are carved in stone.

Sound communication and information sharing are important to reducing resistance to culture change. The advertising of positive aspects of change and the reduction of uncertainty require effective communication.

I recall an attempt at new execution methods and culture change in a medium-size company in which the prime requisite for success was actually considered to be "communication, communication, and communication." Without effective communication about the need for change, top management felt that a negative climate would ensue. Their stated preference was to communicate openly to prevent the development and dissemination of misinformation that could increase resistance and hurt the change process. This emphasis on communication and information proved to be most beneficial and useful.

If people don't have information, they'll make it up to fill the void. Nature abhors an informational vacuum. Rumors thrive in this fertile soil, and most hold negative implications for change. It is far better to be proactive and forthright and focus on communication of the positives of change and the actions required to ameliorate the negatives.

Uncertainty is a terrible thing during episodes of change. The rumor creation and manufacturing of stories or scenarios to reduce it, however, actually increase uncertainty and exacerbate the negative consequences of change. Lying or playing games with the "facts" is also taboo. People ultimately see through these diversions or prevarications, and the result again is resistance to change and a real threat to execution success.

Successful culture change and strategy execution demand a communication plan that stresses positive aspects of the change and informs people honestly about their options and opportunities. A communication plan indicates the individuals who must receive information about changes in execution methods. Individuals directly affected by new execution methods should be communicated with on a face-to-face basis, individually or in small groups. A change in structure, for example, should be communicated to and discussed openly with those directly affected by new reporting relationships or new assignments and responsibilities. Individuals indirectly affected, such as staff personnel who work with or support line managers directly affected by the structural change, can be informed in more efficient ways such as e-mails, mass meetings, company newspapers, and video conferencing.

Massive and purposeful communication is critical to reducing resistance to change. It cannot be left to chance. Without a purposeful plan aimed specifically at those directly affected by new execution methods or by changes in incentives, controls, people, and organizational structure, an organization is courting disaster. Rumors and informal conversations will consume valuable time and detract from ongoing, everyday performance. Misinformation will increase uncertainty and anxiety, further affecting performance negatively.

In the DaimlerChrysler merger, a high premium was placed on communication. Externally directed communications were well planned and orchestrated for maximum impact. A communications "war room" was set up to monitor and control information releases to the press and financial markets. Internally, communications weren't planned as completely and rigorously as were the information outputs coming out of the "war room" and directed to external analysts and stakeholders. Still, some methods or tactics aimed at integration, coordination, and execution had the effect of fostering communication and information sharing. The widespread use of task forces and issue-resolution teams, for example, had a positive impact on communication and information transfer. The bottom line is that effective communication is important for reducing anxieties and uncertainties produced by such a mega-merger.

Finally, leadership is central to the process of reducing resistance to culture change. In fact, the impact of leadership is noticeable along the entire bottom line of Figure 8.1.

Effective leaders play a major role in culture change. They are important to the cause-effect analysis that identifies areas of needed change. They clearly are instrumental in changing and managing key people, incentives, and organizational structure. Leaders play a significant role in controls, as they provide feedback to subordinates and help evaluate individual and organizational performance. Leadership is critical to the task of conducting autopsies and facing the brutal facts when change processes related to execution aren't working.

Perhaps most important of all is the leader's role in reducing resistance to culture change or changes in execution methods supporting the new culture. Managers must lead by example. "Do as I say, not as I do," tolls a death knell for the new behaviors required to effect culture change. Leader behavior is action oriented and instrumental, but it also is intensely symbolic. It tells people what's important. It adds credibility to, or detracts heavily from, the perceived worth and impact of credos, values, espoused ethical standards, and an organization's public persona. Whether or not central leadership figures are seen to be supportive of new execution methods, communication plans, incentives, and different ways of doing business will determine the success of culture change and the reduction of resistance to it.

The wave of recent corporate scandals and stories of top-management greed, impropriety, and less-than-desired ethical standards is reducing public confidence in organizational leadership. It also is affecting the confidence of individuals within organizations in management's choice of strategies and execution methods. More than ever, the role of leadership in supporting new execution methods aimed at affecting cultural change is a central, pervasive, and critical one.

Step 8: The Impact of Change

The effective treatment of steps 5 through 7 in Figure 8.1 will result in culture change. It usually will not occur overnight, however. Culture change will definitely happen if the need for change is well documented and communicated, and an execution focus on incentives, people, controls, and organizational structure is directed toward behavior change and new ways of doing business.

Excessive "speed" or moving very fast when it comes to culture change sometimes sounds desirable but is dangerous. Occasionally, speed kills. A new culture cannot easily be legislated, coerced into being, or ordered on demand. People must see and believe in the need for change and the logic of the new execution methods to support it. New values, norms, ways of doing things, and propensities to act can be developed, but these results usually take some time.

Assume, however, that a company feels it is in dire need of speed when it comes to culture change. Assume that top management wants quick results. What elements of steps 5 through 7 on the bottom line of Figure 8.1 can be eliminated in the name of speed?

The short answer is that none of them can be eliminated. Cause-effect analysis and the need for change still must be clearly documented and communicated. A focus on behavioral change via new people, incentives, controls, and structure is still necessary. However, there are risks associated with speed, and they must be kept squarely in mind.

Hiring a bunch of new people—for example, an entirely new top-management team—can facilitate new values, norms, and ways of doing things. However, it also can create apprehension and increase resistance to change. Sudden and massive leadership changes create uncertainty. They can cause a retrenching of sorts as individuals in middle-management positions play a game of wait-and-see to determine which way fair and foul winds might blow. While new people can speed up culture change, the reactions of others may actually slow down the change process.

A related problem was mentioned in Chapter 7. If many changes are made very quickly and simultaneously in people, incentives, controls, and organizational structure, the result is a complex change. If the change fails—people resist, a new culture is rejected—then what? Cause-effect analysis explaining the failure is difficult, if not impossible. What caused the failure? Was it the new incentives? The new controls? The new people? The new structure? Was it a combination of factors in interaction? Which ones? In brief, excessive speed can inhibit learning and increase resistance to change. Moving fast may obscure the underlying forces at work, making it difficult to explain failures and learn from mistakes.

There will be times when management feels that speed is essential. There will be instances when "quick" culture change is needed. Even here, the steps in the bottom line of Figure 8.1 cannot be ignored. They must be attended to effectively, and care must be taken to manage the complex change carefully. Doing many things at once can challenge coordination, control, and learning, as

Chapter 7 showed. Focusing on the key aspects of culture change, while relaxing other performance criteria against which people are usually held accountable, is absolutely essential for success.

SUMMARY

Changing culture is difficult, but it can be accomplished. Here are the "rules" or steps for managing culture change that can be derived from Figure 8.1 and the preceding discussion.

RULE 1: THE REASONS FOR CHANGE MUST BE CLEAR, COMPELLING, AND AGREED UPON BY KEY PLAYERS

Cause-effect analysis and learning are vital to successful change. Explaining poor prior performance is a *sine qua non*, an essential ingredient, before changes in execution methods or the logic of culture change is accepted as legitimate and necessary.

RULE 2: FOCUS ON CHANGING BEHAVIOR—NOT DIRECTLY ON CHANGING CULTURE

Appeals to individuals to change rarely work. Requests to change beliefs, values, or ways of doing things rarely achieve the desired results. It is better instead to focus on changing behavior, which can lead to culture change. New people, incentives, controls, and organizational structures can motivate behavioral change and lead to changes in organizational culture.

RULE 3: EFFECTIVE COMMUNICATION IS VITAL TO CULTURE CHANGE

A communication plan must be developed. People directly affected by changes must be communicated with directly, face-to-face or in groups. Information sharing is important to controlling or squelching rumors and other sources of misinformation that can inhibit change. There can never be too much communication when managing culture change.

RULE 4: ADEQUATE EFFORT MUST BE EXPANDED TO REDUCE RESISTANCE TO CHANGE

Effective communication of the positive aspects of change helps to reduce resistance. Communications dealing with potential "negatives" of change can reduce their impact. Methods aimed at improving participation and involvement in defining or defusing change and its consequences can also help, such as "Work Out" sessions at GE and other companies that identify key issues and collectively and openly reduce the resistance to new execution methods or culture change. The instrumental and symbolic roles of leadership are also important to the reduction of resistance to change.

RULE 5: BEWARE OF EXCESSIVE SPEED

Speed in managing culture change may be desirable or necessary. It is, however, fraught with problems. Changing too many things simultaneously and immediately can confuse the change process and make coordination and communication difficult. Excessive speed can breed uncertainty and increase resistance to change. Moving too fast can hurt the learning process and cloud the need for change, with dire consequences. If excessive speed is absolutely essential, the approach to managing complex change developed in Chapter 7 must be adhered to closely.

Managing and changing culture are difficult tasks. They are part and parcel of the overall process of managing change. It is recalled once again that the ability to manage change effectively was listed by managers surveyed for this research as the most critical requirement for the successful execution of strategy. Managing culture and culture change clearly share this criticality and importance in the execution of strategy.

Only one more major topic must be handled before trying to summarize the content of this approach to making strategy work: the role of power and influence in the execution process. The impact and importance of this role already has been suggested, but it is time now to consider this topic in greater detail. This is the goal of the next chapter on power, influence, and execution.

ENDNOTES

   i. "More Problems for Mitsubishi as Six are Arrested," *Philadelphia Inquirer,* June 11, 2004.

  ii. "Enron's Watkins Describes 'Arrogant' Culture," *The Wall Street Journal,* February 15, 2002.

 iii. William Joyce, N. Nohria, and Bruce Roberson, *What (Really) Works,* Harper Business, 2003.

  iv. Jim Collins, *Good to Great,* Harper Business, 2001.

   v. L.G. Hrebiniak, *The We-Force in Management: How to Build and Sustain Cooperation,* Lexington Books, 1994.

  vi. See *Webster's New World Dictionary* or *Webster's New Collegiate Dictionary* for these and additional definitions of culture.

 vii. "When Disparate Firms Merge, Cultures Often Collide," *The Wall Street Journal,* February 14, 1997; "The Case Against Mergers," *Business Week*, October 30, 1995.

viii. "Disney Posts 71% Jump in Earnings," *The Wall Street Journal,* May 13, 2004.

  ix. "A Novel Cancer Drug, a Biotech, Big Pharma, and Now a Bitter Feud," *The Wall Street Journal,* February 7, 2002.

   x. "AMD Says Intel Intimidates Clients," *The Wall Street Journal,* September 24, 2003.

  xi. "Ed Zander Faces Go-Slow Culture at Motorola," *The Wall Street Journal,* December 17, 2003.

 xii. An excellent early discussion of avoiding and embracing error can be found in Donald Michael's *On Learning to Plan and Planning to Learn,* Jossey-Bass, 1973; see also L.G. Hrebiniak's *The We-Force in Management*, op. cit.

xiii. See, for example, Herbert Meyer's "Intelligence Tenets," an editorial in the *The Wall Street Journal,* June 14, 2002.

xiv. Jim Collins, *Good to Great,* op. cit.

9

Power, Influence, and Execution

Introduction

Successful strategy execution indicates an ability to gain support for a particular course of action or execution plan. Making strategy work often entails getting others to perform in certain ways or change their behavior. Leading execution and culture change presupposes an ability to influence others.

Power is social influence in action.[i] Power always implies a relationship. It normally involves some likelihood that one actor in the relationship can influence another actor. In similar terms, power defines the probability that one person or organizational unit can carry out its own agenda, despite resistance from another person or unit.

Strategy execution and managing change imply the importance and use of social influence or the exercise of power. The influence structure of an organization can seriously affect the success of execution efforts.

Opinions of managers actively involved in execution lend credence to these assertions. Respondents in both the Wharton-Gartner and Wharton Executive Education surveys noted the impact of power or social influence. Their message was that attempts to execute a strategy that "conflicts with the existing power structure" face a dim prognosis for success. Attempts at execution and organizational change that go against the fabric of influence face a steep, uphill battle.

Power and influence clearly are important for execution and organizational change. It is far easier to execute a strategy that has the support of powerful people than one that breeds and fuels the ire of influential players. This seems patently obvious. Yet, as important and obvious as the ability to influence others is, interviews with managers still uncovered important questions in need of clarification.

1. What is power, and where does it come from? What creates differences in power or influence in organizations, especially among "equals," people of the same rank or at the same hierarchical level?

2. How can knowledge of the power structure be used to improve the success of execution efforts?

The first questions are important, as managers sometimes cannot adequately explain power beyond the obvious aspects of hierarchy or personality. "I'm the VP, and he reports to me; that's all you need to know," was one manager's statement to me about power in his functional area.

There's much more to power beyond hierarchy, however. Mid-level managers often have influence far greater than their position in the organization would suggest. People at exactly the same hierarchical level on the organization chart often enjoy different levels of influence. Though formally they are "equals," some of the people are "more equal" than their peers. Years ago, David Mechanic wrote about the power of lower-level participants on execution outcomes in organizations, and his findings about power still hold sway today.[ii] It is simply vital to understand the sources of power to foster and succeed in execution attempts.

The second question follows logically from the first and is especially important for all managers below C-level and top-executive positions, meaning virtually everyone else in the organization. The issue here, especially for upper or middle managers charged with making strategy execution work, is how to use power effectively, even if one doesn't possess it personally. The issue basically is how to tap into others' influence and use it as your own to facilitate execution.

The purpose of this chapter is to shed light on the origins and use of power in making strategy work. The goal is to understand power beyond the obvious explanations of hierarchy or personality and show its relation to execution and important outcomes.

A VIEW OF POWER AND INFLUENCE

Hierarchical position certainly affects power or influence. There's no denying the impact of position. The CEO outranks his or her direct reports, and the same is true of VPs and their subordinates. Yet we all have seen or met "weak" CEOs and VPs. They have the position, but they have little influence over others. They are figureheads with limited power.

Personality also comes into play. "Natural" or charismatic leaders exist, and they certainly wield a ton of influence over their followers, sometimes well beyond the bounds of their formal authority. For years, the influence of Jack Welch, Lee Iacocca, or Percy Barnevik was much more than even their lofty formal position would indicate.

There's much more to power, however. All power differences simply cannot be explained by hierarchical position and personality. Other factors are at work. The present view is that:

Power or social influence both affects, and is affected by, strategy formulation and execution in organizations. Planning and execution rely on and are affected by power, but they also create power differences, thereby affecting power.

Let's analyze this statement further. Let's determine what power is, where it comes from, and how it relates to strategy execution.

Figure 9.1 provides an overview or model of power and influence in organizations. For discussion purposes, let's begin with strategy formulation.

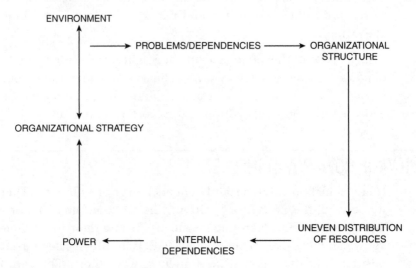

Figure 9.1   Power in Organizations

STRATEGY AND ENVIRONMENT

Organizations confront environments of varying complexity and uncertainty. They must deal with or co-opt them in order to survive. Strategy, in effect, defines how an organization positions itself to allow it to deal with its environment effectively.

At the business level, for example, organizations analyze industry forces, competitors, and their own capabilities to determine how best to position themselves and compete. The resultant strategy defines how the organization plans to cope with its environment. The double-pointed arrow in Figure 9.1 suggests that some organizations have enough market strength within their industries to affect their environment (for example, a monopoly or a large firm in an oligopolistic industry), while others are virtually helpless before environmental forces (for example, a firm in a perfectly competitive market).

PROBLEMS OR DEPENDENCIES

For all organizations, the formulation of strategy defines problems or dependencies that must be solved or handled for the strategy to work. In General Motors (GM), for example, the introduction of robotics was part of a strategy to lower costs while improving product quality. The relationship between the use of robots and outcomes such as cost reduction and product improvement was well documented. Cause-effect relations were clear and compelling: Using robots had predictable positive effects.

But the road to robotic heaven was strewn with potholes. There were critical problems or dependencies that had to be dealt with. Unions, for example, at first resisted the introduction of robots because, in addition to increasing efficiency, they also led to layoffs or the displacement of workers. The unions, of course, represented a critical dependency for GM. The company depended on the unions for its labor supply, a key factor of production. A strike called by the UAW in objection to the robots could curtail or cease production. Labor represented a critical dependency or problem that had to be resolved for the low-cost strategy to work.

A consideration of the pharmaceutical industry reveals similar problems or dependencies related to strategy. In this industry, innovation and product development are critical concerns. The potential of a company's "pipeline" is a driving force in its economic or market valuation. A strategy of differentiation in the marketplace based on product development depends mightily on innovation. A critical dependency on R&D clearly is central to making strategy work.

Companies have experimented with new ways of finding drugs because of this huge dependency and the problems that ensue if new drugs aren't found. For example, pharma companies have spent billions of dollars on machines to create thousands of chemical compounds and then test them with robots. The goal in doing this is to generate a flood of new products and profits to the pharma industry. Yet the U.S. Food and Drug Administration approved only 21 new drugs in 2003, representing a steady decline since a peak of 53 new drugs in 1996. Some of the world's largest pharma companies failed to win U.S. approval for even a single new drug in 2003.[iii]

Most critics are calling this machine- or technology-based incursion into R&D an expensive failure. Machines have turned out compound after compound with no useful results. Replacing a dependency on real scientists with machines simply hasn't worked. The example does show emphatically, however, that pharma companies realize that a critical problem or dependency exists. Innovation must occur if their strategy is to succeed. The formulation of strategy creates demands for the development of critical capabilities (see Chapter 3), as well as problems or dependencies that must be solved or confronted if the strategy is to work.

ORGANIZATIONAL STRUCTURE

How does an organization respond to the critical dependencies or problems defined by strategy? A typical way is to create or adapt an organizational structure to respond to the demands of strategy, as Figure 9.1 notes. This is a logical extension of the argument made in Chapter 4 that strategy affects the choice of structure. Structure now is responding specifically to the problems or dependencies created by the strategic plan.

In the GM case, a unit responsible for industrial relations or collective bargaining handled the union "problem" when introducing robotics into the manufacturing process. Without the dependency on labor, such a unit would never exist. Structure clearly is a response to the existence of a union and the dependencies on it that developed over time.

In the pharmaceutical case, R&D units respond to the need for innovation and product development. Reliance on the opinion, hunches, experiences, and research prowess of scientists in multiple R&D units around the globe has been the typical response to the strategic need for new drugs. The structure of the organization—R&D units—reflects the demands of strategy and the needs created by it.

The result is a dependency on scientists to solve the innovation-related problems necessary for survival. Indeed, the typical large pharma company has multiple R&D facilities as part of its structure. J&J, for example, has approximately 200 SBUs or operating companies, some of which are designated as "prime companies," sources of innovation and new product development. The redundancies and extra costs associated with multiple R&D units in this form of structure obviously must be seen as worth it, given the need to make an innovation strategy succeed. With the failure to date of the machine- or technological-based approach to drug creation previously mentioned, the dependency on R&D units and scientists can be expected to grow even stronger.

Other examples abound, but the point is clear: Structure serves an important function, given the problems or dependencies created by strategy. Its creation and adaptation over time reflects and responds to the problems or critical strategic dependencies needed to gain competitive advantage.

UNEVEN RESOURCE ALLOCATIONS

Not all structural units are equal, however. Over time, some elements or units of organizational structure are seen as solving bigger problems than other units. Some are seen as responding to critical dependencies, whereas others are seen as responding to less critical issues. Some units simply provide more value-added to the organization than other structural units.

The result is inevitable: an uneven distribution or allocation of scarce resources, as Figure 9.1 indicates. Units seen as confronting critical dependencies facing the organization benefit from this uneven allocation of resources. Important units simply get more: bigger budgets, more people, greater access to top management, participation in key strategic-planning sessions, a heavy impact on policy decisions, and more IT support. These units, in effect, get more control over scarce resources and their deployment.

Where does all of this lead? What results from this uneven distribution of scarce resources favoring structural units that confront and solve the critical dependencies or problems facing the organization?

INTERNAL DEPENDENCIES AND POWER

The answer to these questions, as shown in Figure 9.1, is that these favored structural units create internal dependencies. Others depend on the units for a host of things—information, new products, sales forecasts, profits, prestige or brand enhancement, engineering solutions—depending on the function's or unit's task and expertise.

R&D units, for example, create internal dependencies. The rest of the organization relies on them for new products and continued competitive advantage, points emphasized in the pharmaceutical example. Recall, too, the centrality and importance of Bell Labs in its heyday at AT&T. Bell Labs was special. It made scientific discoveries at the leading edge of technology, gave AT&T new products, and enhanced the reputation of the company. Other units needed and depended heavily on Bell Labs. The research unit enjoyed an abundance of resources and used them well. The virtual destruction of a powerful and productive Bell Labs within AT&T over time indeed has been painful to observe.

When I was a manager at Ford Motor, marketing was king of the hill. In an extremely competitive environment in which a market share point translated positively and heavily to the bottom line, the company depended on marketing for sales and share. Marketing received virtually all the resources it asked for because of its centrality and importance to sales and profits. Ford Division was basically a marketing-oriented organization.

Because of its favored position, other units depended heavily on marketing. This function's performance supported other functions' budgets and reason for being and controlled the work done elsewhere in Ford Division. Marketing, for example, made up the production schedule for cars and often changed the product-line mix of units to be built, usually to the chagrin of manufacturing. There were complaints but usually to no avail, as marketing was relied on for its valuable contributions and, consequently, had the upper hand. Marketing had created powerful dependencies on itself within Ford Division.

Definition of Power

It is now possible to define power, or at least the potential for power, in a useful way for practicing managers. Consistent with this discussion, especially the notion of dependency created by strategy, structure, and the resource-allocation process, the following definition of power is feasible and realistic:

> *Power is the opposite of dependency. If B is totally dependent on A, A has power and influence over B.*

Let's clarify this notion of dependency and power and then provide some examples. Assume the existence of two individuals or structural units in an organization, A and B. The preceding definition suggests two conditions that give rise to power differences between A and B.

1. **A has power over B in direct proportion to A's having something B needs.**

   If an individual or structural unit owns or controls something that another individual, unit, department, or function needs to perform a job or achieve its goals, then the potential for power exists. If A has or controls something B requires—information, technological knowledge, human resources, money, or other capabilities or core competencies—then A has the potential for power and can exert influence over B. The phrase "potential for power" is used because this first condition, while *necessary*, is not *sufficient*. Another condition exists that affects power.

2. **A's power is also related to its ability to monopolize what B needs.**

   If an individual or structural unit, A, has or controls something that another individual, unit, or function (B) sorely needs, and B cannot get it elsewhere, then B is totally dependent on A. A has power over B. A's ability to exercise influence over B is extremely strong and compelling because of the dependency *and* monopoly relationship.

Power, then, is the opposite of dependency. Dependency can be observed when one unit or individual copes with uncertainty or provides scarce resources to other individuals or units. If the degree of substitutability is low, meaning the valued resources or knowledge cannot be easily obtained elsewhere from another individual or unit, then dependency is strong, and the power of one individual or unit over the other is consequently also very strong and unilateral.

USING POWER AND INFLUENCE

Individuals or units with power certainly can wield it. Other individual factors may come into play, however, affecting how those with a potential for power actually exercise it.

The celebration of the fortieth anniversary of the Mustang in April 2004, and Ford's revamping of the continued hot seller to boost its recent tepid car sales, takes me back to an interesting anecdote about power and influence.

The great success of the Mustang in the 1960s really could be attributed to two individuals: Lee Iacocca and Don Frey. Iacocca was in marketing and Frey was in engineering, and both collaborated heavily on the design and introduction of the car. Yet, when one thinks of Ford and the Mustang, Frey's name never comes to the fore. It is Lee Iacocca whom people associate with the car's success. His flamboyant and dominant personality enjoyed the exercise of influence and being in the spotlight.

In contrast, while Frey certainly shared a high potential for power or influence, he eschewed the limelight, preferring to work behind the scenes. He very likely exercised his influence in technical circles, but he never achieved the name recognition, standing, and breadth of influence of Iacocca. Frey had a low need for power and attention, and that affected how he chose to use or not use his power position.

Top managers such as Iacocca and Jack Welch certainly used their influence to affect strategy and the direction of a company, as Figure 9.1 shows. What happens, of course, is that the chosen strategy often reflects and perpetuates the organizational power structure. Those in power create strategies that support or feed off their bases of power.

For years, top people in Ford came from marketing, a logical occurrence because of that function's power within Ford Division, a marketing-oriented organization. In contrast, the track or path to top management at GM was traditionally through the finance organization. Clearly, strategy formulation within the companies reflected and supported the prevailing power bases. Those in power developed strategies that would build on their power position and perpetuate their influence over the strategy-making process. Power begets and perpetuates power; those who have it strive to keep it.

In the heydays of DEC, Ken Olsen once told me that his company was basically "an engineering company." Olsen's top people were engineers, whom he trusted for the right answers to DEC's strategic problems. This reliance on engineering worked well for years. However, the inability to develop a sound marketing group because of engineering's power did come back to haunt the company. The marketing of the company's first major PC—the "Rainbow"—was disastrous. Marketing simply couldn't get things done, especially when engineering disagreed with aspects of the product development and marketing plan. DEC wasn't a marketing organization, and the lack of this function's influence was readily apparent to outside observers.

Motorola, too, has traditionally been an engineering-dominated company. Interviews I conducted with key managers prior to one of the Vice Presidents' Institutes—a key executive development and leadership program—stressed what people saw as a growing negative aspect of the company's traditional engineering strengths and influence on strategy.

New product development, a critical aspect of strategy, was driven too much by engineering, these managers argued. Product development was too much of an "inside-out" process. New "toys," technologies, or a new "box" would be driven into production, often without someone ascertaining adequately whether or not customers wanted the new product. An "outside-in" approach would have ascertained that customers wanted certain problems solved. They wanted an integrative approach, using existing technologies, to solve problems and make their companies more effective. They didn't desire new, standalone "boxes" or technologies that didn't get to the core of their problems. Some managers in Motorola felt that it was time for customers to exert more influence on strategy formulation rather than having engineering dominate the product-development process.

Ed Zander, of course, is confronting many problems and opportunities as the new CEO of Motorola. The problem of a complacent culture has already been noted, along with the need for "urgency" in strategic and operational matters. In addition, a focus on culture surely will have Zander changing people, incentives, and organizational structure, which will also have a major impact on the power structure at Motorola. (Recent performance in Motorola's cell phone business suggests that Zander's initiatives may be having a positive impact on the company.)

COMING FULL CIRCLE: CONCLUSIONS ABOUT POWER

Discussion of the impact of power *on* strategy and the perpetuation of power by those involved in strategy formulation brings us full circle in Figure 9.1, where we began with a consideration of the effects *of* strategy. The major conclusions of the analysis thus far are as follows:

1. Power is the opposite of dependency. Differences in dependency denote differences in power.

2. Power both affects, and is affected by, the processes of strategy formulation and execution in organizations.

Power is social influence that arises from differences in dependencies. It's affected by choices of strategy and structure, and the resource allocation decisions that follow logically from these choices. Power, in turn, drives the choice of strategy and consequent execution needs. Individuals in power usually wish to retain or perpetuate it, so choices of strategy clearly reflect the power of individuals creating it. Power, then, both affects and is affected by strategic processes in organizations.

Although this is interesting, we must take the analysis one step further. It's important that managers involved in execution understand power. It's absolutely vital, however, that managers also know how to use the power structure to further the ends of strategy execution. Let's consider next what Figure 9.1 and the preceding discussion are telling us about the relationship between power and execution.

POWER AND EXECUTION

Managers must note and profit from the following three important takeaways about the relationship between power and execution:

1. The need to define power bases and relationships in their organizations
2. The importance of forming coalitions or joint ventures with those in power to foster execution success
3. The need to focus on value-added, measurable results to gain influence and achieve successful execution outcomes

DEFINE POWER BASES AND RELATIONSHIPS

This is a necessary first step in an attempt to use power effectively. Using a model or approach similar to that in Figure 9.1, the first step for managers at any level of the organization is to "map" out the key dependency relationships affecting power or social influence.

Who are the main players affecting what I do in my job? What departments, functions, or other structural units does my department, function, or unit interact with and depend on? Which units depend on my unit's provision of knowledge, technical support, or physical outputs? What are the points of dependency or needed cooperation? Are there other sources of the needed knowledge, technical support, or physical materials besides the unit(s) providing these important inputs?

These and similar questions are intended to ascertain the key factors affecting power or influence in organizations. Consistent with this discussion, these key factors are as follows:

1. **Dependency relationships.** Who is dependent on whom and for what? Is the dependency mutual or reciprocal, or is it unilateral? Unilateral dependencies denote strong power relationships. Those who totally depend on others for vital knowledge or other resources are in a vulnerable position, with low bargaining power and little influence.

2. **Degree of substitutability.** Are there many sources of the needed information or resources, or does a particular unit or individual have a monopoly over the information or resources? Recall that the ability to monopolize the vital resources that others need is an important contributor to power and influence.

3. **Centrality of an individual or unit.** The degree to which an individual or unit is linked to others in the flow of communications or resources is often linked to power. Organizational units that routinely interact with many other units are highly *pervasive*. Units that can cause an organization to literally shut down by not performing their tasks or functions are highly *essential*. An accounting department is typically pervasive; all units need and rely on accounting information. However, it may not be as essential as a technical service department that has the skills and knowledge needed to repair an important computer-based technology or manufacturing process that keeps the organization functioning. Being essential is usually more strongly related to power and influence than being well connected.

4. **Coping with uncertainty.** Many organizations routinely face high levels of uncertainty. Individuals or units that cope with and reduce uncertainty for other individuals or units usually increase the dependency of others on them, thus increasing their power. This "uncertainty absorption" allows for the definition of "facts" or information that others need to do their job. It also reduces tensions or problems related to ambiguity, thereby providing a kind of psychological benefit, again increasing dependency and power.

The marketing function within Ford Division derived some of its power from uncertainty absorption. It provided sales forecasts to production and other units, which reduced uncertainty and provided the facts needed for those units to operate.

A CEO of a company or president of a country has valuable advisors and "insiders" who provide important information and intelligence. These advisors reduce uncertainty and provide data that the CEO or president can use to make critical strategic decisions. The top person's reliance or dependency on the key people increases their standing and power in the organization.

These four conditions or behaviors, in effect, are valuable assets in an organization. Reducing uncertainty, having low substitutability, and enjoying high centrality lead to dependencies and, consequently, differences in power.

Individuals and units in an organization benefiting from these dependencies affect execution. They can get others to buy into their agenda and execution plans. Other individuals and units need the powerful individuals and units to execute their own plans, actually intensifying the power relationship but simultaneously achieving desired execution outcomes for the company.

FORM COALITIONS OR DEVELOP JOINT VENTURES WITH THOSE IN POWER

The previous discussion suggests that forming coalitions or joint ventures with those in power is an effective way to gain support for an execution plan or methods. Cooperation around a common execution goal can foster positive results. Getting powerful people on your side or in your corner can help to overcome resistance to new execution methods or processes.

The most basic coalition is formed between a manager and his or her boss. Selling a superior on the merits of a new strategy or methods of executing that strategy is necessary for success. Convincing the boss of the merits of execution gains hierarchical support, a base of power and influence. Convincing the boss to intercede with his or her boss to support the execution plan locks three different hierarchical levels into the execution process. Gaining the backing of three levels lends credibility to execution and its intended results, and it advertises to others the viability of actions directed toward making strategy work.

Other coalitions and joint ventures also support power. An attempt by nurses at a large Philadelphia hospital to make sweeping changes in procedures was doomed to failure until they were successful in gaining the support of a large block of physicians. Demands made by the combined nurse-physician coalition were met within a reasonable period of time with only a few modifications to the original nurse-only generated demands. The joint venture simply created a larger power base that couldn't be ignored.

Changes in product specifications proposed by sales stand a greater degree of success if engineering supports the modifications. Manufacturing may resist if sales alone is pushing for the changes. Shutting down production to experiment with new products or to develop prototypes of new models clearly reduces efficiency and takes away from the volume, standardization, and repetition needed to achieve low-cost production. The added urging of a respected or powerful engineering unit may convince manufacturing sooner about the logic and feasibility of sales' requests.

Powerful coalitions can affect the execution process and organizational change immensely. Joining forces creates power bases by combining the potential for power of individuals and units, allowing for more effective execution than the individuals or units could achieve acting alone.

FOCUS ON VALUE-ADDED, MEASURABLE RESULTS

The driving force implicit in the model of power in Figure 9.1 and the discussion of key power-related factors or conditions is basic yet extremely important:

> *Individuals or units that create value obtain power. Results clearly count. An execution plan must show the benefits that will accrue to the organization from effective execution for it to be taken seriously.*

To gain power and facilitate execution, execution plans or methods must focus on value-added, measurable results. There must be a positive cost-benefit outcome. Individuals in power won't support execution if they don't see recognizable benefits for the organization. Coalition formation won't occur if parties to a potential joint agreement don't see a "win-win" situation, a sharing of positive results. It is easier to marshal support for execution when higher-ups and others in the company believe that measurable benefits are forthcoming.

A key word here is "measurable." Execution plans that promise "soft" outcomes—greater support, more management commitment, cooperation, a friendlier culture—are usually doomed to poor support and failure if the soft outcomes are not translated into hard metrics. This is not to say that soft measures aren't good or desirable. It simply means that measurable outcomes that people value and can touch, see, and feel usually generate greater backing than poorly defined or less certain execution outcomes. Let me use a recent example taken from a Wharton Executive program to support the point.

The Case of the Frustrated VP

As mentioned previously, in my Wharton executive program on execution, managers bring real problems for participants to attack and solve. Emphasis in the program is on practical and common execution problems, their actual solution, and on making strategy work. One such participant presenter I've labeled as the "frustrated VP."

This woman was the first female to achieve the rank of VP or higher in her company. She described the company as having a "tough, male-dominated, cigar-chomping, scotch-drinking culture." After a few good-natured ribs from male program participants about the company "sounding like a great place to work," she presented her problems, one of which I'll try to summarize as succinctly as possible.

At a meeting with the company's Executive Committee, she and a few of her male colleagues presented their strategic functional plans—including plans for execution—for the committee's approval. According to her:

> "The sales/marketing guy presents his plan, real fast, 'boopity-boop,' over and done. The reaction of the committee? Real positive. Notification of full funding and commitment soon followed.

> "Next, the manufacturing VP presented his plan, with basically the same result. A fairly quick presentation, bang-bang, with quick consensus about the value of the functional plan and the proposed execution process.

> "Then it was my turn. As the new VP of HR, I presented a few interesting and important strategic thrusts and talked about implementation. I was really prepared. I was new to the officer group, and I wanted to impress my peers with my knowledge, careful preparation, and sound planning.

> "So, what happened? There was little visible enthusiasm during my presentation. There were quite a few probing questions and even a couple of snide remarks that generated a few chuckles at my expense. The Executive Committee said it would consider my plan and let me know its recommendation ASAP. The bottom line is that I didn't get close to what I was asking. They didn't like my plan, and it's frustrating."

This represents the gist of her story. Her plan had a rocky journey through the approval process and was "clearly underfunded." The "old-boy" network took care of its own, in her opinion, but she suffered indignity and frustration at what she saw as a major setback.

As is typical, the other participants in the Wharton program and I had questions. We probed, wanting to know the details of her and the other managers' plans. The questions and ensuing discussion were blunt, factual, and to the point, as a more complete picture of her company's plan-approval process came into focus. For present purposes, I'll take one small portion of the discussion and summarize the main issues.

The first questions from us dealt with the quick approvals of the plans of the manufacturing and marketing VPs. After a lot of probing, it was clear that their presentations weren't shallow, "boopityboop," incomplete plans at all. The manufacturing VP discussed introduction of a new technology, closing an outdated plant, and the need to work with the union on execution. Basically, his presentation, pieced together from the probing questions and answers, went something like this:

"My main recommendation is introduction of (new technology) in four of our five plants, with a gradual cessation of operations in the fifth. Here are the important facts. The purchase cost of the technology amortized over X years is $_____. The benefits include a reduction in variable cost per unit produced over that time period of $_____, reducing overall yearly cost of operations by Y percent. If we look at the net present value (NPV) of expenditures vs. cost savings over the life of the new machines, the NPV is positive and actually winds up returning a hefty positive Z percent ROI over the period. In addition, besides the cost reductions, we can expect a significant improvement in product quality, which will improve drastically our position with customers, especially in the mid-market where we've had tough times with (a named competitor) over the last few years."

The presentation (as did that of the marketing VP) focused clearly on facts and measurable results. Discussions focused on costs and benefits, including increased margins. The NPV model was analyzed, including determination of the appropriate discount rate. Measures of quality were discussed, including the determination of quality improvement at the production levels envisioned. The real costs of closing the fifth plant were clarified, the result being a slight reduction in the NPV figure, which was still positive. The additional costs of an elaborate plant-closing process were juxtaposed against the benefits of goodwill with the union (an intangible) and the costs of avoiding a strike or work slowdowns (a real, tangible number).

Though there were additional questions, the essence of the presentation hopefully is clear. The Wharton program participants' probing revealed that there was real "meat" in the VP of manufacturing's remarks. It focused on costs, quality, and NPV, outcome measures that the executive committee could see clearly and understand fully. Now let's consider our beleaguered VP of Human Resources's presentation and draw some parallels or distinctions. I'll take only one portion of her plan for illustration purposes.

Part of her proposed plan dealt (appropriately!) with executive education. She wanted to increase spending dramatically because of the obvious benefits of training and investing in management talent. "People are our most important asset," she argued, and expenditures on increased executive education will only strengthen the value of this asset. She proposed, too, that training be expanded to include more mid-level manager programs to increase the managerial pool for the future. The cost of the expanded training was significant but well worth it, she insisted, because of the benefits, including a better-trained, happier, and more loyal workforce.

Can we identify a problem here? The basic gist of her argument is that executive education is good, a worthwhile expenditure, and that benefits include happier, more loyal employees. But, she is saying, these benefits come at a significant, high cost. The measures of the beneficial outcomes are subjective, at best, with no real metrics provided. The executive committee could see and measure the *costs* in her presentation very easily, but they had to grapple a bit with the supposed *benefits*.

The bottom line is that they saw an increase in expense with no verification of the increase in benefits. They primarily saw costs and a budget increase. Period. Their reaction was to say that her plan was too expensive and that full funding was quite impossible. She needed to revise her budget requests accordingly.

So, what was the advice of the Wharton executive program participants? What did we suggest she do to change her plan and approach to the executive committee while simultaneously reducing her anxiety and frustration level? Rather than reiterate all the advice and discussion that ensued, let me tell you what our VP of Human Resources actually did to follow our advice.

First, she defined a real problem that all members of the executive committee—indeed, all significant stakeholders—could agree with. She focused part of the new plan on turnover. She pointed out correctly that turnover in the company was exceedingly high. In fact, she provided data to show that turnover was the second highest in the entire industry.

Second, she provided data on the cost of turnover. Some of these data were real and hard and some were estimates, but even they nonetheless could be translated into real, hard numbers. For example, replacing a top-level manager who left for a position else-where usually meant hiring the services of a job placement or "headhunter" firm. The service such a firm provides is not cheap: a fee of up to 100 percent of the found executive's annual salary. This fee clearly is a cost of turnover. Similarly, it takes a while for the new manager to get up to snuff in the new job. Clearly, the manager's salary and fringe benefits during the learning period can be treated as a cost of turnover. The suggestion to her was to con-sider six months of salary and fringe benefits as a real cost of turnover. (Six months is an estimate, of course. The logic is real, however, and it's now up to the executive committee to prove she is wrong, a task not easily done.) Other costs were similarly defined as costs attributed to turnover.

Third, she did some extensive research and found that articles in professional journals and popular magazines alike had discovered links between turnover and managerial education and training programs. Devoting time, money, and attention to managers actu-ally increases their commitment to a company, sometimes con-tractually (for example, an agreement not to leave the company for X years after completing a company-paid-for executive MBA program), sometimes psychologically (committing to the company because of a perceived inducements-contributions "contract"). This link between turnover and managerial education programs was critical, as it allowed her to take her plan to a new level.

Fourth, she rewrote her original HR plan and budget with a different thrust and tone. A goal of the new plan was to reduce managerial turnover. Why? Because reduction of turnover would reduce the real costs of turnover. More specifically, the new plan contained a specific objective to:

> *Reduce the cost of turnover by X dollars by reducing the actual turnover among middle- and upper-level managers by Y percent over a period of three years.*

One of the action plan items or methods of reducing turnover and its costs was to increase the number of middle- and upper-level managers participating in management training or executive development programs, in-house and out-of-house. In essence, she defined the following causal link:

Executive Education ⟶ Reduces Turnover ⟶ Lowers Costs

Her terms were well defined, including the costs of turnover. The link between management education and turnover was spelled out and supported substantially. The NPV of the future cash flows from training and cost reduction was shown to be positive. She showed that education and training were not expenses to be eschewed at all costs, but rather were investments in cost reduction and the building of core capabilities in management for the years ahead.

The new budget and HR plan were approved unanimously by the executive committee. (She kept me abreast of things well after the Wharton program was completed.) Committee members remarked about the plan's logic and the compelling relationship between training or education and cost reduction. Her new plan clearly had a different impact than the prior one.

The point of the example, first, is to show that any plan, strategic or operating, must have an execution focus on measurable results and clear value-added outcomes. Approvers of the plan must be able to see and measure real costs and benefits for the execution plan to be accepted.

Second, power in organizations depends on these real value-added contributions. Individuals and units that add value increase their influence. High-performance individuals and units create dependencies on themselves while also increasing their centrality and importance, leading to enhanced power and influence. Power depends on one's perceived contributions to an organization's bottom line or competitive position in an industry.

Finally, a history of successful execution and positive results not only increases power or influence, it also helps future plans and future requests for funding get approved more easily. Power positively affects future planning and execution. People and units with solid track records find that their influence within the organization facilitates the development and execution of future strategic and operating plans. Power can positively affect execution in many ways, including generating the needed support for future plans.

Table 9.1 summarizes the main lessons learned from the case of the frustrated VP. Comparing the original, rejected plan to the accepted one reveals some basic points about performance, power, and execution success. Basically, the example stresses the importance of (a) agreed-upon, measurable factors (turnover and its cost), (b) clear cause and effect (how actions reduce turnover), (c) a strong cost-benefit analysis (positive NPV), and (d) the importance of solid metrics (measurable outcomes).

Table 9.1 The Frustrated VP: Lessons Learned

The Rejected Plan	The Accepted Plan
Seen as an "expense," raising costs.	Focuses on a real, costly problem—turnover.
No clear cause-effect relationship between plan and outcomes.	Cause and effect are clear; execution of proposed plan affects turnover.
No value-added outcomes or benefits.	Cost-benefit analysis is shown with positive net present value.
Lack of metrics, no measurable objectives or outcomes.	Use of solid metrics, agreed-upon measurable outcomes, or measures of value added.
The result of the accepted plan?	Delivery of positive, measurable outcomes increases power or influence and positively affects present and future execution success.

Execution plans fail when these basic elements are lacking. Increased power or social influence usually accrues to individuals whose execution plans are marked by the elements on the right side of Table 9.1. Performance affects influence. Plans that deliver positive, measurable outcomes benefit both the organization and the individuals responsible for them.

A FINAL NOTE ON POWER: THE DOWNSIDE

Power is important for execution. It can facilitate the accomplishment of an execution plan. Power differences are inevitable, given the assumptions and discussion of Figure 9.1, and these differences reflect the results of positive contributions to an organization's ability to compete effectively and prosper. Power, then, has an upside that cannot be denied or denigrated.

There also is a potential downside to power, however. The first and most obvious problem is that power perpetuates itself, a point stressed previously. People in power tend to want to stay there. They formulate and execute strategies that support their skills, power bases, and contributions to the organization. Obviously, this is not a problem if those in power are doing the right things. If the strategy is wrong, however, if the power elite doesn't respond adequately to environmental changes calling for a different competitive strategy, then major problems can occur. If the individuals in charge persist in doing what they've always done primarily to maintain their position, this may lead to competitive disadvantage.

GM in the 1970s and 1980s was very slow to adapt to changing competitive conditions. The incursions by the Japanese carmakers into its market were huge and devastating. Market share was being lost consistently. Profits were disappearing at an alarming rate. Yet change at GM was slow, despite many external outcries for action. Inertia ruled the period, as the company plodded along doing most of the things it had always done.

Part of this inertia and reluctance to change was likely due to a fairly rigid power structure and reliance on hierarchy that was totally ingrained in the company culture. Roger Smith and his top-management team, for example, were not very innovative in their response (or lack thereof) to the many threats facing the company. The recommendations of people such as Mike Naylor and Jim Powers in Corporate Strategy Planning often were not heeded, despite their logic and appeal to those inside and outside the company calling for strategic and operating changes.

The case of Ken Olsen at DEC is another case in point. The dominant group in DEC for years was engineering. It ruled the strategic roost. The dependencies on engineering were strong, and that ultimately proved to be a problem. When the need for marketing and customer service grew more acute in an increasingly competitive PC market, DEC couldn't respond effectively. Engineering still ruled, and some individuals in this function actually believed that other "soft" functions such as marketing were not very important or useful.

Olsen had built a very effective and powerful top coalition around engineering. This worked well when the main strategic problems were technical and dependency on engineering paid huge dividends. When the market changed, demanding more of the soft skills such as marketing, the same power structure proved burdensome. The engineering-dominated structure reared its ineffective head and created massive problems for the company. Marketing didn't have the resources or enjoy the political clout that would have enabled the company to respond to competitive pressures from increasingly sophisticated and demanding customers. Many of DEC's later problems can be attributed to its power structure.

At least some of the problems currently being faced by DaimlerChrysler in the first six years of the merger can be attributed to inertia and a slowly evolving power structure. The German company's model of power and influence was based on hierarchy, top-down command and control, and the huge influence of "silo" functions, especially engineering. Chrysler's power structure was more informal and decentralized, focusing on lower-level participation in decision-making and more transparent boundaries across functions. The two power models have been clashing, regardless of what company press releases and PR bulletins are saying. Many of the Daimler-Benz people wish to perpetuate their model and run the company consistent with their top-down approach. This reluctance to change the company's power structure and *modus operandi* has certainly complicated the integration of the two industrial giants a great deal. It very likely has affected aspects of company performance as well.

> *Power is usually slow to change. Those in power normally wish to maintain it. Power can support execution, which is a positive aspect of it. Power, however, can also create inertia, negatively affecting change and organizational adaptation.*

The Critical Role of CEO Leadership

Changing the power structure when it is wrong and dysfunctional depends very much on top-management leadership, especially that of the CEO. The CEO and the top-management team can change strategy, people, structure, responsibilities, and the allocation of scarce resources, decisions or actions that affect the power structure. Indeed, some of these high-impact decisions can only be made by a CEO or executive committee. Only such a high-level person or executive team can affect the dependencies among major operating units, thereby determining who has influence over whom. This obviously is not an easy task. It often is an unpopular one. Still, it must be done.

In this situation, the CEO must rely on sound cause-effect analysis to explain performance problems and the need for change (see Chapter 7). The reasons for change must be clear and compelling. Communication of the changes, especially those involving resource reallocations, must be complete and pervasive, cutting off dysfunctional rumors and covert manipulations of information and the "facts." Careful, occasional use of external analysts and consultants may help the CEO prepare and present a case for the changes that will alter the power structure. Similarly, obtaining the support of the board of directors or large shareholders can result in a powerful coalition to push for the necessary changes.

In the absence of strong leadership at the top when organizational performance is poor and strategic change is necessary, other groups will definitely step in, take control, and alter the power structure, sometimes usurping the power of top management. Both shareholders and boards of directors are increasing their influence of late, partly in reaction to company performance and partly due to a perceived need for changes in strategy and the power structure. Consider just a few examples:

- Disney shareholders at their meeting in March 2004 forced the resignation of Michael Eisner as chairman of the board (he did keep his job as CEO). They also let him know that they were unhappy with Disney's performance and that major changes and reforms would be necessary. The Disney uprising seems to have jolted corporate America into a flurry of challenges to top management's position and power.

- In one uprising, a group of large pension funds in effect "declared war" on Safeway Inc., announcing its goals of "overhauling the board, getting rid of the chief executive officer, and setting the company on a drastically new course."[iv]

- The Safeway revolt came soon after Marsh and McLennon Co.'s succumbing to demands from shareholders to appoint a new, independent director to watch over its scandal-plagued Putnam Investments subsidiary.[v] The company had to respond to a powerful, external group.

- At its annual meeting in April 2004, DaimlerChrysler shareholders informed Juergen Schrempp, chairman of the board, of all the things he and the company's top management are doing wrong. Six years of a new strategy have not proved beneficial to the company or shareholders, major mistakes have not been addressed, and changes in strategy and in the power structure may be needed, was the gist of their remarks. The suggestion to Schrempp was that he'd better get his house in order quickly.[vi]

A short while after the shareholders' meeting, Mr. Schrempp was weighing the costs and benefits of injecting more money into a troubled Mitsubishi Motors. However, some top executives would not support the plan, and the supervisory board voted to cut off further financing. The board's decision indicates clearly that it won't tolerate poor performance. It also suggests that the traditional power structure with the chief executive at the helm also won't be tolerated if it causes strategic and operating problems.

- Shareholder proposals at Citigroup, GE, Honeywell, IBM, Pfizer, and other companies are increasingly attacking board composition, altering the company decision-making structure (for example, separation of the jobs of CEO and chairman), and objecting to the use of stock options that overpay executives for poor performance.[vii] Clearly, the increased influence of owners is being felt.

- Boards of directors also have been very active in this recent race to control their companies better. Board members are increasingly looking at CEO pay practices, for example, in response to angry shareholders, regulators, and employees. When Michael Jordan, the former head of CBS, took over as CEO of Electronic Data Systems (EDS), the board placed all sorts of restrictions on his pay, stock options, and the company performance needed to reap their benefits. The board felt "under the gun" to exert more control over the company, in effect changing the power structure away from "imperial" CEOs.[viii]

- The board at Whole Foods Market took the step of capping executive pay at a multiple of what its average worker makes. Besides controlling compensation, the move did much to change the perception of the power structure, removing one aspect of the "us vs. them," or the elite and powerful vs. the "worker bee" culture.[ix] Other companies are expected to follow Whole Foods' example in setting executive pay and perks.

- In December 2003, a small, little-known investment fund (Steel Partners Japan Strategic Fund L.P.) shocked all of Japan when it announced hostile takeover bids for two small Japanese companies.[x] In Japan, with its cozy capitalism and comfortable power structure, this was shocking. One headline in a Japanese news magazine declared "U.S. Fund on Wild Rampage."[xi] The traditional, tightly knit system of sharing within a *keiretsu* and the clear power-based status quo were obviously being challenged. The takeovers didn't succeed, but the point is that, even in Japan, management power structures and cozy relationships or coalitions among companies are no longer safe. Power will increasingly be challenged if it's not producing positive execution results.

- Finally, the list of companies in which the board has shown the CEO the door is growing. Dismissals are on the rise as boards step in and make changes because the CEO has been unable or reluctant to change strategy and the roles of his or her top-management team. A flurry of leadership changes in such prominent companies as Kraft, Delta Air, Motorola, and Boeing indicate clearly that boards are becoming more active in the control of business and their willingness to affect changes in their companies. Indeed, some have said that, more than ever, boards will display a "hair trigger," perhaps reducing the tenure of the average chief executive further below the already low figure of just five years.[xii]

The point of these examples is to show that boards and shareholders will take action if CEOs and their top executives won't change dysfunctional power structures. The advice to these high-level, high-profile managers—indeed, to all managers with responsibility for strategy formulation or execution—is simple and straightforward.

Understand the Power Structure

This is an obvious yet basic need. Analysis of the decisions and forces at work in Figure 9.1, including the effects of structure, resource allocations, and dependencies, is a vital first step. Understanding power is an essential requisite for changing power. Knowing what have traditionally been the bases of power is absolutely essential to altering the influence structure and overcoming resistance to change by those who fear the loss of power.

Be Bold and Make the Necessary Moves

Changing the power structure is very much like changing culture. Appeals to those in power to change and relinquish their influence, thereby eliminating some aspects of a dysfunctional power structure, typically fall on deaf or unsympathetic ears. The only way to change power, similar to changing culture, is to focus on the conditions that bestow power.

To change power, it may be necessary to change strategy, as different strategies make different demands on organizational skills or capabilities (see Chapter 3). Whether or not one changes strategy, it may be necessary to alter structure and integration methods in response to the demands of strategy (see Chapter 4 and Chapter 5). If structure changes, this could lead to different resource allocations and dependencies on different individuals and groups within the organization. The dependencies, in turn, could lead to different levels of centrality and importance of these individuals or units, thereby affecting the power structure.

Not all changes in power demand such big, bold moves. Within departments or functions, managers need not concern themselves with strategy and structure, but can focus on resource allocations and changes in people or decision-making responsibilities and authority. Still, even within divisions, departments, or functions, managers must be aware of the fact that power is the opposite or obverse of dependency. Power cannot be changed until dependencies are changed. Changing dependencies, even at lower organizational levels, is a bold and difficult move. People with power are reluctant to lose it, no matter where they happen to be in the organization.

Overcome Resistance to Change

The manager effecting changes in power must be able to overcome resistance to change. Again, the process and requisite steps are similar to overcoming resistance to cultural change (see Chapter 8). The cause-effect analyses, effective communication, and leadership capabilities documented in the previous chapter come into play once again when considering changes in the power and influence structure. Nothing less than a full commitment to change and a full understanding of the key factors and conditions affecting power will work when contemplating and executing a needed change in power.

If a power structure proves to be dysfunctional and an organization is losing competitive advantage, profitability, and market share, it must be changed. Reluctance by top management to do so will inevitably lead to continued performance problems and steps by shareholders or directors to right the situation. Biting the bullet and instituting change is tough, but it's still better than being the target of outsiders' forced changes.

SUMMARY

A number of important conclusions can be drawn from the present chapter's consideration of power influence and execution. They are the following:

- Power affects strategy execution. The data collected from participants for Chapter 1's survey research indicate that attempts to execute strategy that violate or go against the power structure of the organization always face difficulties and are often doomed to failure.

- Power simply is the opposite of dependency. An individual or unit, A, has power over another individual or unit, B, if two vital conditions are met. A has power over B if (a) A has something (information, resources) B needs and (b) B cannot get it elsewhere. If A has something B needs and is able to monopolize what B needs, then B is totally dependent on A, and A has power over B.

- In organizations, the demands generated by strategy affect structure. The structural units solving the critical problems of the organization are rewarded in an uneven distribution of scarce resources. The uneven distribution of resources leads to the differences in dependencies that create power differences.

- Having power facilitates the formulation and execution of strategy. In the absence of power and social influence, an individual or unit (department, function) can form coalitions with those having influence to foster and support execution methods and plans. The logic is that of the joint venture: Joining forces and creating power bases by combining the potential for power of individuals and units allows for more effective execution than an individual or unit could achieve acting separately.

- To receive support, execution methods and plans must produce clear, measurable, and positive value-added results. Hierarchical superiors or potential joint venture or coalition partners will not support execution if they cannot see and measure its results and value-added contributions to the organization. Individuals and units with a history of producing positive results gain credibility and additional influence over time in the organization.

- The desired perpetuation of power by those who have it creates a potential downside for the organization. People in power may persist in doing what's necessary to perpetuate their powerful positions, even if their actions are inappropriate under different or changing competitive conditions. If this happens, the role of the CEO and his or her executive team is essential to changing the power structure. Emphasis must be on changing strategy, structure, or resource allocations, which in turn can affect dependencies and the definition of new power relationships. Power differences are inevitable. The trick is to ensure that power or social influence furthers the achievement of organizational goals and the execution of strategy.

ENDNOTES

    i. The notion of power as a relational social influence and an ability to act, despite resistance, can be traced back to Max Weber's *The Theory of Social and Economic Organization*, Free Press, 1947. See also Robert Dahl's *Modern Political Analysis*, Prentice-Hall, 1963.

    ii. David Mechanic, "Sources of Power of Lower Participants in Complex Organizations," *Administrative Science Quarterly*, Volume 7, 1962.

    iii. "Drug Industry's Big Push into Technology Falls Short," *The Wall Street Journal*, February 24, 2004.

    iv. "Big Shareholders Flex Muscles," *The Philadelphia Inquirer*, April 6, 2004.

    v. Ibid.

    vi. "Shareholders Grill Schrempp Over DaimlerChrysler Stock," *The Philadelphia Inquirer*, April 8, 2004.

    vii. "Big Shareholders Flex Muscles," op. cit.

    viii. "Here Comes Politically Correct Pay," *The Wall Street Journal*, Special Report: Executive Pay, April 12, 2004.

    ix. Ibid.

    x. "With '80s Tactics, US Fund Shakes Japan's Cozy Capitalism," *The Wall Street Journal*, April 15, 2004.

    xi. Ibid.

    xii. "More Companies Showing CEOs the Door," *The Philadelphia Inquirer*, December 24, 2003.

10

Summary and Application: Making Mergers and Acquisitions Work

Introduction

This book shows how a logical, integrative approach can address execution obstacles and opportunities and lead to execution success. It provides a valuable guide for future execution decisions and actions. This chapter takes yet one more step to show the usefulness of the present approach to strategy execution.

The purpose of this concluding chapter is to apply the book's concepts to a real execution problem. It shows how the present model and insights can actually be used to foster positive execution outcomes for a very complex strategy. It shows how to make mergers and acquisitions work.[i]

MAKING MERGER AND ACQUISITION STRATEGIES WORK

WHY FOCUS ON MERGERS AND ACQUISITIONS?

M&A activities are common, important, and consume huge amounts of resources, including management's time. They are always in the news. They are exciting. These attempts at growth and diversification fuel the imagination as they purport to drive future profitability and shareholder value.

The sad truth is, however, that most mergers and acquisitions fail or founder. They don't deliver on their goals and management's promises. A number of articles and special reports in recent years show convincingly that there is a strong case against M&A. They fail to deliver.[ii] Just consider the following brief list of mergers:

- AT&T and NCR
- Matsushita and MCA
- Quaker Oats and Snapple
- Aetna and US Healthcare
- Wells Fargo and First Interstate
- Upjohn and Pharmacia
- AOL and Time-Warner
- Costco and Price
- Morgan Stanley and Dean Witter
- Glaxo Wellcome and Smith Kline Beecham
- Citicorp and Travelers
- Daimler-Benz and Chrysler
- Disney and Capital Cities/ABC

These are well-known mergers that have had or are having problems with making their combinations work. They all have struggled to some degree, and many have failed to return value on their shareholders' investment. They and countless other examples show how difficult executing M&A strategies can be.

A 10-year study of 340 major acquisitions by Mercer Management Consulting is especially significant and important because it validates the fact that most business marriages do not work. The study found that a full 57 percent of the merged companies lagged behind industry performance averages three years after the transactions had been completed. Many of these mergers destroyed shareholder wealth. They failed to deliver. They wasted valuable resources and presented real and opportunity costs to investors.[iii]

There is additional strong evidence that mergers and acquisitions, at least during the last 30 years or so, have hurt more than helped companies and shareholders alike. A study by Boston Consulting showed that, of 277 deals done between 1985 and 2000, 64 percent resulted in a *drop* in shareholder value.[iv] While large, unwieldy companies such as ITT and Litton Industries have been discredited and broken up, there are still many companies struggling to get out from under the burden of poor and costly M&A activities.

The problems with M&A, moreover, will not go away; they will be around for a long time. Not only have there been failures or problems in the past, there certainly will be many more mergers and acquisitions that will founder in the future. In 2003, investment banks arranged $1.2 trillion in acquisitions. A rising stock market in 2004 and beyond, experts agree, will likely fuel even more M&A activity.[v] The value of mergers may not approach the record $2.9 trillion posted in 2000 for quite a while, but the merger trend and the associated problems will definitely continue. M&A difficulties won't go away in the future, despite the horrendous performance and mistakes of the past.

WHY DO SO MANY MERGERS AND ACQUISITIONS FAIL OR FOUNDER?

The answer to this question is straightforward: They fail because of poor planning and poor execution. The following list shows some aspects of poor planning and poor execution that explain poor M&A results.[vi]

Poor Planning	+	Poor Execution	=	Poor M&A Results
• No Compelling Strategic Rationale		• No Clear, Logical Approach to Execution		• Poor Financial Performance
• Inadequate Due Diligence		• Conflicting Cultures		• Erosion of Shareholders Value
• Overstatement of Expected Synergies		• Poor Integration		• Decreases in Customer Satisfaction
• Too High a Price Paid		• Poor Leadership		
		• Excessive Speed		
		• Poor Management of Change		

Let's summarize briefly some of the main issues and problems that characterize poor planning and poor execution. Time then can be devoted to a discussion of how the present approach to execution can address the problems and help make M&A strategies work.

Poor Planning

Bad planning generates execution problems. It may also doom a merger or acquisition from the outset.

No compelling strategic logic. A rising stock market from the mid-1990s to the early 2000s actually fueled a great deal of M&A activity. High market capitalizations were burning a hole in CEOs' pockets. M&A activities often reflected feelings of "wealth" and a penchant to spend rather than sound strategic analysis of what sustains long-term value.

Related to the previous point is CEO hubris and greed. "Bigger and better" is a driving force that CEOs occasionally succumb to, leading to M&A activities for the wrong reasons. Excessive pride ("I can handle this huge merger easily") and personal benefit also come into play. Once, after asking a CEO why he was pursuing global diversification and after hearing some of his stock answers about growth and shareholder value, he added, "Besides, a CEO of a large, diversified company makes much more money and wields much more influence than a CEO of a smaller, nondiversified company."

This was a great rationale for him, obviously, but not necessarily a sound strategic footing for diversification and an enhancement of shareholder value.

A compelling and logical strategic rationale is needed to justify an M&A strategy. If the rationale isn't clear and compelling, critical stakeholders won't jump on the bandwagon, and execution will be more difficult and problematic.

Inadequate due diligence. This is a critical aspect of planning for M&A. Due diligence, including cultural due diligence, is vital to M&A success. An acquiring company must carefully analyze a target industry and potential candidates. "Hard" data—industry forces, resources and capabilities, industry attractiveness, market power, competitors, and the foundations of expected synergies and costs savings—must be studied carefully. So must the "soft" issues revolving around culture and the similarities and differences between potential merger partners. People, culture, values, and attitudes rarely mesh easily. It is easier to integrate distribution channels than divergent cultures.

Sound planning and due diligence must prepare the merger for the need to handle and integrate hard and soft measures if the M&A strategy is to work. Poor due diligence usually results in poor execution outcomes.

Too high a price paid. Paying a premium for an acquisition in M&A is the rule, not the exception. Paying a high premium means that the probability of earning back the cost of capital is virtually nil. Paying a 50 percent premium, for example, would mean that a company realizing synergies in the second year after purchase would have to increase the return on equity of the acquisition by 12 percentage points and maintain it for nine more years, *just to break even*.[vii] On average, this isn't going to happen.

Good planning is necessary to keep the price in line, given the synergies and other benefits that realistically can be expected from an acquisition. Poor planning increases the costs to everyone, especially the shareholders who entrust their money to managers who, they hope, will look out for their best interests.

Poor Execution

Not having a logical approach to execution. Having a logical approach to execution is necessary for the success of M&A strategies. The importance of this for all strategies was emphasized by managers in Chapter 1's research, and it is especially true for M&A strategies. Executing diversifications without a well-thought-out execution plan and process is simply asking for trouble. This book has developed execution guidelines and a model that will be applied to the case of making M&A work later in this chapter.

Poor integration. This is often the big deal killer. Structural integration must be done well if a merger is to achieve any success.

The melding of organizational functions or divisions and clarification of responsibilities and authority in the merged organizations are important to effective and efficient postmerger performance.

Even more important for M&A success is cultural integration. Due diligence on the planning side can prepare an acquiring company for culture conflicts and related problems. Even with good planning, however, cultural integration is a formidable challenge that, if done poorly, can hurt the execution of M&A strategies. Attempts at making diversification strategies work that ignore the management of culture and culture change are doomed to failure.

Costs of execution. Often overlooked are the costs of execution beyond the obvious expenses incurred by acquisition strategies. Structural and cultural integration demand management's time and involvement. Unclear execution responsibilities can increase decision time and create frustrations. Managers may leave the company or "drop out psychologically" because of the frustrations and unclear direction of change.

Execution activities also create opportunity costs, as time spent on M&A execution means that less time is available for other managerial tasks. Time spent on execution may detract attention from other critical industry forces and competitive conditions, thereby injuring organizational performance. Real and opportunity costs, including management taking its eye off the ball to handle execution bottlenecks, clearly represent a potential problem when trying to make M&A strategies work.

"Speed kills." Moving quickly in M&A transactions and integration is often touted as a good thing. But excessive speed can be dangerous. As heretical as this sounds, speed in integration and culture change can have a serious downside.

A high "velocity of change" and the need to handle many conflicting factors at once when integrating an acquisition can create a highly complex change and lead to disastrous outcomes. Excessive speed can hurt integration and execution success.

Poor change management. Execution of M&A strategies usually involves change, and the ineffective handling of change will thwart or seriously injure execution. Key questions or issues include whether to make changes quickly or manage them over longer periods of time. Obviously, decisions must take the speed or velocity of change into account, including benefits and costs of alternative change approaches to making M&A work. Leadership is also critical here, as managers at all levels of an organization must deal with change and overcome resistance to it.

The issue of trust. One more issue needs to be mentioned—trust. Trust between the parties involved in an acquisition can affect both planning and execution. A lack of trust can affect the sharing of information and the validity of due diligence data. Trust clearly can positively affect cultural integration, the setting of performance objectives, and the structural integration of a new business into the corporate fold. Managers on both sides of an M&A strategy must be open and honest with each other to facilitate execution.

This, then, is a brief summary of planning and execution problems that are related to the performance of M&A strategies. The literature on M&A, opinions of managers in the present research, and my experiences suggest that these problems can seriously affect execution results.

The critical question is where do we go from here? How can we improve the odds of success for the execution of M&A strategies? Given that so many mergers fail, any change in success will save countless dollars and frustrations. But how does one address the huge problems just noted and improve the chances for success?

One answer to these questions is to apply the ideas and concepts developed in this book. The following sections apply the present model and concepts to the critical issue of making acquisitions and consolidation work. They go through the steps, decisions, and actions necessary to confront the execution problems and issues just noted and make M&A strategies successful. Upon completion of this task, you can judge for yourself how useful and practical the present approach to execution really is.

USING THE PRESENT MODEL AND APPROACH TO EXECUTION

CORPORATE STRATEGY

The present approach to execution begins with corporate strategy (see Chapter 2). As was just stressed, planning affects execution outcomes. Poor corporate strategic plans usually beget poor execution results.

Corporate strategy is typically concerned with portfolio analysis, financial issues, and diversification or divestiture strategies, as Chapter 3 stressed. It is concerned with the mix of businesses in the corporation and resource allocations across businesses to maximize shareholder value. When considering M&A strategies, the corporate task or responsibility looks like the following:

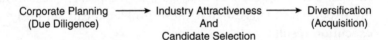

Corporate Planning   ⟶   Industry Attractiveness   ⟶   Diversification
   (Due Diligence)   And   (Acquisition)
                     Candidate Selection

Corporate planning involves due diligence in the analysis of possible target industries and candidates for M&A activity. Industry forces and conditions must be analyzed, including industry concentration, the power of suppliers and customers, the strength of competitors, and the barriers to effective entry.

Philip Morris, for example, really didn't read the forces and conditions well in the soft-drink industry when it bought Seven-Up. The dominance of full-line producers such as Coke and Pepsi made it virtually impossible for Seven-Up to take share from these behemoths, which Philip Morris tried to do. The company did much better when it purchased Kraft to "save" General Foods, a previous acquisition. It knew the industry, felt Kraft's management could help an ailing General Foods, and bet correctly that it could make the acquisition work.

In the case of related diversification, when the candidate company for acquisition is in the same industry as the acquirer, much is already known about industry forces, structure, and competition. Emphasis now is less on learning about the industry and more on analyzing how the acquisition will *alter* market or competitive forces in that industry. The acquisition, for example, may increase market power over suppliers due to the buying power of a larger post-acquisition organization. Larger size may also lead to a low-cost position in the industry. Candidate attractiveness thus is more important than industry attractiveness in the case of stick-to-the-knitting, related diversification. This is an additional reason why the Kraft-General Foods merger made sense at the time.

If an industry or strategic niche within an industry is attractive, a list of suitable acquisition candidates can be drawn up and carefully analyzed. Due diligence requires a thorough examination of the candidate's finances, resources and capabilities, current strategy, potential for growth, and appropriateness as an addition to the corporate portfolio.

Due diligence also demands cultural due diligence of the acquisition candidate (see Chapter 8). What are the driving cultural values? What is the company's credo or vision? Its approach to compensation and how it makes important decisions? Is the candidate vastly different in terms of style, culture, structure, and how it does things? What is the power structure (see Chapter 9), and will it clash or meld easily with the existing corporate power structure?

The importance of due diligence cannot be exaggerated. Due diligence in M&A on the "hard" issues—market position, financial resources, technological assets and capabilities, distribution networks—is important for success. But due diligence on the "soft" issues is also important. Ignoring them is like walking into a minefield of potential culture clashes. Moreover, "hard" issues often breed "soft" issues; focusing on the former while ignoring the latter can spell disaster.

In the BP-Amoco merger, for example, the two companies had different "hard" strengths: One focused upstream on exploration and R&D, the other more on downstream capabilities such as marketing and retail distribution. But the obvious differences also suggested harder-to-detect "soft" issues. The people, skills, attitudes, and culture generated in an R&D-type, "upstream" organization in any industry are quite different than those in an organization dominated by sales, marketing, and a "downstream" market mentality. These differences can affect execution success.

Daimler-Benz certainly knew the "hard" issues of the automotive industry when it went after Chrysler. It might have erred a bit in its analysis of Chrysler's cost structure, but for the most part, due diligence on the "hard" issues was fine.

Where Daimler-Benz faltered was in its due diligence on the "soft" issues. The cultural differences between the German and American companies were huge. The vast differences between compensation schedules caused major cultural and perceived equity problems. A job of due diligence on the "hard" issues was offset by poor cultural due diligence, a fact that still is negatively affecting the execution of the "merger of equals." Due diligence on the "softer" cultural issues is a must for M&A success.

With sound planning and appropriate due diligence of potential candidates, the corporation can decide on a merger or acquisition candidate and a fair price, thereby enacting the diversification strategy.

CORPORATE STRUCTURE

The next major step in executing the corporate M&A strategy is the choice or modification of organizational structure, given the new acquisition. Strategy affects the choice of structure, as was emphasized in Chapter 4 dealing with structure and execution, and Chapter 5 on managing integration and information sharing, and this choice is affected by M&A transactions.

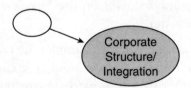

Choice of structure depends on the type of acquisition strategy being executed. The typical related diversification usually involves the melding of two organizations in the same industry that are alike in many ways. Their similarity usually means an execution emphasis on the reduction of duplications and costs and an attempt to attain synergies by consolidating the companies.

Related diversifications in terms of markets and technologies usually call for greater centralization of structure, as like units are combined to service the merged organization. Core central functions provide the scale and scope economies that drive down operating costs. Centralization also allows for the development of centers of excellence to serve the entire organization. Related diversifications, then, typically call for some centralization of structure and the expertise and scale and scope economies it implies.

The case of unrelated or mixed diversification is a bit trickier. An acquired company, though in a different industry, may share similar technologies, manufacturing operations, marketing capabilities, or distribution channels. On the other hand, some or all of these same characteristics may be quite different. The rule developed in Chapter 4 emphasizes that common, similar elements become centralization candidates, while differences usually drive the choice of decentralized structures.

If technologies are similar across the companies, for example, a corporate R&D group or a centralized engineering function may be in order. The postmerger organization simultaneously may be characterized by separate divisions or SBUs to reflect differences in customers, markets, or distribution channels. Centralization and decentralization exist side by side because of the mix of technological and market similarities and differences.

Another example is provided by looking at vertical integration backwards or forward, a typical unrelated diversification. This diversification also raises the question of structural choice: Should the newly purchased unit stand alone, as a separate division or profit center, or should it be melded into an existing corporate function as a cost center?

Retaining the new company as a profit center generates cash and usually maintains focus on R&D, technological change, and product development, as the company continues to compete effectively in its own industry. The fruits of its labor, however, are shared by all, including competitors that buy the acquired company's products and technological advances. Conversely, bringing the new unit in as a cost center reporting to an existing function such as manufacturing increases the acquirer's control, but this option foregoes market share and the R&D capability of a separate profit center. The cost-center move also risks a dramatic drop in production, adversely affecting economies of scale. Another issue is how much autonomy corporate ultimately allows the acquisition within the corporate portfolio.

When Disney bought Capital Cities/ABC, many of these questions had to be addressed. The acquisition was a merger of content (Disney) and distribution (Capital Cities/ABC), both of which are critical to successful performance. How much control would Disney exercise over Capital Cities/ABC, a profit center in the Disney portfolio? Could ABC choose its own content, or could Disney "push" content on ABC that it might not normally choose? Would the content producers at Disney feel the same motivation to produce new and exciting material, given the captive distribution network it now enjoyed? Would other content producers (such as DreamWorks) shun ABC, choosing not to fill the coffers of a major competitor by sending outstanding programming to ABC? Should Disney meld the creative, content-oriented people into one structural unit or leave them as is, in both Disney and ABC? These and other questions were generated by Disney's vertical integration strategy, and the shareholders' revolt of 2004 expressing dissatisfaction with ABC's performance suggests that these and similar issues are still being debated.

A related example involving Disney is its decision in May 2004 not to distribute Michael Moore's award-winning but controversial documentary, *Fahrenheit 9/11*. Miramax, a division of Disney, was overruled by corporate, where people felt the movie was too politically charged to be consistent with corporate strategy. Although Disney's diversifications had created or acquired different autonomous businesses, corporate strategy still clearly is a driving force in the control of subsidiaries and organizational structure.

Structural choice also affects the degree of structural integration required by the acquisition strategy. Under related diversification, the acquisition must be melded into the organization structurally. With unrelated diversification, interdependence is lower and integration requirements are also consequently lower. Structural integration simply isn't as urgent when the acquired company is to remain as a separate, standalone profit center.

The structural integration of two companies is no easy task. The many acquisitions in the banking industry worldwide in the past couple of decades usually had efficiency or cost-cutting goals. The inability to deliver on cost-cutting promises could be attributed in part to poor structural integration. Melding of similar organizational units to reduce redundancies and create synergies sounds straightforward, almost easy. The many problems that exist with related diversification in the banking industry suggest that the consolidation process is not at all easy, but an exacting and difficult one.

Structural integration also holds important implications for organizational power and influence. At the new Citigroup, much time was spent figuring out whether Sandy Weill's group from Travelers or John Reed's charges from Citibank would dominate the critical positions in the combined structure. Recalling from Chapter 9 that structure is related to strategic problem solving, the distribution of scarce resources, and the formation of dependency relationships that lead to differences in power and influence, it is no wonder that structural choice and integration consumed so much attention within Citigroup when executing its M&A strategy.

Structural issues were treated in depth in Chapters 4 and 5. This summary is merely trying to emphasize that, to make M&A strategies work, the corporate level must choose an appropriate structure to realize the benefits of its acquisition strategy. The appropriate mix of centralization and decentralization is needed to maximize the performance, most notably, the efficiency, and effectiveness of the new, combined organization. Structural integration is needed to realize the benefits of cost cutting and avoidance of expensive duplications in the combined organization.

In addition to structural choice and integration, cultural integration of the merger partners is also vital to the execution of diversification strategies. This is another important task confronting corporate decision-makers trying to make M&A work.

CULTURAL INTEGRATION IN M&A

Cultural integration is important for M&A success. Except for pure conglomerate-type mergers in which acquired units are totally independent, standalone entities ("pooled" interdependence; see Chapter 5), cultural integration comes into play.

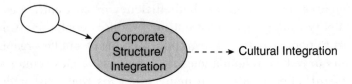

Corporate Structure/Integration - - - - ▸ Cultural Integration

As important as cultural integration is for success, it is often neglected or woefully mismanaged. It often creates problems with making acquisition strategies work.

The poor performance of 57 percent of the companies in Mercer Management's study of 340 acquisitions (cited previously) can be attributed heavily to corporate culture clashes. These consultants and other M&A specialists point to the fact that culture clashes have probably become the leading cause of M&A failure, not just an incremental contributing factor.

Sony and Matsushita's hardware-software dreams may have been grandiose and crazy from the start, almost guaranteeing that they would turn into horrific nightmares. However, the Japanese managers were worlds apart from the "Hollywood smoothies" they chose to run the combined companies.[viii] The culture clash turned out to be one of the big deal killers.

Daimler-Benz and Chrysler again can be mentioned. The vast differences between German and U.S. cultures have already been noted, as have the huge disparities in compensation levels that caused major problems in the merged company. But other important cultural differences also exist. Premerger Chrysler was more informal, often taking a "buccaneering" approach to problem solving and new product development, with cross-functional teams working together and interacting heavily in a reciprocally interdependent setting (Chapter 5). In contrast, Daimler-Benz had a more traditional silo or "chimney" structure in which engineering ruled and marketing or design people mixed infrequently with engineers and played much more of a secondary role.[ix] These differences in style and process make cultural integration difficult, challenging the viability of an acquisition strategy.

How, then, does one achieve effective cultural integration? Table 10.1 summarizes a few practical steps toward this end.

Table 10.1   Achieving Cultural Integration in Mergers and Acquisitions

1. Create an individual job or "SWAT" team responsible for integration:
   - Responsibility for integration
   - Integration objectives defined
   - "Riding herd" and pushing the integration agenda
2. Take immediate steps to help clarify personnel orientations:
   - "How do I answer the phone?"
   - New IDs, business cards, as needed
   - Information regarding the new merged company: phone numbers, e-mail addresses, benefit programs, health plans, stock options, reporting relationships, and communication links
3. Define the new desired culture:
   - Key values and drivers of excellence
   - Results or outcomes desired, as well as strategic rationale
   - Advertise the new, exciting elements of work (growth opportunities, increased responsibility, new promotion possibilities) and other positive aspects of the merger
4. Maintain and reinforce the best characteristics of the old culture:
   - Entrepreneurial climate, informality, client or customer orientation
   - Holding on to familiar "anchors," performance strengths
5. Institute communication programs to reduce uncertainty and facilitate the culture change process:
   - Providing forums for communication and open confrontation of problems
   - Q&A sessions
   - "Work Out" programs
   - Advertise training for new responsibilities

continues

Table 10.1   *Continued*

6. Develop and reinforce incentives and controls that support the new culture:
    ■ Supporting new behaviors and acquisition objectives
7. Manage change effectively:
    ■ Tactics and methods of managing change, including culture change
    ■ Overcoming resistance to change

Assign Responsibility for Integration

The first step is to assign responsibility for the integration task. Assigning an individual or preferably a "SWAT" team with the job of "riding herd" or pushing the integration agenda and ensuring that critical tasks get done is a good initial step. If someone isn't directly responsible for cultural integration and paid to worry about integration success, this important task will not receive sufficient attention.

When choosing members of the "SWAT" team, you must consider the operational strengths and weaknesses, cultural similarities and differences, and the power structures of the two merging organizations. Agreement must be reached on the team's composition. Usually, both organizations are equally represented, but top-management agreement may be reached about greater inclusion of one side or the other based on strategic or operating needs.

This initial step of assigning responsibility, while basic, is critical. Choosing an integration team signals a great deal to members of both companies about the merged company's commitment to making the acquisition strategy work. Assigning accountability for integration emphasizes its importance and its central role in making a merger successful.

Orient Personnel Immediately

There are simple yet critical early steps that the organization or "SWAT" team can take immediately to aid cultural integration. Orientation sessions or messages ("town-hall" meetings, in-house

TV broadcasts, e-mails, and printed flyers) can focus on issues that may seem trivial at first but are important for ease of integration. Clarifying simple things such as "how to answer the phone" in the merged company reduces stress. So does immediately providing new identities and position descriptions via new IDs and business cards. Information regarding the new company—such as phone numbers, e-mail addresses, health plans, benefit programs, reporting relationships, and so on—can reduce uncertainty, define employees' new space in the company, and go a long way toward eliminating small, nitty-gritty annoyances that collectively can stall or injure the process of cultural integration.

Define the New Culture

It is important to be proactive and define the new, desired culture of the merging company, as Table 10.1 indicates. Setting expectations is critical to integration success. Key values, beliefs, and drivers of excellence should be clearly communicated and reinforced. Results or value-added outcomes expected as a result of the merger should be explained, as well as the strategic rationale behind the consolidation. Any new and exciting elements of work or new opportunities created by the merger should be advertised, such as growth opportunities, promotion possibilities, and new positions.

It is vitally important to publicize what the merger means for everyone and not just focus on the aspects of it that are critical only to top management or institutional investors. Doing everything possible to emphasize the widespread positive impact of the merged company can begin to firm up understanding and commitment throughout the organization, smoothing the transition and aiding development of a new climate or company culture.

Save the Best of the Old Culture

Cultural integration doesn't mean automatic rejection of all old values and previous ways of doing things. Positive aspects of the previous company culture should be retained and their retention clearly advertised to all. An entrepreneurial climate, informality, or customer orientation that has always served the organization well should not be automatically discarded. These aspects of the old culture should be advertised and played up strongly.

"It is important to have something familiar to hold on to" is the way quite a few managers have expressed their feelings to me about the importance of cultural or organizational "anchors" in M&A transitions. Even people who can handle change and ambiguity well have emphasized the importance of the security, safety, and familiarity that accompany these "anchors" or points of stability when going through the throes of a merger.

Institute Communication Programs

Good communication is absolutely essential to cultural integration and reducing resistance to change. Rumors develop and fly as a result of M&A activities. Uncertainties abound, especially around job-security issues. These sparks of discontent can easily fuel a blaze of resistance to cultural integration and cause the merged company countless problems.

Providing communication forums is critical to integration success under M&A. Q&A sessions, "work-out" type programs, and open-house discussions allow for fact finding, venting of emotions, and avoidance of misinformation. Training or educational programs do much to advertise new, exciting opportunities created by the merger. They also provide a forum for communication and dissemination of information useful for cultural integration.

It is important to handle negative information openly and directly. If redundancies are likely to result in consolidation and a displacement of personnel, the company should communicate clearly what will be done to mitigate personnel reductions. "No layoff" policies, retraining programs, and processes to help move people into new jobs should be advertised to reduce security concerns.

Establish Appropriate Incentives and Controls

It is important that incentives and controls support the new culture in a merged organization, as Chapter 6 suggests. Incentives must be consistent with and support new behaviors and the achievement of acquisition objectives. They must motivate cooperation and integration in the new organization, not excessive competition or other dysfunctional behaviors.

The uneven compensation schedules in Daimler and Chrysler created problems for the postmerger integration process. Grossly different pay for similar positions in a merger of equals motivated competition and some ill feelings among managers whose work and contributions were undervalued. DaimlerChrysler executives knew that these disparities had to be confronted and annoying differences eliminated if the merger was to get on a solid, cooperative footing. Six years after the merger, these issues, while being addressed, are still causing some problems.

In mergers such as Morgan Stanley–Chase and Citicorp-Travelers, important goals dealt with cross-selling of products and services across supposedly related or interdependent businesses. Yet much of this ballyhooed cross-selling and integration never materialized. One reason is that incentives didn't clearly support or encourage the desired behaviors. Managers and marketing people felt no great urge to work laterally and push other divisions' products and services. Relatedly, incentives and benefits of one-stop shopping weren't clearly communicated to customers, who independently continued to seek and choose a variety of financial services on their own from an array of different companies.

If incentives don't motivate and support the new desired outcomes and behaviors in a merged company, cultural integration will suffer. Chapter 6 emphasized the importance of rewarding the "right things," and this advice is particularly salient when trying to meld two organizations.

Effective controls and strategy reviews are also important to structural and cultural integration. Because these reviews in M&A situations involve business-level objectives and performance in a corporate review, these issues are discussed later in this chapter when considering controls at the business level and reviews of business performance.

Manage Change and Transitions Effectively

This is also a critical step in achieving cultural integration, as Table 10.1 and previous discussions have indicated. Because managing change is so important for many aspects of M&A success beyond just cultural integration, more detailed attention is paid to it in separate sections and discussions later in this chapter where managing change and managing cultural change are the topics of discussion.

The tasks of structural and cultural integration are vital to achieving effective execution of an M&A strategy. Careful planning and dutiful attention to structure and integration are important responsibilities of the top-management team committed to M&A success. Let's now turn to the next steps in making acquisition strategies work.

BUSINESS STRATEGY AND SHORT-TERM OBJECTIVES

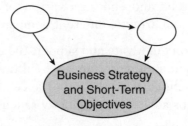

The newly acquired business in the corporate portfolio must formulate or clarify its strategy. Effective integration of corporate and business strategy is impossible if the latter isn't clear and its role or position in the corporate portfolio isn't accepted and well understood.

Business strategy involves analysis of industry forces, competitors, and resources and capabilities, as each business unit attempts to position itself to compete in its industry and attain competitive advantage (see Chapter 3). This summary simply adds that, to make M&A work, the strategy of the acquired unit must support and be consistent with corporate strategy.

The goals of the corporate M&A strategy should already have been laid out as part of the company's compelling strategic rationale for pursuing an acquisition. These goals presumably are clear, drivers of the prior search for and choice of an acquisition candidate. The new organization's role in the corporate portfolio should have been carefully considered by corporate strategists prior to the acquisition.

Much more is needed for execution success, however. Corporate expectations are important, but they must be communicated to the newly acquired business. The role of the new business in the corporate portfolio must be understood and embraced by the acquired company and the parent organization alike.

If corporate expects the acquisition to function as a cash generator, its performance is central to the success of the corporate portfolio strategy. The new company's generation of cash may be critical to resource allocations to other businesses, especially those in emerging or growth industries where cash requirements are high. The poor performance of the acquired organization in this regard can seriously injure the attainment of corporate strategic goals. Consequently, a clear understanding of and commitment to a business strategy is important to the success of the corporate M&A strategy.

The communication between corporate and business executives is also important for the execution of the acquired business's strategy. Expectations surrounding resource allocations to the new business must be hashed out and agreed upon. What the business gets or gets to keep from its own earnings surely has an impact on business-level performance. The goals or performance standards that the new business will be held accountable for also will affect business performance, and these too must be negotiated fully and openly between corporate and business management. Conflicting expectations must be confronted.

There clearly is an interactive, symbiotic relationship between corporate and business strategy and objectives that affects execution outcomes at both levels of the organization. This relationship is shown in Figure 10.1.

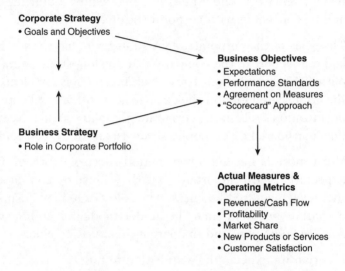

Figure 10.1   Relationship Between Corporate and Business Planning and Execution

Figure 10.1 shows, first, that corporate and business strategies must be integrated and consistent with each other. Good planning and the integration of plans are important to the success of M&A strategies (see Chapter 3).

The figure shows, second, that objectives and performance metrics must be determined for the newly acquired business. Performance standards and measures must be agreed to by both corporate and business management. These objectives are related to a business' role in the corporate portfolio. They also will be used in an evaluation of business performance at a later point in time.

A "scorecard" approach is needed to integrate corporate and business plans and objectives (see Chapter 3).[x] Corporate and business strategies must be translated into performance metrics at the business level, as Figure 10.1 shows. Emphasis is on the data or information that will appear on "dashboards" showing the health and performance of the combined postmerger companies. Corporate and business planning results, then, in a scorecard or set of business-level objectives and performance metrics that can be used to track execution success. The failure to institute these tracking metrics can negatively affect the execution of the M&A strategy.

All this assumes, of course, that there is a clear, coherent corporate strategy for businesses to relate to and help execute. Major problems occur when corporate strategy and its portfolio assumptions are unclear or don't exist to guide and help shape the development of business strategy and objectives. In these cases, execution clearly suffers. The present discussion also assumes that business strategy is consistent with corporate strategy (see Chapter 3). If corporate and business strategies clash or are in conflict, clearly the corporate strategy of the acquirer must prevail. The dog must wag its tail, not the other way around.

Strategic and Short-term Objectives

After corporate and business strategies and objectives are fully developed, communicated, and integrated, it is time to focus on executing business strategy, in this case that of the acquired company.

A scorecard approach again comes into play. The need now is to translate strategic objectives into short-term operating metrics at the business level (see Figure 10.1). The strategic objectives of the acquired business have been hashed out and committed to, as the previous discussion stressed. What must happen next is a cascading or translation of strategic objectives into short-term, measurable, operating objectives within the acquired business.

As was suggested in Chapter 3, formal approaches such as MBO or the Balanced Scorecard can help with this process of translation. If M&A objectives at the business level include cash generation or increased customer satisfaction, for example, these strategic needs must generate operating measures down through the organization that are consistent with the M&A objectives. Higher-level goals must be translated into lower-level goals if execution is to be successful.

This aspect of execution—integrating strategic and short-term objectives within a business or operating unit—is central and important in all attempts to make business strategy work. The role of the business leader is to ensure internal consistency of objectives and efforts in the quest to fulfill the new business's intended role in the corporate portfolio.

BUSINESS STRUCTURE/INTEGRATION

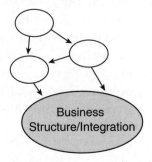

The present approach to execution (see Chapter 2) emphasizes next that strategy and short-term objectives again drive structure, now at the business level. The job of the business management team is to create and manage an organizational structure that is consistent with business strategy (see Chapter 4). Integration and information sharing also must be attended to within the new business, consistent with the points about interdependence and coordination emphasized in Chapter 5. The preceding discussion argued that corporate strategy affects the choice of structure; the present point is that business strategy also affects the choice of structure and integration methods.

An additional aspect of integration that is important is the possible structural integration required between corporate and business levels. The existence of corporate functions or centers of excellence defines the centralized expertise or capabilities that the acquired business unit may have to tap into and employ to execute its business strategy. Information sharing between a corporate R&D function and the newly acquired business' engineering or product-development units, for example, may be critical to the acquisition's ability to develop and deliver new products or technologies.

Steps or methods to facilitate this integration and information sharing include the use of informal and formal methods (see Chapter 5). Rotation of technical people, joint meetings or scientific symposia, or teams comprising members of both groups can facilitate integration. So can "dual" or "matrix" reporting relationships, in which business-level R&D people report to a business leader while simultaneously reporting, solid-line or dotted line, to a centralized R&D group. Effective post-acquisition integration is the need being met by methods such as these.

INCENTIVES AND CONTROLS

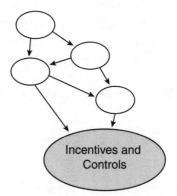

The role of incentives (see Chapter 6) again comes into play. If corporate R&D and engineering at the business level must work together to achieve important product development objectives, the incentive to do so must exist and be positive. Incentives must support important M&A strategies and goals. Perceptions of inequality in incentives certainly can affect the performance of integration teams comprising members from both parties to the merger.

Incentives must also support and reinforce important short-term objectives *within* the newly acquired business. The translation of business strategy into short-term operating objectives must be reinforced, and incentives are important to this reinforcement.

They are vital to execution and achievement of the short-term objectives that the management-by-objectives process or Balanced Scorecard approach identified in a prior execution step.

Controls are also important, especially in the early post-acquisition stages of M&A activities. The strategic objectives and role of the newly acquired organization in the corporate portfolio have been set. Structural and cultural integration have begun and are in process as the new business commences performance in its new role. It is important next that corporate reviews the performance of the new unit to ensure consistency with corporate needs and to provide feedback to the acquisition as to how it's performing its agreed upon role in the corporate portfolio.

The Strategy Review

The importance of the strategy review was noted in Chapters 3 and 6 as an important aspect of control and performance assessment. This review process and its outcomes are also important for the execution of M&A strategies, especially in early stages of the postmerger integration process. The essence of the strategy review, it is recalled, looks something like this:

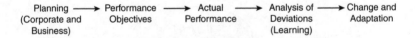

Planning ⟶ Performance ⟶ Actual ⟶ Analysis of ⟶ Change and
(Corporate and   Objectives   Performance   Deviations   Adaptation
Business)   (Learning)

The planning stage in M&A involves both pre-acquisition planning at the corporate level and postmerger planning between corporate and its business acquisition. The importance of the planning stage has already been noted when discussing the integration of corporate and business strategies in the M&A process.

Planning before and immediately after the merger of Chemical Bank and Chase Manhattan was done well, facilitating the M&A strategy. The usual issues of strategy, structure, and operations were discussed. But discussions and processes were also set up to talk about and plan for softer issues such as culture. A policy council, for example, comprised 22 individuals from both banks to help meld the newly created behemoth.[xi] It discussed obvious questions such as definition of businesses and who would run them. But its communications also addressed future competition and what kinds of strategies would work in an increasingly competitive banking industry. The integration team blended business and cultural concerns while planning and communicating business needs. Performance objectives were hammered out based on the two companies' insights into each other's culture and operations.

The critical phase of the strategy review process occurs when actual performance of the new unit is assessed and analyzed.

The analysis of an acquired business' performance against agreed-upon objectives is important for making the acquisition strategy work. Assume for a moment that the performance of the acquired company is *not* up to expectations, meaning that there is a significant deviation between desired outcomes or objectives and actual performance.

One goal of the strategy review as a control device is to analyze and explain what went wrong. Learning is the desired end here. Confronting the brutal facts is essential. Was the strategic plan sufficiently focused? Were competitors' capabilities underestimated? Did the acquired firm have the necessary people, products, distribution, and other capabilities to achieve its goals? Did industry forces change to present unforeseen challenges and increase the intensity of competition in the industry, thereby negatively affecting profits? Was the corporate or business plan too robust, resulting in unrealistic expectations of the new firm in the corporate portfolio?

The purpose of the strategy review, then, is to explain and explicate past performance. This is important, but not sufficient, however. The strategy review has two more functions or purposes. The first function characterizes all such reviews; the second is applicable primarily to a newly acquired company and, thus, is important for M&A success.

The first purpose or function of the strategy review, beyond explaining past performance, is to look ahead and try to understand and shape future performance.

While the term "review" clearly denotes a view of the past, it also must include learning, a look ahead, and potential modification of future strategy and execution efforts. The past must be considered, but future scenarios and strategic thinking must also be the rule. Some typical issues or questions in a review geared to the future include the following:

- How did competitors and customers respond to our products and services in the past? How will they respond in the future? What data support the predictions?

- Are competitors making changes in response to our consolidation that will affect us in the future? Building large, new plants could signal a future emphasis on volume, cost reduction, or a new low-cost strategy with aggressive price competition. Hiring key top management from competitors could also signal a change in strategy.

- Will competitors add new capabilities to compensate for prior shortcomings or to meet our strengths? Adding new salespeople or distribution channels could signal competition on new fronts or in new market segments.

- Are customers' needs or demands changing? Increased competition, especially price competition, could give customers more power to make demands, including for expensive product changes or extensions that challenge a company's cost structure.

- Are new CEOs coming aboard in the industry, promising an industry shake-up and new forms of competition in response to industry consolidation?

- Is anyone in the industry close to a technological breakthrough that can make existing technologies or manufacturing methods obsolete?

These and similar questions force participants in the strategy review to look ahead and anticipate future needs, opportunities, and problems. This is true and valuable in any organization. The review cannot be confined only to an analysis of the past and regurgitation of data that may not be meaningful in future competitive scenarios.

The strategy review involving a newly acquired company has an additional important function. Its purpose is the continued integration of the acquisition and development of a better strategic fit between the new company and its corporate parent.

Planning for the acquisition focused on both hard and soft data. Industry and competitive forces were studied, and the role of the acquisition in the corporate portfolio was carefully weighed. Performance criteria were set, and resource allocations were made. There were also considerations of issues such as cultural integration, the development of managers for their new roles in the merged company, and the leadership and communication skills needed to make the M&A strategy work. The latter issues, too, must be reviewed, discussed, and possibly changed to aid the integration of the new company.

The strategy review provides an opportunity to see where additional new processes or methods could be developed to facilitate communication, uncertainty reduction, and assimilation of new employees. Most, if not all, of these integration issues have already been addressed in a portfolio of older, established companies. Shortly after an acquisition, however, there always are integration issues that weren't considered in the acquisition planning stage. The strategy review allows participants to see which issues are still causing problems and need attention, increasing the review's utility in making M&A strategies work.

As always, the need is to focus on clear, measurable performance metrics. I've been part of post-acquisition reviews in which managers complained about poor morale, uncertainty, conflicts, commitment in the acquired company, and how these issues were affecting postmerger integration and performance. My response has always included, among other things, a demand for greater specificity:

- What are the measures or indicators of poor morale? Has turnover increased? Have exit interviews revealed problems?

- What performance measures are down, indicating problems? What other factors could be affecting performance besides postmerger integration problems? How can one tell if coordination is poor, negatively affecting decision-making and results such as customer satisfaction?

- How does one know that conflicts are real and debilitating? How can their effects be identified, measured, and corrected?

- What are the indicators of poor or insufficient communication that supposedly are hampering postmerger integration? What communication methods or processes should be added and why?

These and similar questions are intended to add value to the post-acquisition strategy review. Reviews should not resemble or degenerate into gripe sessions. They can serve a useful function in the postmerger integration process, provided that they focus on important measures of performance and the factors that impact them.

Analysis of data in the strategy review results in learning. It also identifies areas of change that are needed to fine-tune the execution process and facilitate the achievement of M&A goals.

MANAGING CHANGE

Executing an acquisition strategy always involves change, and managing change well clearly is important for M&A success. Chapter 7 dealt with the tactics and steps that a company can take to execute change over various time intervals. Chapter 8 looked at the softer issues involved in managing culture and cultural change. Both chapters contain important advice for making mergers and acquisitions work. Let's first consider the issues raised in Chapter 7.

Executing change under M&A strategies is a huge task. The first critical decision is to determine how much time the acquiring company has to execute its acquisition strategy. The time available—the implementation horizon—will determine how the large change is managed and controlled and what kinds of problems will likely arise. Questions here include:

- How much time for change is available? Is it important to move quickly to reap the benefits of consolidation? Why?

- Do we have the luxury of time? Can major post-acquisition changes be instituted logically over, say, a one- to three-year period?

- Is it possible to attack the easy changes first, the "low-hanging fruit," and then attack the more difficult changes in a more piecemeal, planned fashion?

Decisions about the time available for change determine whether a sequential change approach is possible when integrating the new acquisition and managing the M&A process, or whether a faster, complex intervention is necessary. The former is more logical and slower, breaking down large changes into smaller, more manageable pieces and executing changes sequentially, with more attention to detail and achieving successes along the way. In contrast, the latter does everything at once, simultaneously changing many things under the short perceived time constraints defining the complex intervention.

Chapter 7 stressed that there are strengths and weaknesses of both sequential and complex change approaches. Sequential change allows for incremental investments, learning, and the celebration of success along the change-management path. It takes longer, however, allowing competing issues to crop up and challenge the change process.

Complex change, in which many things are changed simultaneously, is fast, but coordination is troublesome, learning is difficult, if not impossible, and the prognosis for success is usually poor. If complex change is absolutely essential, the only way to make it work, Chapter 7 stressed, is to relax or eliminate many of the concurrent performance criteria against which people involved in change are normally held accountable. Complex change taxes organizational resources and should not be taken lightly.

Some changes under M&A strategies can usually be done quickly. These often are the smaller changes, the "low-hanging fruit," that can easily be picked in the early stages of post-acquisition integration. Elimination of obvious functional redundancies or sharing established capabilities or competencies right away are examples of issues that management in the merged company can agree with and act on quickly.

Larger changes brought about by the acquisition take more time, planning, and care in execution. Melding entire sales forces or distribution channels and changing invoicing procedures overnight may affect customers negatively, thereby demanding more time and forethought. Elimination of R&D units holds important implications for innovation, and scientific or technical capabilities shouldn't be scrapped without careful analysis. Introducing an entirely new IT system to eliminate disparate legacy systems and achieve communality of information and information processing is a huge task that, if done quickly and poorly, can severely hurt operations, decision-making, and customer satisfaction.

When the shareholders of Bank of America and Fleet Boston approved their companies' merger in March 2004, Bank of America management spent the next day "reassuring employees and customers that change will be slow at Fleet Bank—and for the better."[xii] The nation's new number-three bank announced some quick changes, but it also emphasized that other changes that could negatively affect internal operations or customer service would be executed gradually.

Integration of the banks' complex computer systems would be handled carefully and not be rushed. Deep cuts in branches and personnel would also be handled gingerly. Management stressed that Bank of America would take its time to avoid the problems seen in other banks in their recent mergers, such as those experienced by Wachovia when it made deep cuts quickly in Core States Financial Corp. in 1998 that created major service problems with customers. The bank, then, is talking about slow, deliberate change in major areas. Only time will tell how true it remains to this course of action.

Beware of excessive speed. A popular mantra among M&A analysts is that "speed in integration is good." Yet data reported earlier regarding the vast number of mergers and acquisitions that founder or fail suggest that something is definitely going wrong. One culprit might be that excessive speed, resulting in complex change, does major harm.

The problems with complex change have already been noted in Chapter 7, including the difficulties with coordination and learning and the poor prognosis for the success of change. By stressing speed in the postmerger integration process, proponents of quick integration are actually arguing for complex change and its attendant difficulties. This obviously can affect integration and the execution of M&A strategies.

Excessive speed in the execution of complex M&A strategies may do more harm than good. Speed increases the complexity and velocity of change, which can definitely work against M&A success.

If the merger has major problems or is considered a failure, learning from mistakes and explaining the failure under conditions of complex change are virtually impossible. Future M&A mistakes cannot be avoided; in fact, they are guaranteed.

The case of C. Michael Armstrong's strategic decisions as CEO of AT&T again comes to mind.[xiii] In 1998, Armstrong announced plans to buy cable giant TCI, hoping to integrate phone and cable service. In 1999, AT&T outbid Comcast for MediaOne. In 2000, Armstrong restructured the company, splitting it into three separate entities. While all this was going on, the competitive landscape in AT&T's industries was becoming even more complex and competitive.

Can new acquisitions be integrated effectively in the midst of such turmoil? Can a coherent corporate strategy be developed and executed speedily under such turbulent competitive conditions? Can acquisitions be made to fit into a corporate portfolio with the time pressures Armstrong and Wall Street analysts imposed on the company? Can major structural change also be executed in the midst of all these other changes? Probably not. Armstrong very likely was trying to do too much too fast, and the results were less than favorable.

Reliance on speed in the execution of complex strategies such as M&A may cause yet other problems. The intense focus of managerial time and attention devoted to making strategy work may distract management from other tasks, including tracking and reacting to competitors' actions and changing competitive conditions.

Boeing had a terrible year in 1998, reporting its first loss in 50 years and writing off $4 billion. It easily could have been distracted greatly by the execution of its merger with McDonnell Douglas. Similarly, the Citicorp-Travelers merger, with its huge implementation problems, though handled fairly well, could have deflected attention away from the marketplace and hurt the development of programs to foster cross-selling and the satisfaction of complex consumer needs.

A focus on fast integration in M&A may cover up an inability to plan change carefully and think things through. Worse yet, if speed is associated with decisiveness and "macho" action, while slower planned change somehow is seen as a weakness, then the execution of M&A strategies surely is in jeopardy. Speed doesn't necessarily imply being tough or being able to "bite the bullet" and get things done. Tackling complex change doesn't suggest a positive management style any more than using a slower, sequential change process suggests an overly cautious, timid style.

The effects of speed and complex change must be weighed carefully when executing M&A strategies. The costs and benefits of complex change must be compared to those of a slower, sequential change process. The bottom line is that speed is good for "low-hanging fruit" and other relatively easy, visible execution problems, whereas less speed and more thoroughness are better for larger, more impactful, and more difficult execution-related changes.

MANAGING CULTURE AND CULTURE CHANGE

Executing M&A strategies also demands an ability to manage culture and culture change effectively (see Chapter 8). Southwest airlines spent two months exploring cultural compability with Morris Air before acquiring it. It tried hard to determine whether Morris' employees and style would fit with its can-do attitude and *esprit de corps*, and the effort paid off handsomely. In contrast, the Price-Costco marriage lasted only 10 months due to an inability to create a single unified culture, suggesting a poor attempt at cultural due diligence, change management, and integration in this merger.

Cultural differences abound when executing mergers and acquisitions. These differences are seen in many areas, including the following:

- Style of management
- Centralized vs. decentralized decision-making
- Upstream vs. downstream emphasis on the value chain
- Incentive and compensation packages
- Control systems (risk-averse or risk-accepting companies, different performance appraisal methods)
- Functional competition vs. cooperation
- Entrepreneurial vs. a top-down, command-and-control decision-making climate
- Professional vs. bureaucratic orientation (reliance on rules, standard procedures)
- Internal (production) vs. external (customer) orientation

Managing culture effectively requires that these differences be noted and critical ones targeted for change. Inability to resolve cultural differences will certainly come back to vex or harm the execution of an M&A strategy.

A critical point emphasized in Chapter 8 is that, when changing culture, it is not advisable to focus directly on changing culture itself. Changing culture by appealing to managers to think and act differently is a losing proposition. Examples were provided to show that changing culture is more successful if the focus is on changing people, organizational structure, incentives, or controls.

To change the "decision style" of corporate management after a new acquisition, one can appeal to them to change. For example, an appeal can be made to corporate personnel to assume a more entrepreneurial or decentralized style of decision-making to allow the acquisition to cope with its own industry problems. Will such an appeal for change work, given that a centralized or top-down structure has been the norm for years? Not likely. Such appeals sound good, but they alone rarely produce results.

To change corporate "decision style" as an element of desired culture in managing the new acquisition, Chapter 8 emphasized that changing people, structure, incentives, and controls has a higher probability of success. Increasing spans of control, for example, forces behavioral change because it is more difficult to exercise top-down control when spans are large. Large spans foster a "hands-off" management style. Even if a manager still desires to micromanage, it simply is more difficult to do so, given the larger number of organizational units or subordinates. Changes in behavior would likely occur, defining a new management style. Changing corporate structure or redefining corporate managers' responsibilities can help eliminate close control of an acquired business' activities.

Bringing in new people likewise can effect behavioral change, leading to culture change. New people bring in fresh ideas, motivations, and new capabilities, which can affect decision style and the way things get done. Moving managers internally after an acquisition has been made also can result in cultural change. New people may respond strongly and positively to different incentives developed to foster integration and motivate new behavior consistent with M&A goals. Placing Kraft people in charge of General Foods (GF) operations and GF people in charge of Kraft operations early in their merger did much to signal the importance of integration and the impact new people can have on culture change.

Changing the power structure may also be a necessary ingredient in successfully managing culture and culture change in the post-acquisition organization. Differences in power in the premerger organizations must be addressed after an acquisition. The roots of power and the dependencies that support them (see Chapter 9) must first be understood. If changes in power are necessary, the CEO or top-management "SWAT" team can alter structure and resource allocations, resulting in changes in dependencies and power in the new, post-acquisition organization. The changes in power and influence can be instrumental in changing culture and making the M&A strategy work.

This suggests another problem with the DaimlerChrysler merger. So much time and attention were devoted to the two companies as partners in a "merger of equals" that real power differences in the acquirer-acquiree relationship were overlooked or ignored. It's rare that two companies contribute the same value or have the same power in a combination of companies. The influence and contributions of each must be confronted and discussed to integrate the two organizations effectively. Ignoring the power structure is not wise in M&A activities.

Finally, it is absolutely imperative to reduce resistance to the changes that result from M&A activity and the new company and culture involved. The preceding advice on cultural integration is certainly applicable to the task of reducing resistance to change. The emphasis on personnel orientation, definition of culture, advertisement of the huge opportunities provided by a larger, merged company, and massive doses of communication clearly can help in this regard. Additional discussions of culture change and power relationships in Chapters 8 and 9, respectively, provide yet additional suggestions to help reduce resistance to changes brought about by M&A activities.

THE CRITICAL ROLE OF LEADERSHIP

The importance of sound leadership is vital to all the steps or actions necessary to make M&A strategies work. The critical activities just noted can work only if managers assume an execution-biased role. Aspects of this active and demanding role in M&A include the following:

- An ability to analyze, understand, and "sell" execution needs and decisions
- A need to "ride herd" on the integration of an acquired company to ensure that the steps needed for structural and cultural integration take place
- An ability to develop and use positive incentives for change
- An ability to temper a strong penchant for "numbers" and past performance with strategic thinking and a view toward learning and future performance
- An understanding of power, culture, and resistance to change and how to overcome obstacles in these areas

- A knowledge of managing change effectively, including when to use "speed" or complex interventions and when to proceed incrementally, in a sequential, paced intervention

- Open-mindedness and a high tolerance for ambiguity and uncertainty

Poor leadership can kill or seriously injure execution efforts. Good leadership demands both analytical skills and insights and an ability to handle issues that arise during postmerger or post-acquisition activities. A balance of sorts is needed with an ability to meld the "hard" and "soft" issues critical to execution success. These admittedly are demanding leadership prerequisites, but they're necessary ones when trying to make M&A strategies work.

SUMMARY

Making M&A strategies work is a difficult task. Much is at stake, and success depends very much on managing a complex set of activities or actions. This chapter has applied aspects of this book's approach to the successful execution of M&A strategies, emphasizing the key steps, actions, or decisions it espouses.

The highlights of this approach are shown in Figure 10.2. The execution process begins with sound planning and corporate strategy and then takes a logical, integrated journey through organizational structure, structural and cultural integration, business strategy and its integration with corporate planning, business structure, agreement on performance metrics, strategy reviews, and the inescapable need to manage change and culture effectively. The basic premise is that a practical, unified approach to executing M&A strategies is needed, along with the necessary leadership capabilities to make it successful, and this chapter has provided such an approach.

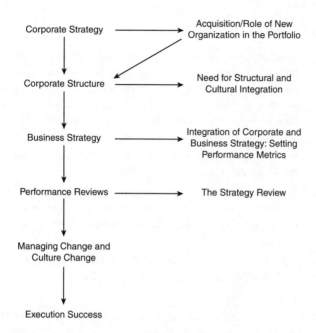

Figure 10.2   Highlights of Process Aimed at Making M&A Strategies Work

Results of M&A activity for the last few decades have been poor. Few mergers have delivered on their promises to achieve synergies and enhance shareholder value. Few have justified their premium prices. Few have been able to integrate disparate or culturally divergent firms to produce positive results. Cultural collisions with negative outcomes have been the rule rather than the exception.

This chapter shows what can be done to make M&A strategies work. Although focusing on the M&A challenge, this chapter also suggests the utility of this material for leading effective execution and management of change across all industries, organizations, strategies, and execution challenges. You can choose and use aspects of this approach to help make strategy work in your own organization.

ENDNOTES

i. Pure "mergers of equals" are relatively rare in the M&A arena. The bulk of transactions are acquisitions by cash, stock, or both. Even pure mergers must go through the steps laid out in this chapter to achieve success—integration, cultural due diligence, managing change, and so on—so no further differentiation between mergers and acquisitions need be made in this discussion.

ii. See, for example, the special report, "The Case Against Mergers," *Business Week,* October 30, 1995.

iii. See the results of the study and related discussion in "The Case Against Mergers," ibid; see also "When Disparate Firms Merge, Cultures Often Collide," *The Wall Street Journal,* February 14, 1997.

iv. "Investment Banks Arranged $1.2 Trillion in Mergers in '03," *The Philadelphia Inquirer,* December 30, 2003.

v. Ibid.

vi. "The Case Against Mergers," op. cit.; see also "How to Merge," *The Economist,* January 9, 1999.

vii. The data on gains, profitability, and time to break even on an acquisition investment are from a study by Mark Sirower, as reported in "The Case Against Mergers," op. cit.

viii. "How to Merge," op. cit.

ix. Ibid.

x. Robert Kaplan and David Norton, *The Balanced Scorecard,* Harvard Business School Press, 1996.

xi. "When Disparate Firms Merge," op. cit.

xii. "Bank of America Vows Slow Post-Merger Change," *The Philadelphia Inquirer,* April 2, 2004.

xiii. "Former Chief Tries to Redeem the Calls He Made at AT&T," *The Wall Street Journal,* May 26, 2004.

Executive Business Panel Questionnaire
GartnerG2 and The Wharton School

PUTTING STRATEGY INTO PRACTICE

INTRODUCTION

Welcome to our survey on strategy execution. The Wharton School of the University of Pennsylvania and GartnerG2, a research service for business strategists, are seeking to understand challenges faced by managers as they make decisions and take actions to execute strategic plans to improve their company's competitive advantage.

The survey should take about 5 minutes to complete (Responses to open-ended questions may take longer). You are part of a carefully selected group that has been asked to participate in this survey, and we appreciate your assistance. As with all surveys we conduct, your responses are confidential. Should you have any difficulties in responding, please contact us at websupport3@gar.com or call our panel support line at +1-800-xxx-xxxx.

To start, click on "Start Questionnaire." Thank you for your participation!

QUESTIONNAIRE

Q01)   We've identified 12 obstacles or hurdles to successful strategy execution. In your experience, how big a problem for execution is each of the following for your company? Use a 7-point scale, where a 1 means *not at all a problem* and a 7 means *a major problem.*

		Not at all a problem						A major problem	Don't know
1.	Poor or vague strategy	1	2	3	4	5	6	7	DK
2.	Not having guidelines or a model to guide strategy execution efforts	1	2	3	4	5	6	7	DK
3.	Insufficient financial resources to execute the strategy	1	2	3	4	5	6	7	DK
4.	Trying to execute a strategy that conflicts with the existing power structure	1	2	3	4	5	6	7	DK
5.	Inability to generate "buy in" or agreement on critical execution steps or actions	1	2	3	4	5	6	7	DK
6.	Lack of upper management support of strategy execution	1	2	3	4	5	6	7	DK
7.	Lack of feelings of "ownership" of a strategy or execution plans among key employees	1	2	3	4	5	6	7	DK
8.	Lack of incentives or inappropriate incentives to support execution objectives	1	2	3	4	5	6	7	DK
9.	Poor or inadequate information sharing between individuals or business units responsible for strategy execution	1	2	3	4	5	6	7	DK
10.	Unclear communication of responsibility and/or accountability for execution decisions or actions	1	2	3	4	5	6	7	DK
11.	Lack of understanding of the role of organizational structure and design in the execution process	1	2	3	4	5	6	7	DK
12.	Inability to manage change effectively or to overcome internal resistance to change	1	2	3	4	5	6	7	DK

Executive Business Panel Questionnaire
GartnerG2 and The Wharton School

Q02) Strategy execution requires information sharing and coordination. Please rate the effectiveness of the following coordination methods for strategy execution between functions, business units, and key personnel within your company. Use a 7-point scale, where a 1 means *highly ineffective* and a 7 means *highly effective*.

		Highly ineffective						Highly effective	Not applicable	Don't know
1.	Use of teams or cross-functional groups	1	2	3	4	5	6	7	NA	DK
2.	Use of informal communication (i.e. person-to-person contact)	1	2	3	4	5	6	7	NA	DK
3.	Use of formal integrators (e.g., a project management or quality assurance organization)	1	2	3	4	5	6	7	NA	DK
4.	Use of a matrix organization or a "grid" structure to share resources or knowledge	1	2	3	4	5	6	7	NA	DK

Q03) Based on your perceptions of knowledge and information sharing within your company during strategy execution, please indicate the extent to which you agree or disagree with the following statements. Use a 7-point scale, where a 1 means *strongly disagree* and a 7 means *strongly agree*.

		Strongly disagree						Strongly agree	Not applicable	Don't know
1.	Employees are reluctant to share important information or knowledge with others	1	2	3	4	5	6	7	NA	DK
2.	Some sources of information are unreliable	1	2	3	4	5	6	7	NA	DK
3.	Managers are reluctant to trust information generated from sources outside their own departments	1	2	3	4	5	6	7	NA	DK
4.	Information fails to reach people who need it	1	2	3	4	5	6	7	NA	DK
5.	Employees fail to understand or evaluate the usefulness of available information	1	2	3	4	5	6	7	NA	DK

Executive Business Panel Questionnaire
GartnerG2 and The Wharton School

Q04)   I know there are problems with strategy execution in my company when....

		Strongly disagree						Strongly agree	Not applicable	Don't know
1.	Execution decisions take too long to make	1	2	3	4	5	6	7	NA	DK
2.	Employees don't understand how their jobs contribute to important execution outcomes	1	2	3	4	5	6	7	NA	DK
3.	Responses to customer problems or complaints take too long to execute	1	2	3	4	5	6	7	NA	DK
4.	The company reacts slowly or inappropriately to competitive pressures while executing strategy	1	2	3	4	5	6	7	NA	DK
5.	Time or money is wasted because of inefficiency or bureaucracy in the execution process	1	2	3	4	5	6	7	NA	DK
6.	"Playing politics" is more important than performance against strategy execution goals for gaining individual recognition	1	2	3	4	5	6	7	NA	DK
7.	Important information "falls through the cracks" during execution and doesn't get acted on	1	2	3	4	5	6	7	NA	DK
8.	We spend lots of time reorganizing or restructuring, but we don't seem to know why this is important for strategy execution	1	2	3	4	5	6	7	NA	DK
9.	We're unsure whether the strategy we're executing is worthwhile, effective, or logical, given the competitive forces we face in our industry	1	2	3	4	5	6	7	NA	DK

APPENDIX

Executive Business Panel Questionnaire
GartnerG2 and The Wharton School

Q05)   Managers have told us that *executing* strategy is more challenging than *formulating* strategy.
        Please tell us whether you agree with this view and briefly explain your answer.

Q06)   Finally, what other factors not mentioned in this survey make the execution process challenging
        or difficult in your company?

INDEX

B

Balanced Scorecard, 87, 345
Ballmer, Steve, 125
Bank of America (BOA), 237
  merger with Fleet Boston, 354
Barnard, Chester, 77, 140
behavior changes, changing culture,
  272-274, 286. *See also*
  performance
benefit measurement, impact of
  corporate structure, 110-115
Bethlehem Steel, 66
binary objectives, 191-192
blueprint. *See* model of strategy
  execution
BOA (Bank of America), 237
  merger with Fleet Boston, 354
boards of directors, influence of,
  315-317
Boeing, integration example, 143, 356
Bossidy, Larry, xx, 29, 70, 214
Boston Consulting Group, 325
BP, merger with Amoco, 331
Bristol-Myers, 264
British Air, 76
brutal facts, learning from mistakes,
  201-202
Burke, James, 259
business roles, problems with
  unclear business roles, 79-80
business strategy, 44-48
  impact on strategy execution, 71,
    74-77
  integration with corporate strategy,
    78-85, 213-215
  and mergers and acquisitions,
    342-346
  short-term operating objectives,
    49-50
  and strategy review, 212-213

business structure, 50, 53
  and mergers and acquisitions,
    346-347

C

capabilities to support strategy,
  development of, 89-98, 127,
  130. *See also* corporate
  structure
Capital Cities/ABC, aquisition by
  Disney, 40-41, 334
cause-effect analysis
  complex change management,
    247-248
  and culture change, 270-272, 286
  in strategy review, 217-218
"centers of excellence" (corporate
  center staff), 125-126
Centocor, 59
centralization versus decentralization, 41, 115-126, 132-137
change management, 225, 228
  complex change, 243-245
    benefits of, 245
    GE example, 252-254
    General Motors example,
      250-251
    National Hurricane Center
      example, 250
    problems with, 246-251, 254
  for cultural integration in mergers
    and acquisitions, 342
  execution-related problems,
    231-235
  mergers and acquisitions, 352,
    355-356
  as opportunity for success, 24, 58
  sequential change, 235-237
    benefits of, 237-238, 243
    Kraft and General Foods
      example, 238-240

functional organization, costs and
benefits, 111

G

Galbraith, Jay, 183
Gartner Group, Inc. *See* Wharton-
Gartner survey
GE, 201
complex change management
example, 252-254
"Work Out" (reciprocal
interdependence example),
156-157
GE Capital, flat organizational
structure example, 119-121
General Foods, sequential change
example, 238-240
General Motors (GM), 312
complex change management
example, 250-251
corporate structure and strategy
execution example, 104-106
dependencies, 293
Gensler, Robert, 244
Gillette, 67
global strategies
corporate structure choices,
130-131
"demands" of strategy, 96-98
GM (General Motors), 312
complex change management
example, 250-251
corporate structure and strategy
execution example, 104-106
dependencies, 293
Google, 227
growth of organization, corporate
structure choices, 136-137
guidelines. *See* model of strategy
execution

H-I

Hartman, Amir, 183, 249
Head, Howard, 133
Hewlett-Packard, 227
Hrebiniak, L.G., 64, 87, 101, 183,
223

Iacocca, Lee, 298
IBM, 76
ImClone, 264
imitation, 75
Immelt, Jeffrey, 55, 155, 189
restructuring of GE Capital, 119
implementation. *See* execution
of strategy
incentives, 53-56, 187-194. *See also*
controls
changing culture, 273, 276
for cultural integration in mergers
and acquisitions, 341-342
demotivation, 187-188
importance to reciprocal
interdependence, 155
and mergers and acquisitions,
347-348
and performance criteria, 192-194
role of, 186
types of, 188-192
inertia, flat organizational structure
problems, 121
influence. *See* power
informal contact, methods for
information sharing, 165, 168
information sharing. *See also*
communication
Citibank example, 160-161
factors affecting, 168-169
absorptive capacity (AC),
172-173
codified knowledge versus tacit
knowledge, 169-170
organizational structure, 173-175
trustworthiness of information
sources, 170-172

> "Great schools have…endeavored to do more than keep up to the respectable standard of a recent past; they have labored to supply the needs of an advancing and exacting world…"
>
> — **Joseph Wharton,** *Entrepreneur and Founder of the Wharton School*

The Wharton School is recognized around the world for its innovative leadership and broad academic strengths across every major discipline and at every level of business education. It is one of four undergraduate and 12 graduate and professional schools of the University of Pennsylvania. Founded in 1881 as the nation's first collegiate business school, Wharton is dedicated to creating the highest value and impact on the practice of business and management worldwide through intellectual leadership and innovation in teaching, research, publishing and service.

Wharton's tradition of innovation includes many firsts—the first business textbooks, the first research center, the MBA in health care management—and continues to innovate with new programs, new learning approaches, and new initiatives. Today Wharton is an interconnected community of students, faculty, and alumni who are shaping global business education, practice, and policy.

Wharton is located in the center of the University of Pennsylvania (Penn) in Philadelphia, the fifth-largest city in the United States. Students and faculty enjoy some of the world's most technologically advanced academic facilities. In the midst of Penn's tree-lined, 269-acre urban campus, Wharton students have access to the full resources of an Ivy League university, including libraries, museums, galleries, athletic facilities, and performance halls. In recent years, Wharton has expanded access to its management education with the addition of Wharton West, a San Francisco academic center, and The Alliance with INSEAD in France, creating a global network.

Academic Programs:

Wharton continues to pioneer innovations in education across its leading undergraduate, MBA, executive MBA, doctoral, and executive education programs.

More information about Wharton's academic programs can be found at:
http://www.wharton.upenn.edu/academics

Executive Education:

Wharton Executive Education is committed to offering programs that equip executives with the tools and skills to compete, and meet the challenges inherent in today's corporate environment. With a mix of more than 200 programs, including both open enrollment and custom offerings, a world-class faculty, and educational facilities second to none, Wharton offers leading-edge solutions to close to 10,000 executives annually, worldwide.

For more information and a complete program listing:
execed@wharton.upenn.edu (sub 4033)
215.898.1776 or 800.255.3932 ext. 4033
http://execed.wharton.upenn.edu

Research and Analysis:

Knowledge@Wharton is a unique, free resource that offers the best of business—the latest trends; the latest research on a vast range of business issues; original insights of Wharton faculty; studies, paper and analyses of hundreds of topics and industries. *Knowledge@Wharton* has over 400,000 users from more than 189 countries.

For free subscription:
http://knowledge.wharton.upenn.edu

For licensing and content information, please contact:
Jamie Hammond,
Associate Marketing Director,
hammondj@wharton.upenn.edu • 215.898.2388

Wharton School Publishing:

Wharton School Publishing is an innovative new player in global publishing, dedicated to providing thoughtful business readers access to practical knowledge and actionable ideas that add impact and value to their professional lives. All titles are approved by a Wharton senior faculty review board to ensure they are relevant, timely, important, empirically based and/or conceptually sound, and implementable.

For author inquiries or information about corporate education and affinity programs or, please contact:
Barbara Gydé, Managing Director,
gydeb@wharton.upenn.edu • 215.898.4764

The Wharton School: http://www.wharton.upenn.edu
Executive Education: http://execed.wharton.upenn.edu
Wharton School Publishing: http://whartonsp.com
Knowledge@Wharton: http://knowledge.wharton.upenn.edu